Winning Research Skills

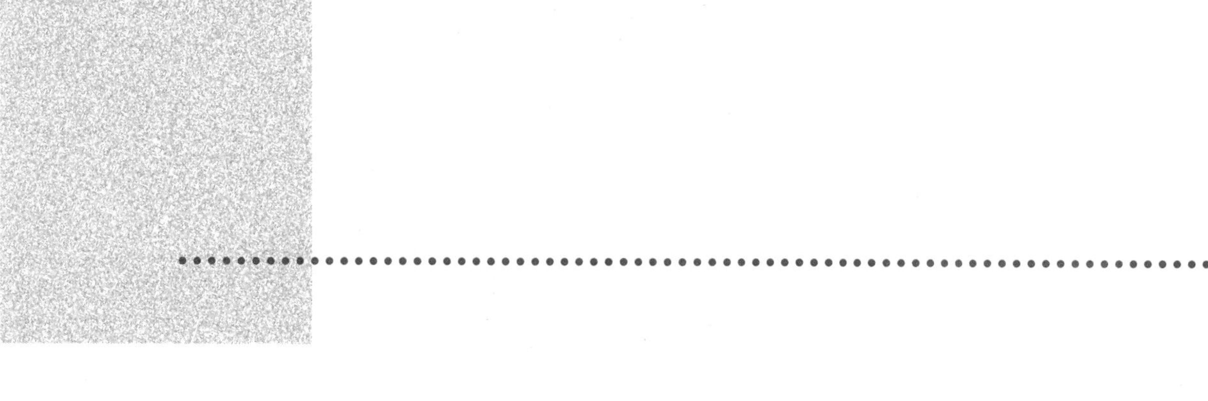

Nancy P. Johnson

Director of the Law Library and Professor of Law
Georgia State University

Robert C. Berring

Director of the Law Library and Professor of Law
University of California, Berkeley

Thomas A. Woxland

Director of the Law Library and Associate Professor of Law
Northern Illinois University

WEST PUBLISHING COMPANY
St. Paul *New York* *Los Angeles* *San Francisco*

Copyediting: Patricia Lewis
Interior Design: Roslyn Stendahl, Dapper Design
Illustrations: Rolin Graphics
Composition: Parkwood Composition

Printed in the United States of America

98 97 96 95 94 93 92 91 8 7 6 5 4 3 2 1 0

ISBN 0–314–89354–7

About the Authors

NANCY JOHNSON has been the Director of the Law Library at Georgia State University since 1986. Previously, she served as a Reference Librarian at Georgia State, the University of Illinois Law Library, and the University of Chicago Law Library. She teaches courses in legal research. She is the co-author of the *Legal Research Exercises* and the author of the *Sources of Compiled Legislative Histories*. Johnson received her B.A. from Marycrest College, M.L.S. from the University of Illinois, and J.D. from Georgia State.

BOB BERRING has been the Director of the Boalt Hall Law Library since 1982. Previously, he held positions at the University of Washington Law Library, Harvard Law Library, the University of Texas Law Library, and the University of Illinois Law Library. He is the co-author of several legal research texts, including *How to Find the Law*. He teaches courses in legal research, in person and on video tape. Berring is a past president of the American Association of Law Libraries. Berring has a B.A. from Harvard and a M.L.S. and a J.D. from the University of California at Berkeley.

TOM WOXLAND joined the faculty of the Northern Illinois University College of Law in 1989. Prior to that he spent ten years on the staff of the University of Minnesota Law Library, where he was the assistant director for public services. He teaches courses in legal research. He has published several articles on research topics and on the history of legal publishing. He is also the co-author of instructional software used nationally for computer-assisted legal research training. Woxland has a B.A. from St. Olaf College and an M.A.L.S. and a J.D. from the University of Minnesota.

ACKNOWLEDGEMENTS

The authors thank their staff at the Georgia State University Law Library, the Boalt Hall Law Library, and the Northern Illinois Law Library. Nancy Johnson specifically thanks Rhonda Rosenberg who helped with the initial phases of the book. A project of this kind is, in a genuine sense, a joint effort; we are grateful to all of the individuals at West Publishing Company who worked on this book. Several persons at West helped with various stages of preparation and completion of this work: Bill Lindberg, Craig Runde, Ann Possis, Sharon Kavanagh, and Kara Johnson. Finally, we thank each other for still being friends.

Contents

INTRODUCTION

Legal research is largely a matter of sex, drugs, and rock 'n' roll. Well, not really, but at least we have caught your attention. The point is, legal research is not the dull, plodding enterprise that it is often made out to be. Unfortunately, many law schools still do not have the resources to teach research well. Some students assume that the research training that is crammed into the first few weeks at those schools represents the full picture of legal research. Nothing could be further from the truth. The structure of how one finds the law is really the *center* of the legal educational enterprise.

This is a book for first-year law students. If you are one, you have probably already heard more than once that one of the main goals of the first year is to teach you how to "think like a lawyer." Most of your first-year courses will be concerned with teaching you methods of analyzing the law and facts in a particular situation. It is this type of *thinking* that is most important. Although the same core courses—Contracts, Torts, and Property—have been taught for over a hundred years, the *content* of these courses is not really as important as the way it is analyzed. In most of these first-year courses, you are being taught to think, question, and analyze. The specific rules of law that you discuss are just part of the process, not the point. This is why you will know very little real "law" at the end of your first year. It is only in the *legal research* enterprise, and the legal writing experience, that you are actually taught how to *do* things. That's why we are here.

There are a number of books devoted to the enterprise of legal research. They include large textbooks that explore everything in minute detail and friendly paperbacks that provide a broad overview of the research process and its bibliography. This book falls into neither of those categories. It is an attempt to introduce you to basic research materials and methods, and especially to the products of the nation's leading and most comprehensive law publisher, West Publishing Company. We will devote much attention to one particular product, WESTLAW, West's computer-assisted legal research (CALR) service. We are not going to make any attempt to argue that WESTLAW (or West books for that matter) are substitutes for all of the other materials, nor would we pretend that using these West products is the only way to do intelligent research. But we do see them as very important parts of the complete research picture. As such, they need to be placed in that context. That is the aim of this book.

West books have been an essential part of any lawyer's library for more than a century. But during the last twenty years, the computer revolution has reached law libraries. A major purpose of this book is to show you how computer-assisted legal research relates to the materials in a traditional law library. One reason we have presented the information in this way is to make clear that the on-line databases are more than simply auxiliary case-finding mechanisms. Lots of people think this, but trust us, they are wrong. Both LEXIS and WESTLAW, the two major services, are, in themselves, *law libraries* filled with information.

A generational change is going on in the way people think about legal information. Many lawyers who graduated from law school more than five or ten years ago will always think of law as printed on a page. They may use computers, but in their own minds, they will not *really* be reading law until they see something on the page of a book or in a loose-leaf service. We believe that your generation of law students is riding the crest of what may become a flood tide of change. Information in on-line services is indeed information. A service like WESTLAW contains primary sources, secondary sources, and links between them. With a modem, you can sit at your home personal computer and access much of the world of legal information.

In a way, this book is a hybrid product. It provides a little background on legal information in general and introduces you to relevant ways of using WESTLAW as well as traditional print sources. It is a one-legged enterprise, however, and does not stand alone. It should be used with other tools, as a part of other courses, where it should be a legitimate help for you. WESTLAW offers enormous advantages to users. You should be able to make the most of those advantages. You should also understand the context in which they operate. No one should graduate from law school without understanding what a case reporter is, both in its traditional printed format and in its on-line manifestation. Nor should you leave law school without understanding how statutory materials are organized and why using them on-line might be different or better—or worse. You should know why administrative rules and regulations are important and how you can find them on-line. And you should also be aware of the role secondary sources and indexes play in the real world of legal research.

Of course, a book of this size must necessarily omit a great deal, and, believe it or not, we don't always agree on every point. Our goal, however, is to provide you with something that helps. We recognize that we can only present a tip of the iceberg of legal research materials, and we'll try not to take ourselves too seriously as we present the information. If we were to leave you with only one injunction, it would be to look beyond the four corners of the research enterprise and see that understanding how the tools work, how the pieces fit together, and how the body of research materials function as a whole may be the most important piece of the puzzle.

A Little History

Let's begin with a short history of legal research and go back to the earliest days of the American republic. Finding the law was pretty simple for the small group of American lawyers who practiced two hundred years ago. Legal research was much easier then. It is only a slight overstatement to say that all you needed to practice law in 1800 was the American edition of Blackstone's *Commentaries on the Laws of England*—the great, multivolume, comprehensive law text of the eighteenth century. With Blackstone, an inkwell, and a desk, you were a lawyer.

By the end of the nineteenth century, both the law and legal research were getting more complicated. Back in 1810, there had been only eighteen volumes of American court reports; a lawyer of the time could literally read *all* the cases. But by 1885, a comprehensive law library had 3,500 volumes of reports, and not even with Evelyn Wood's assistance could you have read all the cases. Speed reading courses might not help, but law book publishers did.

Responding to lawyers' needs, large legal publishing companies developed during the last quarter of the nineteenth century to compile, and provide access to, the explosive growth in legal sources. Many of the commercial legal publishers whose books you will use for the rest of your careers began their work during this period. Among the best known are West Publishing Company, the Lawyers Co-operative Publishing Company, and the Frank Shepard Company (now Shepard's/McGraw-Hill, Inc.).

Between 1875 and 1900, these publishers introduced many of the now-familiar types of law books, including regional reporters and comprehensive digests from West; citators from Shepard's; and annotated reporters from Lawyers Co-op. Along with a few other publishers, they also introduced most of the common features of today's legal publications. For example, during this time, publishers developed the basic types of modern supplementation techniques: pocket parts, advance sheets, and—slightly later—loose-leaf services.

In effect, then, in answer to the anguished complaints of lawyers about the outpouring of law from the courts and legislatures, the legal publishers said: "Don't worry. We will publish all of it. And, not only will we publish it, but we will read and organize it for you as well. We will give you indexes and annotations and summaries and digests."

During the second half of the twentieth century, the lawyers' old lament has been heard again. Now there were even more courts and they were deciding ever more cases. To make matters worse, to the steady stream of statutes coming out of the legislatures was added a river of regulations flowing from administrative agencies. *Three million* appellate cases had been published. Federal statutes and regulations filled hundreds of thousands of pages. Fifty states multiplied this torrent by fifty times. The storage capacities of many law libraries were strained. Book budgets were burdened. New and competing publications confused lawyers, not to mention law librarians.

The publishers responded again. This time their answer was high technology. One of the first solutions was to use microfiche for mass storage. A filing cabinet of fiche could replace a whole library of books.

But the computer brought about the biggest change. Computer-assisted legal research systems, principally the WESTLAW service of West Publishing and the LEXIS service from Mead Data Central, were developed in the 1970s and improved in the 1980s. These services contain hundreds of thousands of legal documents, including cases, statutes, regulations, and legal periodical articles, many of which can be fully displayed. Together, these documents contain tens of millions of words, each of which (with the exception of a few very common words) is searchable. The ability to search the "full-text" of documents has made virtually every word in the databases a possible search term and a possible indexing term. In the legal publishing revolution of the nineteenth century, professional editors and indexers read and summarized cases for attorneys. The computer revolution of the twentieth century has added a different type of indexing tool for attorneys to use. The speed and capacity of a service such as WESTLAW provide us all with a new and fantastic level of access to the law's many sources.

The modern law library is a collection of old and new publishing technologies, books and computers, working together. Neither WESTLAW nor LEXIS is the panacea for all of your research needs. For some types of research, the old ways are still the best. For example, searching for broad concepts, such as negligence or proximate causation, is most effectively begun with treatises or digests. For other types of research, the speed, ease, and accuracy of computerized legal research should make WESTLAW your starting point.

A Few Helpful Hints

Before we begin looking more specifically at the tools and techniques of legal research, we offer some general hints to remember about legal publications, either paper or electronic: (1) When the same material is published both by a government printer and a commercial publisher, the latter is almost invariably more useful. (2) Different commercial publishers have different publishing philosophies—knowing the "philosophy" helps you understand the scope and content of their publications. (3) You will often find the same legal materials published in both a chronological arrangement and a subject-based arrangement. (4) Finally, the forms of publication for the law of the various states are very similar to the forms of publication of federal law; if you understand the system on the national level, you will understand it on a local level.

Governments—both state and federal—often print the text of the primary sources of their law. They publish the statutes enacted by their legislatures, the decisions handed down by their appellate courts, and the regulations promulgated by their administrative agencies. All of these materials, of course, are in the public domain. Commercial publishers, like West Publishing or Lawyers Co-op, publish the same statutes, decisions, and regulations as the government printers. These "unofficial" publications are usually more helpful than the "official" government publications for two reasons.

First, the commercial publications are usually more up-to-date than the government publications. Laws change, new decisions appear. Government printers frequently are several years behind in their publications. In contrast, the commercial publishers will publish new cases or statutes in "advance sheet" form within only a few weeks or months of their occurrence.

Secondly, the commercial publishers frequently add other useful information to their publications. For example, the officially published *United States Code* prints only the text of the federal statutes, but the commercially published "annotated" codes also include summaries of judicial cases that have construed or explained those statutes as well as references to other helpful interpretive sources.

Perhaps it seems strange to think of law book publishers as having "philosophies." But it's true. The two biggest publishers of law books have very different philosophies, which were enunciated more than a hundred years ago and are still valid. In 1890, John West, the founder of West Publishing, said of his company's publications: "The profession has now the immense advantage of being able to turn to a single set of reports and digests, and be sure of finding *everything* which the courts have said on any given subject." James Briggs, the first president of Lawyers Co-op, responded: "Much is said by certain contemporaries about 'completeness,' referring simply to the agglomeration of all the opinions of the various jurisdictions of the United States into masses of what are, in fact, largely made up of useless repetitions. . . . [The] work undertaken by my Company . . . is to give that most valuable in the most elaborate form, and that least valuable in the most condensed." The two companies continue to adhere to their founders' statements. When West and Lawyers Co-op publish equivalent products—legal encyclopedias or annotated codes are good examples—the West set will invariably be more voluminous. West still provides "completeness," and Lawyers Co-op still "condenses."

Similar differences in philosophy exist between publishers of computer-assisted legal research services. While both WESTLAW and LEXIS include cases in their databases, WESTLAW adds the traditional West editorial enhancements—the headnotes, key numbers, and other features that we will soon tell you about—to the text of court opinions in its computerized documents. It also applies the same editorial scrutiny to the on-line form that it does to the printed form, assuring accuracy in matters of citations, spelling, and the like. LEXIS, on the other hand, provides the language of the court alone, without the "added value" of any editor's or indexer's work. In addition, largely because WESTLAW was created by a traditional book publisher and LEXIS was not, WESTLAW has emphasized the interconnectedness of books and databases, while LEXIS sees the on-line service as central to the research process.

Our third hint concerns chronological arrangement versus subject arrangement. Most primary sources, whether judicial, legislative, or administrative, are initially published in a chronologically arranged series. As more cases or statutes or regulations appear, another volume or pamphlet is published. If these chronological materials were the only ones available, research would be impossible. How, in three million cases, would you be able to find cases on a certain topic? Publishers have recompiled this material by subject. Case *digests* are subject arrangements of points of law in cases. Statutory and administrative *codes* are topical arrangements of *session laws* and *administrative registers*.

Finally, the forms of legal publication are common throughout different jurisdictions. Federal laws are published chronologically as *session laws* and recompiled as a *statutory code*. Federal regulations appear in a *register* and then in an *administrative code*. Federal cases are published in *reporters* and indexed in *digests*. The same is true, more or less, for each of the fifty state jurisdictions. Therefore, once you've learned the research tools for one jurisdiction, you've learned them for all.

Where to Go for More Help

This book is not going to answer all of your legal research questions. No one book could, and certainly not one as short as this. There are several much more exhaustive (and exhausting) research guides. Two very good and very comprehensive ones are *How to Find the Law* and *Fundamentals of Legal Research*. Both of them will be in your law school library and will also probably be in your law school's bookstore. Every truly compulsive legal researcher will constantly consult those books. Take a look at them. That research maniac who sits next to you in Torts already has.

If you want to know more about the wide range of West's books and services, look at *West's Law Finder*. You have probably already received a complimentary copy. It is handy, helpful, and thin enough to keep in your briefcase.

If you have specific questions about WESTLAW, your best bet is the *WESTLAW Reference Manual*. It is both informative and *well written* (unlike many computer manuals, which appear to have been written by people who scored 800 on the SAT math section and 350 on the SAT verbal). The *Reference Manual* is not only readable and informative, it has a good index. You can find answers in it.

If you have questions that the manual doesn't answer, you can call West Customer Service toll-free at 1-800-WESTLAW. For a really tough question about query formulation, ask to speak to one of the West Reference Attorneys. Or if you have a really complex technical question—something like "Will WESTMATE be adversely affected if I install it on a turbo PC, running a TSR 'carbon-copy,' that, while using a local modem, will also have a network adaptor card?"—you may be referred to the Technical Specialists (West's "computer jocks"). Don't be afraid to call. The call is free, and these people are paid to answer your questions. Go ahead and make their day.

What Follows

We have tried to keep this book short. You have a lot to read during this year, and while we think that a book on legal research should be at the top of the list, we have known enough law students to realize that it won't be. So we will be as brief as possible.

Chapter 1 will introduce you to the basics of case reporting—how cases are published in hard-copy reporters as well as in the WESTLAW service. Chapter 2 explains how to *find* cases, and Chapter 3 how to *update* cases. Later chapters examine statutory and administrative sources and secondary materials; finally, Chapter 7 reviews the entire research process. Sprinkled liberally along the way are illustrations from both the hard-copy materials and the on-line databases. Even the most careful reader should need only a couple of hours to reach the end.

One last note: Throughout this book are suggestions on how WESTLAW can be used in various research contexts. If you know nothing about the mechanics of full-text searching, you might want to look at the appendix on WESTLAW query formulation before you begin reading Chapter 1.

1 Case Law

Since the ability to find and read cases is fundamental to legal study as well as to legal practice, we will begin with a description of how cases are organized. You will be introduced to the kind of information that is included in the hard-copy case reporters. You will also learn how cases are organized on WESTLAW. The "stuff" of the cases—that is, the words of the judge or justice authoring the opinion—is the same in the hard copy and on WESTLAW, but there are important differences in the way the cases are arranged and presented.

From reading this chapter, you should acquire certain basic skills. You should be able to locate the correct case in a reporter from a legal citation. You should also be able to find parallel citations, a mandatory part of the proper citation form. And you should be able to recognize and understand the various elements of a case in a reporter volume and the different fields of a case on WESTLAW.

We will begin by explaining what a court reporter is, how cases are issued and published, and how cases are arranged within the different levels of the court system.

Court Reporters

Reporters or reports are the books that contain the text of court opinions. These are *real* cases, not the edited versions that you find in your casebooks. In fact, you can often learn a great deal about a case in your casebook by reading the "unexpurgated" version in the reporter. Try it. You will notice that the title of the reporter in a citation will be abbreviated. All of the reporters have standard abbreviations. For example, F.Supp. and F.2d are abbreviations for the *Federal Supplement* and the *Federal Reporter* second series, respectively. You will memorize these pretty quickly whether you want to or not. You can easily decipher the abbreviation by checking the last pages of *Black's Law Dictionary* or the *Uniform System of Citation,* better known as the "Bluebook." A typical F.2d citation, such as 516 F.2d 924 (5th Cir. 1975), includes the following components:

516	F.2d	924	(5th Cir.	1975)
↓	↓	↓	↓	↓
Volume	Reporter	Page	Court	Year

One of the trickiest things about finding the right reporter is making sure you have the correct series. Many of the reporters are published in two or possibly three series. For example, the first series of the *Federal Reporter* goes up to Volume 300, and the second series starts over at Volume 1. Lots of old series stopped at 300, but no one seems to follow that practice now.

It may come as a surprise to you that the great majority of judicial opinions are not published at all. Most state trial-level cases are not reported. A very high percentage of federal district court opinions is not reported either. In fact, not even all appellate cases are reported. The trend has been to publish considerably fewer opinions on a percentage basis. But since the absolute number of cases being decided continues to skyrocket, plenty are still published. Many are not reported though because the courts deem them to be redundant of previous decisions; others are not reported because they are determined to have no precedential value.

The court rules of each jurisdiction state when publication of an opinion is appropriate. An appellate judge consults with the judges who participated in the opinion on whether it is desirable or necessary to publish the opinion. Occasionally, an editor will recommend that a case not be published, or that an accompanying order not be published.

Many cases that are not selected for publication in print do go into the WESTLAW service, however. Both published and unpublished opinions appear on both WESTLAW and LEXIS.

There is great debate in legal circles as to whether these unpublished opinions, which may only appear on-line, may serve as precedent; that is, whether they can be cited as "law." The argument goes as follows: since all persons, even those represented by attorneys, do not always have access to the computerized services, they could not possibly follow these unpublished rulings. The upshot of the argument is that, in most jurisdictions, unpublished opinions cannot be used as precedent or may be used only under certain guidelines requiring ample notice to the court and the opposing counsel. Even if unpublished opinions may not be useful as precedent, they may be very helpful in determining judicial thinking in similar cases. Think strategically—if you are going before Judge Smith in a products liability case, it may be valuable to know what Judge Smith has done in products liability cases in the past even if you do not use them as precedent. In practice, cases have *many* uses.

The cases that are reported are organized by court, jurisdiction, or geographic proximity. The arrangement of cases is determined by the editors. For example, in a regional reporter the cases from a single state are published together. The arrangement of cases may also be based on a hierarchy of courts within a state. The on-line service WESTLAW organizes its cases into "databases." For example, WESTLAW has state databases, federal databases, and specialized topical databases (Figure 1.1).

The capacities of electronic information storage allow for much more flexibility in the arrangement of materials than the hard-copy reporters do. A database of electronically stored information can be reorganized repeatedly.

Opinions do not appear immediately in bound volumes. Instead, they appear first in official slip opinions issued by the court itself (Figure 1.2).

Figure 1.1 WESTLAW Databases

```
                 WELCOME TO THE WESTLAW DIRECTORY                P1
 GENERAL MATERIAL   TOPICAL MATERIAL   TEXT & PERIODICAL  SPECIALIZED MAT'L
Federal       P2   First Amend.  P157 Law Reviews, P211 Gateways (Dow  P257
State         P5   Gov't Cont.   P158  Texts & CLE        Jones, D&B,
 TOPICAL MATERIAL  Health Serv.  P161    CITATORS         Dialog, etc.)
Admiralty     P122 Immigration   P164 Insta-Cite,   P241 Historical     P258
Antitrust     P124 Insurance     P166 Shepard's PreView  Newspapers     P273
Bankruptcy    P126 Intell. Prop. P170  and Citations     Other Pubs     P274
Civil Rights  P129 International P172  SPECIALIZED MAT'L Tax Management P278
Communication P132 Labor         P174 ABA           P242 TaxSource      P279
Corporations  P134 Legal Service P181 AJS           P244 WESTLAW        P280
Crim. Justice P137 Military Law  P184 BNA           P245  Highlights
Education     P140 Products Liab P186 Callaghan     P249 Other Services P282
Energy        P143 Securities    P189 C. Boardman   P250  & Databases
Environmental P147 Social Secur. P196 CCH           P252  (NEW, FIND,
Family Law    P152 Taxation      P199 Dictionary    P253  etc.)
Financial     P155 Transport     P206 Directories   P254  EZ ACCESS     P283
                   Worker Comp.  P208 Envtl L Inst  P256  CUSTOMER INFO P284

If you wish to:
   View another Directory page, type P followed by its NUMBER and press ENTER
   Select a known database, type its IDENTIFIER and press ENTER
   Obtain further information, type HELP and press ENTER
```

Figure 1.2 A Slip Opinion

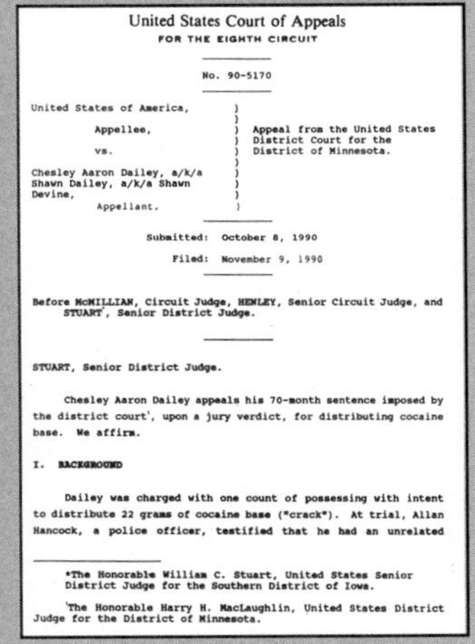

United States Court of Appeals
FOR THE EIGHTH CIRCUIT

No. 90-5170

United States of America, Appellee, vs. Chesley Aaron Dailey, a/k/a Shawn Dailey, a/k/a Shawn Devine, Appellant.

Appeal from the United States District Court for the District of Minnesota.

Submitted: October 8, 1990

Filed: November 9, 1990

Before McMILLIAN, Circuit Judge, HENLEY, Senior Circuit Judge, and STUART*, Senior District Judge.

STUART, Senior District Judge.

Chesley Aaron Dailey appeals his 70-month sentence imposed by the district court[1], upon a jury verdict, for distributing cocaine base. We affirm.

I. BACKGROUND

Dailey was charged with one count of possessing with intent to distribute 22 grams of cocaine base ("crack"). At trial, Allan Hancock, a police officer, testified that he had an unrelated

*The Honorable William C. Stuart, United States Senior District Judge for the Southern District of Iowa.

[1]The Honorable Harry H. MacLaughlin, United States District Judge for the District of Minnesota.

Opinions of the U.S. Supreme Court first appear in slim pamphlets published by the U.S. Government Printing Office. Most law libraries do not collect slip opinions from courts other than the U.S. Supreme Court.

Slip opinions and unreported cases generally do not contain editorial enhancements. When West receives slip opinions, it adds them to WESTLAW immediately. Therefore, the fastest way for you to read a new opinion is on-line. In fact, U.S. Supreme Court opinions are in the WESTLAW U.S. Supreme Court database (SCT) within a few hours of filing. Slip opinions from the other courts are on-line within different time periods, depending on the court.

The case is then scrutinized by the West manuscript staff who check over one million citations per year. They also add parallel citations to cases. The statute citations in the case are also checked, and many are corrected. All of the other editorial enhancements, which will be explained in this chapter, are added at this time.

Slip opinions are next gathered into softbound advance sheets (Figure 1.3). Advance sheets allow you to read the decision in the reporter format without having to wait until enough opinions are accumulated to make an entire bound volume. Most of West's advance sheets are published on a weekly schedule. As you have learned in your classes, the rule of *stare decisis* demands access to the latest cases; law publishing has kept pace with this need for current cases either in print or on-line.

At the third stage of publication, the bound case reporter volumes appear (Figure 1.4). The bound volumes contain a large number of decisions arranged in the same sequence as they appeared in the advance sheets. The citation will be identical in the advance sheet and in the bound reporter so you do not have to recheck your citation once the opinion appears in the advance sheet format.

There is a distinction in case reporting between official and unofficial reporters. When a statute or a court order directs the publication of court reports, they are called official reports. The official reports are no more accurate than the unofficial reports; in fact, the unofficial reports came into existence because they could be published more quickly than the official re-

Figure 1.3 An Advance Sheet

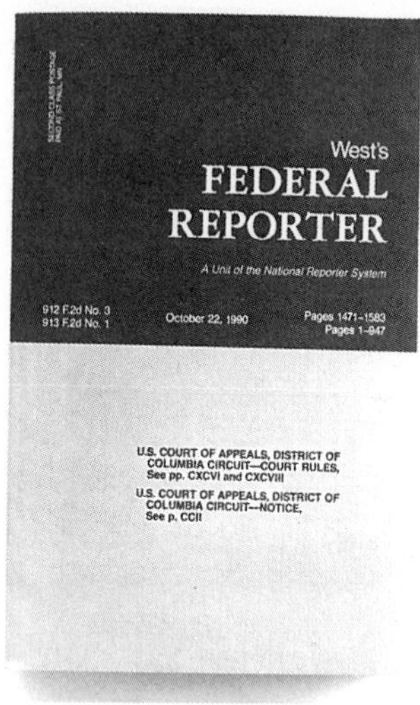

ports. Additionally, West editors may contact the court if clarification or corrections are needed, or if it appears that text has been omitted. Many times the corrections are initiated by the court itself. However, the official citation of a case, if available, should be cited. This is a citation format rule. If the unofficial reporter is also cited, remember to cite the official report first.

In re Green, 448 Pa. 338, 292 A.2d 387 (1972)
Official Unofficial

U.S. Supreme Court and Lower Federal Court Decisions

You will study the jurisdiction of the federal courts during your first year of law school. At the top of the federal judicial pyramid is the Supreme Court of the United States (Figure 1.5). Almost all of its business consists of reviewing the judgments of lower courts. These may be the judgments of state courts of last resort that dealt with questions of federal law, or they may be the decisions of lower federal courts. If a federal question arises in state litigation, that question must be pursued on appeal up through the state court system—to the *state courts of last resort*—before the case is eligible for review by the U.S. Supreme Court. The *lower federal courts* are the federal circuit courts of appeals and the federal district courts. Generally, the Supreme Court hears only cases that have already been appealed through a state appellate court or to one of the thirteen federal circuit courts of appeals.

The Supreme Court could not possibly hear all of the cases that come before it. It disposes of most appeals summarily by denying petitions for a *writ of certiorari.* This is a device used by the Court in choosing the cases it wishes to hear.

Figure 1.4
A Bound Case Reporter

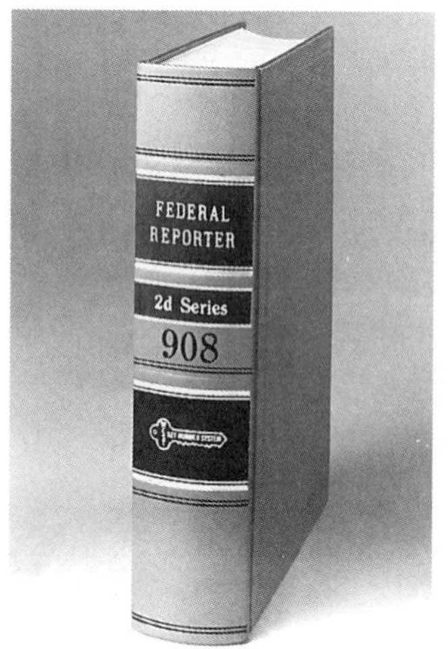

The decisions of the U.S. Supreme Court appear in published form in one official reporter and two unofficial reporters. The *United States Reports* (U.S.) is the official reporter for the Supreme Court. It is published by the U.S. Government Printing Office. As with many official publications, the advance sheets and bound volumes of the *United States Reports* appear very slowly. Almost two years pass between the announcement of a decision and its appearance in the advance sheet, and yet another year passes before it is included in a bound volume. The decisions of the U.S. Supreme Court also appear in the *Supreme Court Reporter* (S.Ct.) published by West and in the *United States Supreme Court Reports, Lawyers' Edition,* (L.Ed. and L.Ed.2d) published by Lawyers Co-operative Publishing Company. The WESTLAW SCT databases contain the Supreme Court decisions from the inception of the Court (1790). Although the citation format book, *A Uniform System of Citation,* requires only the official citation to the *United States Reports,* most citations include all three sources:

Figure 1.5
The Federal Judicial Pyramid

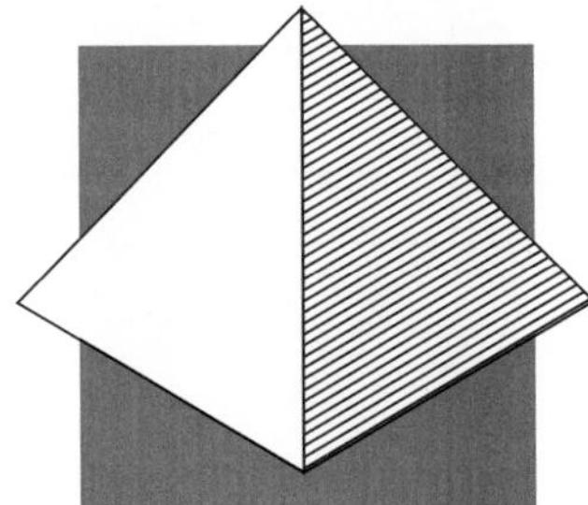

	Official Government reporter	West reporter	Lawyers Co-op reporter	
Hustler Magazine v. Falwell,	485 U.S. 46,	108 S.Ct. 876,	99 L. Ed.2d 41	(1988)
	U.S. Reports	*Supreme Court Reporter*	*Lawyers Edition*	

Many law firm libraries and some court libraries have only one of the bound sets available, so parallel citations can be a big help.

Another source for Supreme Court decisions is *United States Law Week (U.S.L.W.)* published on a weekly basis by the Bureau of National Affairs, Inc. *U.S.L.W.* is published in two volumes: One volume contains all of the U.S. Supreme Court decisions as well as other actions taken by the Court. The second volume publishes abstracts of what it considers important lower federal and state court opinions. Other than the on-line services, *U.S.L.W.* is the first place to find the full text of recent Supreme Court decisions in print format. *U.S.L.W.* is also available on WESTLAW.

Below the Supreme Court in the federal system are thirteen federal courts of appeals and numerous federal district courts (Figure 1.6). The jurisdiction of the federal courts of appeals, or circuit courts, is really very simple. It consists of appeals from decisions by district courts, together with appeals from decisions by federal administrative agencies, such as the Federal Communications Commission. The decisions of the federal courts of appeals since 1880 are published in West's *Federal Reporter* (F. and F.2d). West has also published a collection of earlier cases in a set called *Federal Cases*. Decisions of the courts of appeals, from the beginning of the court, are in the CTA databases on WESTLAW. You can also search in individual courts of appeals databases.

The jurisdiction of the district courts is the most complex part of the federal jurisdiction. For example, a case will be tried in district courts if it "arises under" federal law for purposes of federal trial court jurisdiction. In addition to these "arising under" cases, federal courts also have jurisdiction over civil cases involving parties from different states; these are known as diversity cases.

The criminal jurisdiction of the district courts includes all prosecutions for federal crimes. The decisions of the federal district courts since 1924 are published in West's *Federal Supplement* (F.Supp.). Decisions of district courts are in the DCT database in WESTLAW. Since the district courts are the federal trial courts and only a small percentage of their cases are reported in the West reporters, the DCT database on WESTLAW includes both cases that appear in the West reports and those that are unreported.

West's *Federal Rules Decisions* (F.R.D.), which began in 1940, is a specialized reporter that contains selected opinions of the U.S. district courts on matters related to the Federal Rules of Civil Procedure and Criminal Procedure. In addition to these decisions, the *Federal Rules Decisions* reporter includes articles dealing with federal rules. These articles from the West reporter are in the WESTLAW database Federal Rules Decisions (FEDRDTP), and the cases themselves appear in the DCT database.

Figure 1.6 The Federal Judicial Circuits

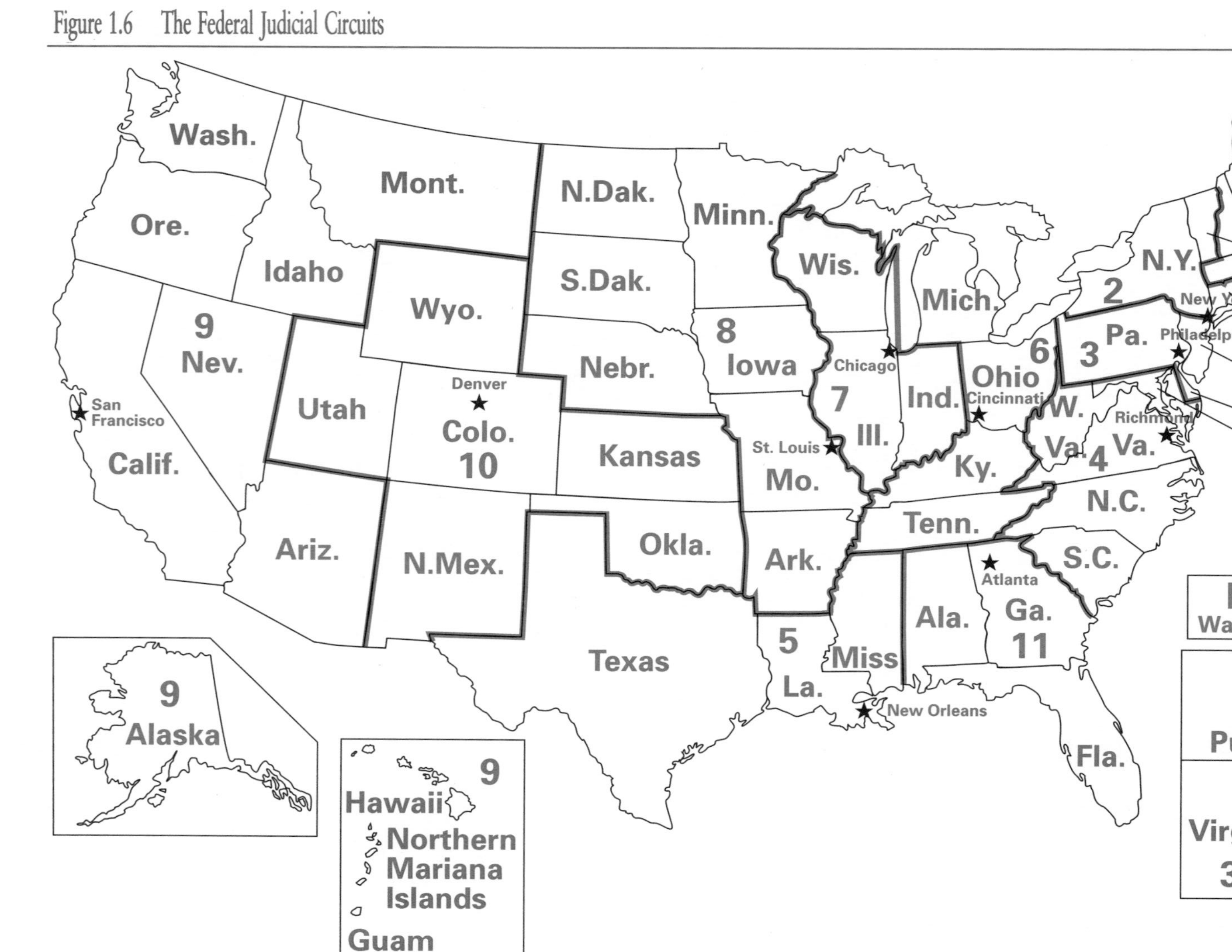

Decisions of Special Courts

A few special federal courts, such as the Tax Court, publish their own decisions. West publishes the *Bankruptcy Reporter,* which includes cases from the federal bankruptcy courts plus district court bankruptcy cases not reported in the *Federal Supplement.* West also publishes reporters compiling federal and state decisions in subject areas, such as the *Education Law Reporter.* The decisions from these reporters also appear on WESTLAW.

State Court Decisions

It is difficult to generalize about the structure of state courts since each state has a different structure. Suffice it to say that each state has either a triple-layered or a two-tiered hierarchy of courts.

About half the states still publish their own "official" reporters. Many states have ceased publishing their official reports, and attorneys rely on West's National Reporter System for reporting cases. In some states, the legislature or the courts have designated the West volumes as the official repository of state opinions. In other places, this has been done by default. It is surprising how informal much of this process is. Many states have discontinued their official reports because of long publication delays and untimely publication of new opinions. Even when states publish their own reporters, attorneys often use the West reporters because of the many editorial enhancements and because the headnotes link the researcher with the key number system, which we will discuss in the next chapter.

West's National Reporter System (NRS) is a set of reporters that divide the fifty states and the District of Columbia into seven national regions: Atlantic, North Eastern, North Western, Pacific, South Eastern, South Western, and Southern (Figure 1.7). The National Reporter System covers the appellate courts of all the states. The decisions of New York's highest court are reported in the *North Eastern Reporter* and the *New York Supplement.* The opinions of New York's lower courts, as well as those of the highest court, are reported in the *New York Supplement.* Similarly, California Supreme Court decisions appear in both the *Pacific Reporter* and the *California Reporter.* The opinions of California's lower courts, along with those of the California Supreme Court, are published in the *California Reporter.* The federal reporters published by West are also part of the National Reporter System.

The reporters in West's National Reporter System contain several special features. The advance sheets include a number of tables that later appear in the bound volume. The table that you will use most frequently is the Table of Cases Reported (Figure 1.8). If you are looking for a very recent case, you could search either WESTLAW or the National Reporter System advance sheets. Remember that the Table of Cases Reported in the advance sheets is cumulative for each volume. That means you only have to check the table in the most recent advance sheet for that volume.

Figure 1.7 West's National Reporter System

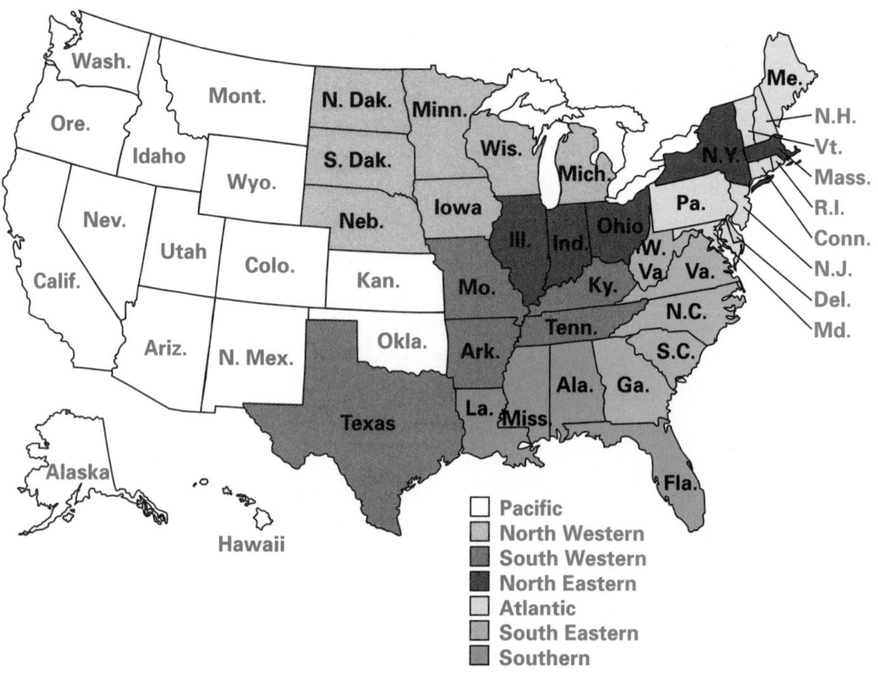

Take a few minutes to look at the special tables in the advance sheets in your library. You may one day need to find a listing of all judges sitting on a particular court or a listing of cases that cite the American Bar Association's Standards for Criminal Justice, for example. These tables can be found in the first few pages of each reporter following the Table of Cases Reported.

Cases from the regional reporters are also available on WESTLAW (Figure 1.9). Decisions of every state are also on-line in their own databases. The individual databases are retrospective to different dates so you need to check the WESTLAW *Database List* or type SCOPE when you enter a database. The SCOPE command tells you the type of documents available in a database and the scope of coverage for these documents. To search in a state court database, for example, you use the state postal abbreviation for that state, followed by **–CS** (Figure 1.10).

Deciphering a Case Citation

If someone hands you the legal citation of a case, you should be able to head to the correct volume and turn to the correct page without checking any indexes or asking for help. Cases that appear in reporters have a citation that consists of the name of the case; the volume of the reporter; the name of the reporter;

Figure 1.8 A Table of Cases Reported from an Advance Sheet

CASES REPORTED

	Page
Abboud v. Viscomi (Mem.)—N.J.	1286
Abington School Dist.; McCloskey by McCloskey v. (Mem.)—Pa.	329
Abington School Dist. v. Sportmaster (Mem.)—Pa.	329
Aceta; State v.—N.J.Super.A.D.	1317
A Child By Benigno-White, Matter of Adoption of—N.J.Super.Ch.	1345
Acmat Corp.; Gilbane Bldg. Co. v. (Mem.)—N.J.	1293
Adamar of New Jersey, Inc., Petition of—N.J.Super.A.D.	704
Adams v. Leager (Table)—Md.	272
Adderly; State v. (Mem.)—N.J.	1288
A.D.H., State in Interest of (Mem.)—N.J.	1303
Advanced Living, Inc. v. Montgomery County Bd. of Assessment Appeals—Pa.Cmwlth.	948
Advisory Committee on Professional Ethics No. 545, Matter of (Mem.)—N.J.	1274
Advisory Committee on Professional Ethics Opinion No. 562, Matter of (Mem.)—N.J.	1286
American Communication Installations, Ltd. v. Emory (Table)—Del.Supr.	203
AFSCME, Council 4, Locals 196, 318, 355, 478, 538, 562, 610 and 704; State v.—Conn.App.	517
A.N.; M. v.—D.C.App.	579
A.N.; R.N.M. v.—D.C.App.	579
Anam v. W.C.A.B. (Hahneman)—Pa. Cmwlth.	932
Andersen v. W.C.A.B. (Nat. Forge Co.)—Pa.Cmwlth.	971
Andrea W., In re—Me.	596
Anne Arundel County; Chu v.—Md.	250
A.P. Development Corp. v. Band (Mem.)—N.J.	1293
Arlequin; State v. (Mem.)—N.J.	1290
Armen; State v.—Me.	1143
Associated Mountain Top, Inc. v. Greate Bay Hotel and Casino, Inc. (Mem.)—N.J.	1294
Associated Mountain Top, Inc. v. Sands Hotel and Casino (Mem.)—N.J.	1294
Atlantic Home Insulation, Inc. v. James	

Figure 1.9 Regional Databases on WESTLAW

```
                          COPR. (C) WEST 1990 NO CLAIM TO ORIG. U.S. GOVT. WORKS
___WESTLAW DIRECTORY WELCOME SCREEN_______________________________P1______
 ___GENERAL STATE DATABASES:  WEST'S REGIONAL REPORTERS           P7______

                                CASE LAW
 ATL      Atlantic Reporter (CT DE DC ME MD NH NJ PA RI VT)
 NE       North Eastern Reporter (IL IN MA NY OH)
 NW       North Western Reporter (IA MI MN NE ND SD WI)
 PAC      Pacific Reporter (AK AZ CA CO HI ID KS MT NV NM OK OR UT WA WY)
 SE       South Eastern Reporter (GA NC SC VA WV)
 SO       Southern Reporter (AL FL LA MS)
 SW       South Western Reporter (AR KY MO TN TX)
Note:     Regional Reporter databases include quick opinions and any unreported
           cases.

 Related Databases:  To see a list of individual state case law databases,
 enter P6


If you wish to:
   Select a database, type its IDENTIFIER, e.g., ATL and press ENTER
   View information about a database, type SCOPE followed by its IDENTIFIER
     and press ENTER
   View the INDEX to State Databases, type P5 and press ENTER
```

Figure 1.10 A State Court Database on WESTLAW

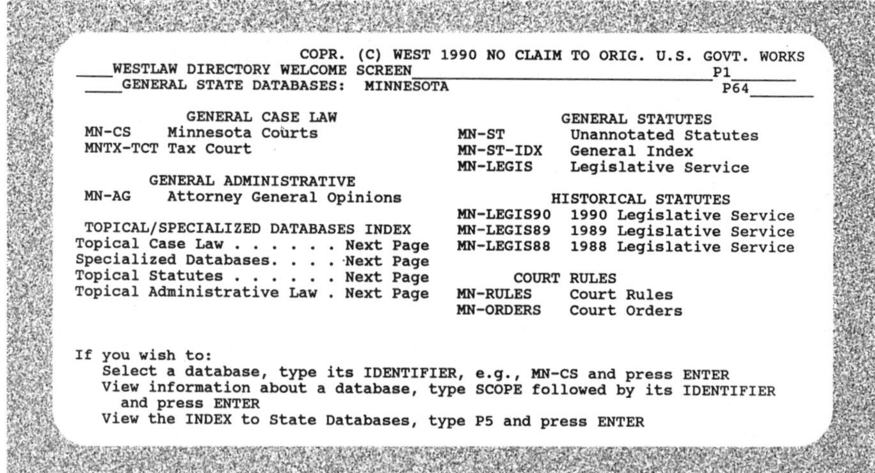

```
                    COPR. (C) WEST 1990 NO CLAIM TO ORIG. U.S. GOVT. WORKS
___WESTLAW DIRECTORY WELCOME SCREEN___________________________P1______
___GENERAL STATE DATABASES:  MINNESOTA________________________P64_____

         GENERAL CASE LAW                            GENERAL STATUTES
MN-CS     Minnesota Courts                MN-ST       Unannotated Statutes
MNTX-TCT Tax Court                        MN-ST-IDX   General Index
                                          MN-LEGIS    Legislative Service
     GENERAL ADMINISTRATIVE
MN-AG     Attorney General Opinions                 HISTORICAL STATUTES
                                          MN-LEGIS90  1990 Legislative Service
 TOPICAL/SPECIALIZED DATABASES INDEX      MN-LEGIS89  1989 Legislative Service
Topical Case Law . . . . . . Next Page    MN-LEGIS88  1988 Legislative Service
Specialized Databases. . . . Next Page
Topical Statutes . . . . . . Next Page          COURT RULES
Topical Administrative Law . Next Page    MN-RULES    Court Rules
                                          MN-ORDERS   Court Orders

If you wish to:
   Select a database, type its IDENTIFIER, e.g., MN-CS and press ENTER
   View information about a database, type SCOPE followed by its IDENTIFIER
     and press ENTER
   View the INDEX to State Databases, type P5 and press ENTER
```

the page number in the reporter where the case begins; and the year the case was decided:

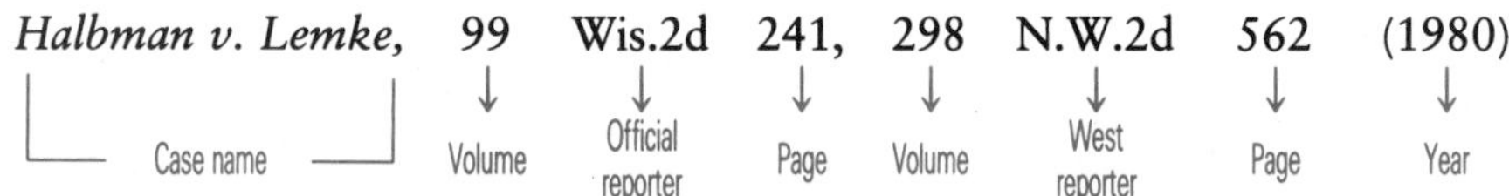

The citation may include a notation of the court deciding the case, or the court may be obvious from the reporter abbreviation, such as Wis.2d. A citation to a particular paragraph or sentence may also include the number of the page of the quotation:

298 N.W.2d 562, 564

↓ 562: Page case begins

↓ 564: Page of quotation

Although books may be your first choice, when the volume that you are looking for is not available, access WESTLAW and use FIND. You do not need to access a database identifier, simply type FI and your citation; for example, type **FI 298 N.W.2d 562** to find *Halbman v. Lemke.*

If cases appear only on WESTLAW (a very recent opinion or a case that does not appear in the West reporters), the citations will consist of WESTLAW cites. A WESTLAW cite appears on the screen in the upper left corner of slip opinions and unreported cases. Each WESTLAW cite consists of four parts: the year of the decision, WL (identifying WESTLAW as the place the document is located), a unique document number, and the jurisdiction in which the case was decided (Figure 1.11).

All of the rules for writing and deciphering legal citations appear in *A Uniform System of Citation,* published by the Harvard Law Review Associ-

Figure 1.11 A WESTLAW Cite of an Unreported Case

WESTLAW Cite

```
Citation                                 Page(P)        Database   Mode
Not Reported in F.Supp.      FOUND DOCUMENT P 1 OF 8    DCTU       P
(CITE AS: 1987 WL 9398 (E.D.PA.))

                          Derrick JONES
                               v.
    Superintendent Charles ZIMMERMAN and Deputy Superintendent Vaugh.
                        Civ. A. No. 86-6425.
            United States District Court, E.D. Pennsylvania.
                          April 15, 1987.
 Derrick Jones, in pro. per.
                      MEMORANDUM AND ORDER

 SHAPIRO, District Judge.

 *1 Plaintiff has filed a pro se 42 U.S.C. s 1983 civil rights action,
accompanied by a motion for leave to proceed in forma pauperis.  As it appears
plaintiff is unable to prepay the costs of commencing this action, leave to
proceed in forma pauperis is granted.
 Plaintiff, an inmate at Graterford prison, alleges that on or about October
20, 1986, following the death of a fellow inmate, he was locked in his cell
"without any written notice or reason given...." Plaintiff does not say how
long he was confined to his cell.  He claims that he was discriminated against
```

ation (Figure 1.12). It is commonly called the "Bluebook." The Bluebook has many shortcomings; it is sometimes more a hindrance than a help, and it does not yet handle citations to on-line databases well. Nevertheless, you will have to use the Bluebook during your entire legal career, so you should become acquainted with it now.

Parallel Citations

As we noted earlier, you will often find a string of citations after the case name:

In re Baby M, 109 N.J. 396, 537 A.2d 1227 (1988)

(109 N.J. 396: Official reporter; 537 A.2d 1227: Unofficial reporter)

A citation to the same case published in a different reporter is called a *parallel citation.* Parallel citations are different citations to the same exact case and not to different stages of a case. According to the Bluebook, a proper citation should always include parallel citations (except for the U.S. Supreme Court where only the official citation is required).

There are several ways to find a parallel citation if you only know one citation:

1. West's reporters provide the official citation if it is available (Figure 1.13a). However, since the official reporters are generally slow to be published, the official citation is not usually available at the time the regional reporter is published. Some of the official state reports cite to West's reporters. The reporters of the U.S. Supreme Court cases published by West and Lawyers Co-op both provide citations to the official *United States Reports* and to each other. The *United States Reports* does not supply any parallel citations.

Figure 1.12 A Page from A *Uniform System of Citation*

Cases 10

Basic Citation Forms 10.1

(a) United States (federal and state), Commonwealth, and other common law jurisdictions.

	In law review footnotes	In briefs and legal memoranda
filed but not decided	Smith v. Forbush, No. 90-345 (D. Mass. filed Sept. 18, 1990)	Smith v. Forbush, No. 90-345 (D. Mass. filed Sept. 18, 1990)
unpublished interim order	Smith v. Forbush, No. 90-345 (D. Mass. Oct. 25, 1990) (order granting preliminary injunction)	Smith v. Forbush, No. 90-345 (D. Mass. Oct. 25, 1990) (order granting preliminary injunction)
published interim order	Smith v. Forbush, 725 F. Supp. 1395 (D. Mass. 1990) (order granting preliminary injunction)	Smith v. Forbush, 725 F. Supp. 1395 (D. Mass. 1990) (order granting preliminary injunction)
unpublished decision	Smith v. Forbush, No. 90-345, slip op. at 6 (D. Mass. Dec. 4, 1990)	Smith v. Forbush, No. 90-345, slip op. at 6 (D. Mass. Dec. 4, 1990)
decision published in service only	Smith v. Forbush, 1990 Fed. Sec. L. Rep. (CCH) ¶ 102,342 (D. Mass. Dec. 4, 1990)	Smith v. Forbush, 1990 Fed. Sec. L. Rep. (CCH) ¶ 102,342 (D. Mass. Dec. 4, 1990)
decision published in newspaper only	Smith v. Forbush, N.Y.L.J., Dec. 5, 1990, at 1, col. 5 (D. Mass. Dec. 4, 1990)	Smith v. Forbush, N.Y.L.J., Dec. 5, 1990, at 1, col. 5 (D. Mass. Dec. 4, 1990)
published decision	Smith v. Forbush, 727 F. Supp. 1407, 1412 (D. Mass. 1990)	Smith v. Forbush, 727 F. Supp. 1407, 1412 (D. Mass. 1990)
appeal docketed	Smith v. Forbush, 727 F. Supp. 1407 (D. Mass. 1990), *appeal docketed*, No. 90-567 (1st Cir. Dec. 20, 1990)	Smith v. Forbush, 727 F. Supp. 1407 (D. Mass. 1990), appeal docketed, No. 90-567 (1st Cir. Dec. 20, 1990)
brief, record, or appendix	Brief for Appellant at 7, Smith v. Forbush, 925 F.2d 314 (1st Cir. 1991) (No. 90-567)	Brief for Appellant at 7, Smith v. Forbush, 925 F.2d 314 (1st Cir. 1991) (No. 90-567)
disposition on appeal	Smith v. Forbush, 925 F.2d 314, 335 (1st Cir. 1991)	Smith v. Forbush, 925 F.2d 314, 315 (1st Cir. 1991)
disposition in lower court showing subsequent history	Smith v. Forbush, 727 F. Supp. 1407, 1412 (D. Mass. 1990), *aff'd*, 925 F.2d 314 (1st Cir. 1991)	Smith v. Forbush, 727 F. Supp. 1407, 1412 (D. Mass. 1990), aff'd, 925 F.2d 314 (1st Cir. 1991)
petition for certiorari filed	Smith v. Forbush, 925 F.2d 314 (1st Cir. 1991), *petition for cert. filed*, 60 U.S.L.W. 3422 (U.S. Jan. 14, 1992) (No. 92-212)	Smith v. Forbush, 925 F.2d 314 (1st Cir. 1991), petition for cert. filed, 60 U.S.L.W. 3422 (U.S. Jan. 14, 1992) (No. 92-212)

Figure 1.13 Four Ways of Finding Parallel Citations

(a) A West Reporter

Official Citation — 109 N.J. 396

MATTER OF BABY M N.J. **1227**
Cite as 537 A.2d 1227 (N.J. 1988)

In the Matter of BABY M, a pseudonym for an actual person.

Supreme Court of New Jersey.

Argued Sept. 14, 1987.
Decided Feb. 3, 1988.

Natural father and his wife brought suit seeking to enforce surrogate parenting agreement, to compel surrender of infant born to surrogate mother, to restrain any interference with their custody of infant, and to terminate surrogate mother's parental rights to allow adoption of child by wife of natural father. The Superior Court, Chancery Division/Family Part, Bergen County, 217 N.J.Super. 313, 525 A.2d 1128, held that surrogate contract was valid, ordered that mother's parental rights be terminated and that sole custody of child be granted to natural father, and authorized adoption of child by father's wife. Mother

2. Infants ⚷**19.4**

Adoption of child through private placement is very much disfavored in New Jersey, although permitted.

3. Contracts ⚷**105**

Surrogate parenting contract's provision for payment of money to mother for her services and payment of fee to infertility center whose major role with respect to contract was as "finder" of mother whose child was to be adopted and as arranger of all proceedings that led to adoption, was illegal and perhaps criminal, under laws prohibiting use of money in connection with adoptions. N.J.S.A. 9:3–54.

4. Adoption ⚷**7.3**

Surrogate parenting contract's provision for termination of mother's parental rights violated laws requiring proof of parental unfitness or abandonment before termination of parental rights is ordered or

(b) A Digest

Baby M, Matter of, NJ, 537 A2d 1227, 109 NJ 396, on remand 542 A2d 52, 225 NJSuper 267.—Adop 7.3, 7.5, 7.6(1); App & E 843(2); Child 20; Const Law 82(10), 225.1; Contracts 105, 108(2); Infants 19.2(2), 19.3(2), 19.4, 85, 155, 156, 157, 232; Parent & C 2(16), 2(17).
Baby M, Matter of, NJSuperCh, 542 A2d 52, 225 NJSuper 267.—Child 20; Inj 96.
Baby M., Matter of, NJSuperCh, 525 A2d 1128, 217 NJSuper 313, certification gr 526 A2d 203, 107 NJ 140, aff in part, rev in part 537 A2d 1227, 109 NJ 396, on remand 542 A2d 52, 225 NJ-Super 267—Abort .50; Child 20; Const Law 70.1(9), 82(10), 224(1), 225.1, 274(5), 276(1); Contracts 1, 10(1), 94(1), 95(1), 110, 143.5, 147(2), 152, 169, 187(1); Fraud 3; Infants 155, 200;

2. If you know the name of the case, check the Table of Cases in the digest that covers the jurisdiction where your case was published, and you will find all of the parallel citations (Figure 1.13b). Digests will be discussed in the next chapter.
3. You can easily find parallel citations by using either *Shepard's* citators (either in print or on WESTLAW) or Insta-Cite, which is part of the WESTLAW service (Figure 1.13c). These services will be explained in a later chapter.
4. When you have the official citation and need the West citation, use the *National Reporter Blue Book,* published by West. It will provide you with parallel citations to West's National Reporter System. Just look up your citation, and you will find the West citation (Figure 1.13d).

Parts of a Case

Since you will be spending most of your waking moments, or at least your semiconscious moments, in law school reading cases, it is important that you understand the structure of a case. We will discuss the parts of a case in a reporter and on WESTLAW.

Figure 1.13 Four Ways of Finding Parallel Citations (continued)

(c) *Shepard's* and Insta-Cite

```
                                 SHEPARD'S  (Rank 1 of 2)          Page 1 of 3
CITATIONS TO: 537 A.2d 1227
CITATOR: ATLANTIC REPORTER CITATIONS
COVERAGE: First Shepard's volume through Dec. 1990 Supplement
Retrieval                                     Headnote
   No.     --Analysis-- -----Citation------     No.
              Same Text (109 N.J. 396)
              Same Text ( 77 A.L.R.4th 1)
    1      SC Same Case 525 A.2d 1128
           SC Same Case 526 A.2d 203
    2                   543 A.2d at 45           16
    3                   543 A.2d 925, 932         2
    4                   543 A.2d 925, 932         3
    5                   543 A.2d 925, 939         4
    6                   547 A.2d 691, 696        26
    7                   549 A.2d 792, 813
    8                   555 A.2d 1149, 1157      20
    9                   555 A.2d 1149, 1158      21
   10                   558 A.2d 1377, 1381       6
   11                   558 A.2d 1377, 1386      31

NOTE:  Check Shepard's PreView, Insta-Cite, and WESTLAW as a Citator
Copyright (C) 1990 McGraw-Hill, Inc.; Copyright (C) 1990 West Publishing Co.
```

```
                                 INSTA-CITE                   Page    1 of     2
CITATION: 537 A.2d 1227
      1  Matter of Baby M., 107 N.J. 49, 526 A.2d 138 (N.J., Nov 21, 1986)
           Related Reference
      2  Matter of Baby M., 107 N.J. 66, 526 A.2d 150 (N.J., Dec 16, 1986)
           Related Reference
      3  Matter of Baby M., 217 N.J.Super. 313, 525 A.2d 1128, 55 U.S.L.W. 2544
              (N.J.Super.Ch., Mar 31, 1987) (NO. FM-25314-86E)
           Certification Granted by
      4  Matter of Baby M., 107 N.J. 140, 526 A.2d 203 (N.J., Apr 07, 1987)
           AND Judgment Affirmed in Part, Reversed in Part by
 =>   5  MATTER OF BABY M, 109 N.J. 396, 537 A.2d 1227, 77 A.L.R.4th 1,
              56 U.S.L.W. 2442 (N.J., Feb 03, 1988) (NO. A-39 SEPT TERM 1987)
           On Remand to
      6  Matter of Baby M, 225 N.J.Super. 267, 542 A.2d 52
              (N.J.Super.Ch., Apr 06, 1988) (NO. FM-25314-86E, A-39-87)


Note: DIRECT HISTORY: Coverage begins - Federal 1754, State 1938.
      PRECEDENTIAL HISTORY: Coverage begins 1972.  For earlier history use
      Shepard's (SH).  Check Shepard's PreView (SP) and WESTLAW as a citator.
(C) Copyright West Publishing Company 1990
```

(d) The *National Reporter Blue Book*

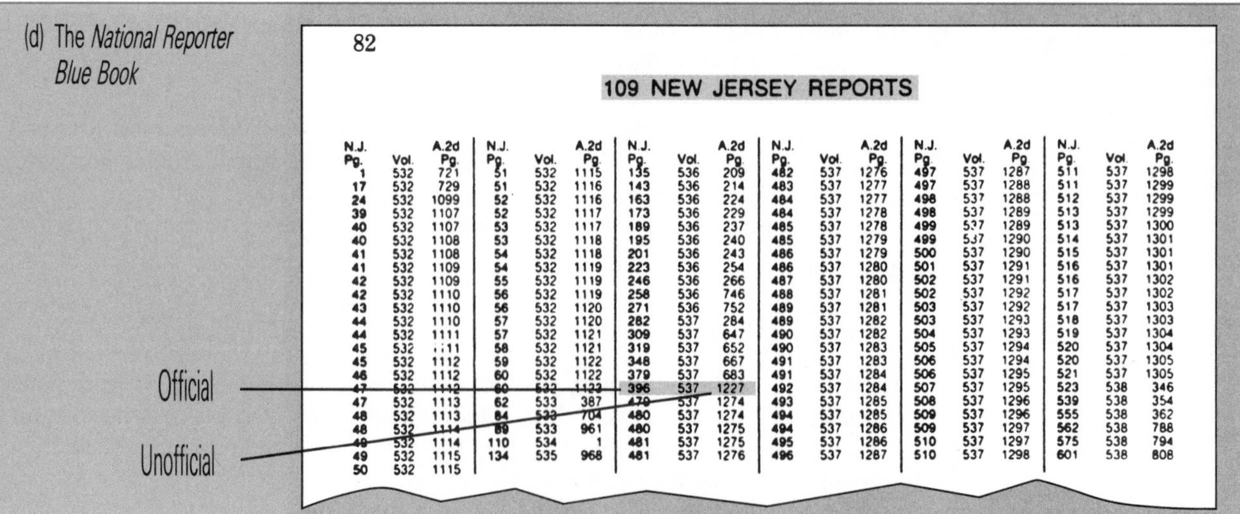

82

109 NEW JERSEY REPORTS

N.J. Pg.	Vol.	A.2d Pg.	N.J. Pg.	Vol.	A.2d Pg.	N.J. Pg.	Vol.	A.2d Pg.	N.J. Pg.	Vol.	A.2d Pg.	N.J. Pg.	Vol.	A.2d Pg.	N.J. Pg.	Vol.	A.2d Pg.
1	532	721	51	532	1115	135	536	209	482	537	1276	497	537	1287	511	537	1298
17	532	729	51	532	1116	143	536	214	483	537	1277	497	537	1288	511	537	1299
24	532	1099	52	532	1116	163	536	224	484	537	1277	498	537	1288	512	537	1299
39	532	1107	52	532	1117	173	536	229	484	537	1278	498	537	1289	513	537	1299
40	532	1107	53	532	1117	189	536	237	485	537	1278	499	537	1289	513	537	1300
40	532	1108	53	532	1118	195	536	240	485	537	1279	499	537	1290	514	537	1301
41	532	1108	54	532	1118	201	536	243	486	537	1279	500	537	1290	515	537	1301
41	532	1109	54	532	1119	223	536	254	486	537	1280	501	537	1291	516	537	1301
42	532	1109	55	532	1119	246	536	266	487	537	1280	502	537	1291	516	537	1302
42	532	1110	56	532	1119	258	536	746	488	537	1281	502	537	1292	517	537	1302
43	532	1110	56	532	1120	271	536	752	489	537	1281	503	537	1292	517	537	1303
44	532	1110	57	532	1120	282	537	284	489	537	1282	503	537	1293	518	537	1303
44	532	1111	57	532	1121	309	537	647	490	537	1282	504	537	1293	519	537	1304
45	532	1111	58	532	1121	319	537	652	490	537	1283	505	537	1294	520	537	1304
45	532	1112	59	532	1122	348	537	667	491	537	1283	506	537	1294	520	537	1305
46	532	1112	60	532	1122	379	537	683	491	537	1284	506	537	1295	521	537	1305
47	532	1112	60	532	1123	396	537	1227	492	537	1284	507	537	1295	523	538	346
47	532	1113	62	533	387	479	537	1274	493	537	1285	508	537	1296	539	538	354
48	532	1113	84	533	704	480	537	1274	494	537	1285	509	537	1296	555	538	362
48	532	1114	89	533	961	480	537	1275	494	537	1286	509	537	1297	562	538	788
49	532	1114	110	534	1	481	537	1275	495	537	1286	510	537	1297	575	538	794
49	532	1115	134	535	968	481	537	1276	496	537	1287	510	537	1298	601	538	808
50	532	1115															

As we walk through the parts of a case, we will compare the parts in a West reporter to the fields on WESTLAW (Figure 1.14). In the published reporters, we will refer to the *parts* or *components* of a case. On WESTLAW, the parts of a case are called *fields*. A field is a unique section in a case, such as a case name or the name of the court. It is more efficient and more economical to limit your search to a particular field when using WESTLAW. Field searching will be discussed in more detail in the next chapter.

Court

Particular reporters generally correspond to particular courts. When you choose a particular reporter, for instance, the *Federal Supplement*, you will be choosing a particular court of jurisdiction; that is, cases from the federal district court. Generally, the reporters are organized by jurisdiction.

Figure 1.14 Parts of a Case

(a) Parts of a Case and Fields on WESTLAW

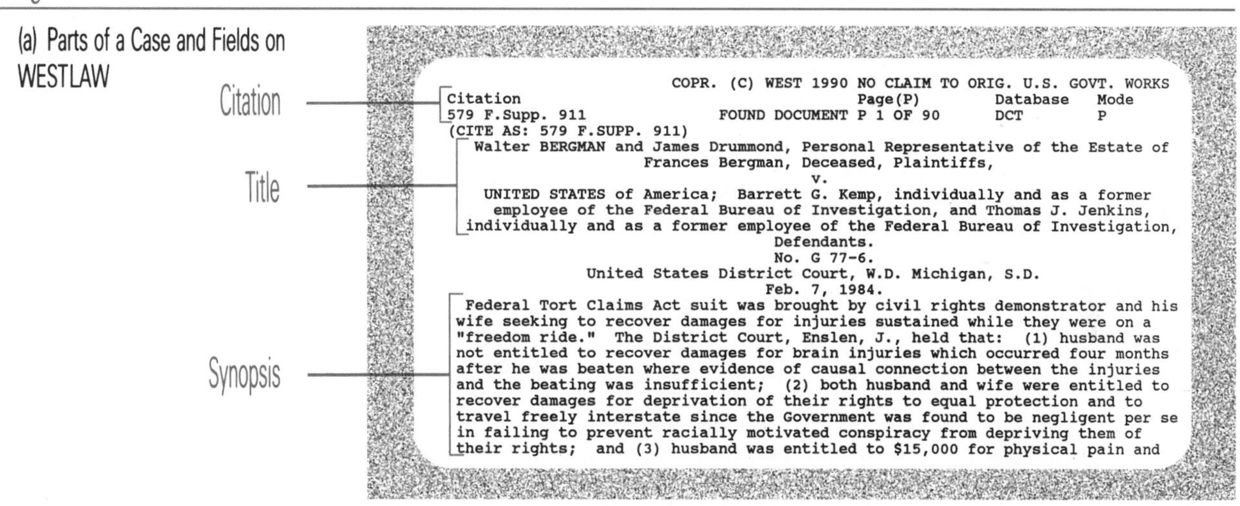


```
                    COPR. (C) WEST 1990 NO CLAIM TO ORIG. U.S. GOVT. WORKS
Citation                                   Page(P)       Database   Mode
579 F.Supp. 911             FOUND DOCUMENT P 1 OF 90     DCT        P
(CITE AS: 579 F.SUPP. 911)
  Walter BERGMAN and James Drummond, Personal Representative of the Estate of
                 Frances Bergman, Deceased, Plaintiffs,
                                   v.
   UNITED STATES of America;  Barrett G. Kemp, individually and as a former
    employee of the Federal Bureau of Investigation, and Thomas J. Jenkins,
 individually and as a former employee of the Federal Bureau of Investigation,
                              Defendants.
                              No. G 77-6.
             United States District Court, W.D. Michigan, S.D.
                             Feb. 7, 1984.
 Federal Tort Claims Act suit was brought by civil rights demonstrator and his
wife seeking to recover damages for injuries sustained while they were on a
"freedom ride."  The District Court, Enslen, J., held that:  (1) husband was
not entitled to recover damages for brain injuries which occurred four months
after he was beaten where evidence of causal connection between the injuries
and the beating was insufficient;  (2) both husband and wife were entitled to
recover damages for deprivation of their rights to equal protection and to
travel freely interstate since the Government was found to be negligent per se
in failing to prevent racially motivated conspiracy from depriving them of
their rights;  and (3) husband was entitled to $15,000 for physical pain and
```

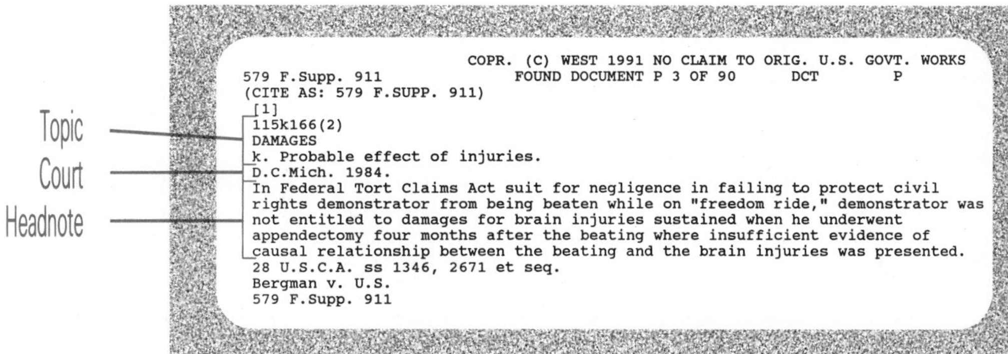


```
                    COPR. (C) WEST 1991 NO CLAIM TO ORIG. U.S. GOVT. WORKS
579 F.Supp. 911             FOUND DOCUMENT P 3 OF 90     DCT        P
(CITE AS: 579 F.SUPP. 911)
[1]
115k166(2)
DAMAGES
k. Probable effect of injuries.
D.C.Mich. 1984.
In Federal Tort Claims Act suit for negligence in failing to protect civil
rights demonstrator from being beaten while on "freedom ride," demonstrator was
not entitled to damages for brain injuries sustained when he underwent
appendectomy four months after the beating where insufficient evidence of
causal relationship between the beating and the brain injuries was presented.
28 U.S.C.A. ss 1346, 2671 et seq.
Bergman v. U.S.
579 F.Supp. 911
```

Figure 1.14 Parts of Case (continued)

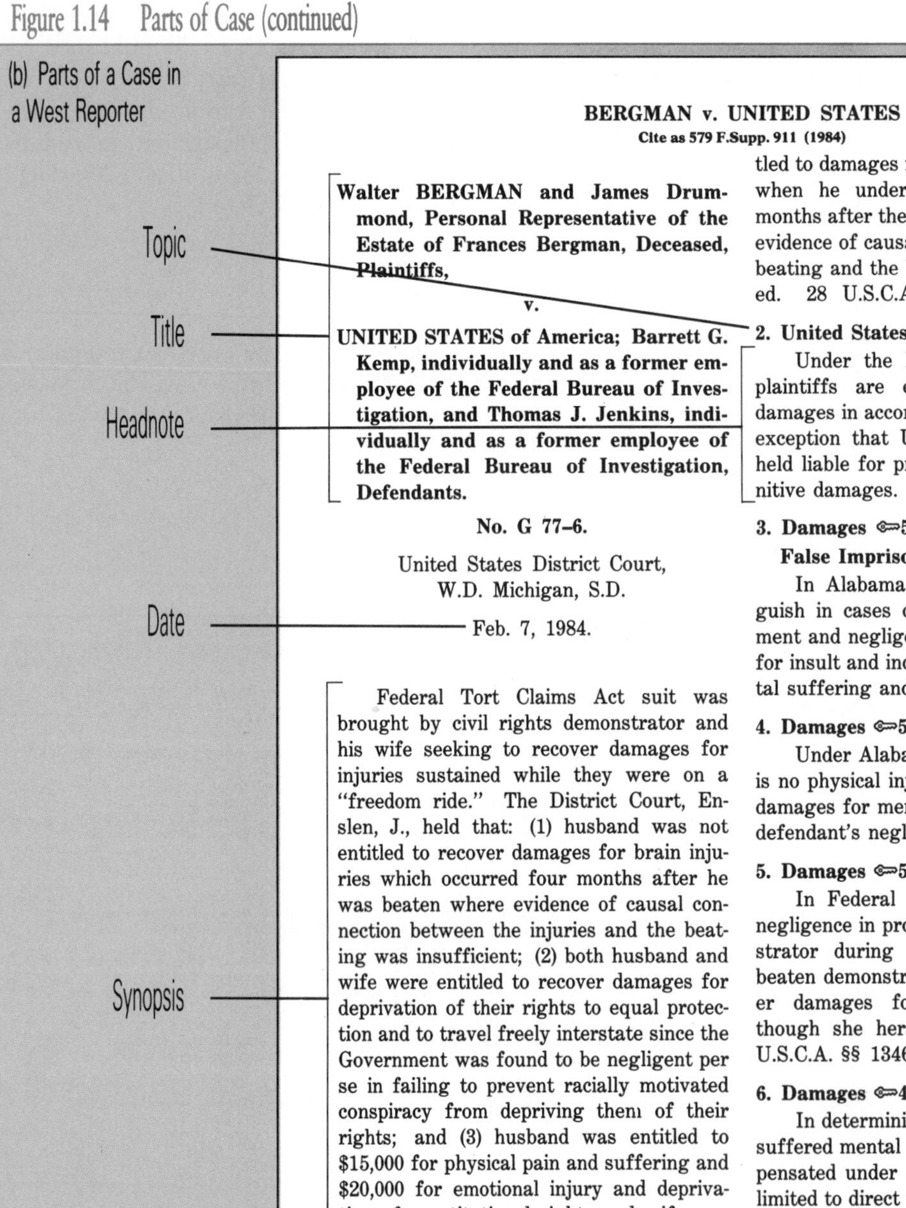

BERGMAN v. UNITED STATES 911

Cite as 579 F.Supp. 911 (1984)

Walter BERGMAN and James Drummond, Personal Representative of the Estate of Frances Bergman, Deceased, Plaintiffs,

v.

UNITED STATES of America; Barrett G. Kemp, individually and as a former employee of the Federal Bureau of Investigation, and Thomas J. Jenkins, individually and as a former employee of the Federal Bureau of Investigation, Defendants.

No. G 77–6.

United States District Court, W.D. Michigan, S.D.

Feb. 7, 1984.

Federal Tort Claims Act suit was brought by civil rights demonstrator and his wife seeking to recover damages for injuries sustained while they were on a "freedom ride." The District Court, Enslen, J., held that: (1) husband was not entitled to recover damages for brain injuries which occurred four months after he was beaten where evidence of causal connection between the injuries and the beating was insufficient; (2) both husband and wife were entitled to recover damages for deprivation of their rights to equal protection and to travel freely interstate since the Government was found to be negligent per se in failing to prevent racially motivated conspiracy from depriving them of their rights; and (3) husband was entitled to $15,000 for physical pain and suffering and $20,000 for emotional injury and deprivation of constitutional rights and wife was entitled to recover $15,000 for emotional injury and deprivation of her rights.

Judgment accordingly.

1. Damages ⚷166(2)

In Federal Tort Claims Act suit for negligence in failing to protect civil rights demonstrator from being beaten while on "freedom ride," demonstrator was not entitled to damages for brain injuries sustained when he underwent appendectomy four months after the beating where insufficient evidence of causal relationship between the beating and the brain injuries was presented. 28 U.S.C.A. §§ 1346, 2671 et seq.

2. United States ⚷78(14), 110, 142

Under the Federal Tort Claims Act, plaintiffs are entitled to compensatory damages in accordance with state law, with exception that United States may not be held liable for prejudgment interest or punitive damages. 28 U.S.C.A. § 2674.

3. Damages ⚷52, 54

False Imprisonment ⚷34

In Alabama, damages for mental anguish in cases of assault, false imprisonment and negligence, include compensation for insult and indignity, hurt feelings, mental suffering and fright.

4. Damages ⚷50

Under Alabama law, even where there is no physical injury, plaintiff may recover damages for mental anguish occasioned by defendant's negligence.

5. Damages ⚷51

In Federal Tort Claims Act suit for negligence in protecting civil rights demonstrator during "freedom ride," wife of beaten demonstrator was entitled to recover damages for mental anguish even though she herself was not beaten. 28 U.S.C.A. §§ 1346, 2671 et seq.

6. Damages ⚷48

In determining whether or not plaintiff suffered mental anguish which can be compensated under Alabama law, court is not limited to direct testimony relating feelings of indignity, mental suffering and fright; mental anguish may properly be inferred as natural and usual consequences from all of the circumstances.

7. Damages ⚷49.10

In Federal Tort Claims Act suit for negligence in protecting civil rights demonstrator during "freedom ride," demonstrators were entitled to damages for mental anguish. 28 U.S.C.A. §§ 1346, 2671 et seq.

Case Name

Every case has a name. Most cases are named for the parties (usually two) involved in the lawsuit to indicate who is suing whom (e.g., *Bergman v. United States*). Some cases may have only one name with a Latin phrase attached (e.g., *In re Seiferth*). In a criminal case, since the state brings the action, the first party will often be the jurisdiction itself (e.g., *State v. Birditt*).

When a case begins in the trial court, the first name is the plaintiff, or the party bringing the suit, and the name after the "v." is the defendant. On appeal, the name of the petitioner or appellant will be listed first, the name of the respondent or appellee will be listed second. Therefore, if the defendant in the trial court brings an appeal, his or her name may be listed first in the appellate case.

When you read a case in one of the reporters or on WESTLAW, you will often find several plaintiffs, defendants, or cross-complainants. Correct citation form requires that only the first-named plaintiff and the first-named defendant be listed. The case name that appears at the top of each page in the reporters is not in correct citation format and should not be followed as an example of Bluebook format. For example, the following appears at the top of the page for the case at 441 F.2d 1061:

Local 13, Int. Longshoremen's & W.U. v. Pacific Mar. Ass'n

The correct Bluebook format for the case name would be *Local 13, Int'l Longshoremen's & Warehousemen's Union v. Pacific Maritime Ass'n.*

Docket Number

When a case is filed in the court clerk's office, it is assigned a docket number that remains with the case until it is decided. Typically, the first two numbers indicate the year that the case was filed. The docket number is printed below the name of the case. On WESTLAW, you can search for a case by docket number by simply typing the number in the correct database.

Date

A reporter or WESTLAW will indicate the exact month, day, and year that the case was decided. For citation purposes, cite only the year.

Synopsis

Editors at West write a synopsis or brief description of each case that appears in the West reporters. You will find the synopsis below the date. Most synopses contain the following information: the facts of the case, the name and holding of the lower court judge, the holding of the court, and the name of the judge writing the opinion. If you have many cases to read, you can quickly scan the synopses to weed out the irrelevant cases, but be advised that the synopsis is not part of the opinion. It is a helpful editorial enhancement prepared by the publisher. If you are looking in a jurisdiction that has an official reporter in which the court writes a synopsis, you may get *two* synopses—one from West and one from the court.

Judge

The judge is listed both in the synopsis or syllabus of a case and on a separate line preceding the opinion. There is no manual index of judges' names that lists all cases decided by specific judges, but you can search for an opinion written by a particular judge by using an on-line service. On WESTLAW, you simply search in the judge (JU) field.

Headnotes

Court decisions typically contain at least one legal issue. An issue is the question raised where the rules of law impinge on the facts of the case. The West editors decipher the legal issues from cases and summarize each issue in a headnote.. Each headnote is usually one sentence. Headnotes appear in the case after the synopsis, but before the opinion. A headnote in a West reporter begins with a number in boldface type followed by a topic and then by a key number (Figure 1.15a). Headnotes are numbered so you can use them as a table of contents to the case. Numbers, corresponding to the headnote numbers appear in brackets in the text of the opinion. The number in brackets indicates that this is covered by that particular headnote (Figure 1.15b).

The next part of the headnote after the number is a term or phrase, which is the topic under which West has classified that particular legal issue. After the topic is a key number. The key number represents a specific aspect or subsection of the topic. For example, under the topic Damages, key number 50 covers "Physical injury, symptoms, or impact." The West editors classify a case under all the applicable topics and key numbers. To find out what the key number stands for, consult a West digest. Digests are books that group headnotes from cases under different topics of law; they are arranged by topics and key numbers. Once you find a relevant topic and key number, you can continue with the digests, or you can search for the topic on WESTLAW (as explained in the next chapter). The lines of text in the digest are actually the headnote itself; that is, they are an annotation of one of the legal issues in the case.

Writing headnotes is an art, not a science. Two different editors will see different sets of legal issues in a case. As in the debate over whether Hank Aaron or Babe Ruth was the greater ballplayer, there is no "correct" answer. Look at the headnotes in each of the three versions of a U.S. Supreme Court case (from the three reporters discussed earlier in this chapter) and see how different they are (Figure 1.16a–c). Note that the West reporter contains thirteen short headnotes while the Lawyers Co-op reporter contains two longer headnotes and a set of references to other related materials. The official *United States Reports* does not contain any headnotes per se, but it does include a long synopsis of the case.

Figure 1.15 Headnote Numbers

(a) Headnote at Beginning of case

912 579 FEDERAL SUPPLEMENT

8. Conspiracy ⚿13

In Federal Tort Claims Act suit for negligence in protecting civil rights demonstrators during "freedom ride," demonstrators were entitled to damages for deprivation of their constitutional rights to equal protection and freedom of interstate travel where United States was found to be negligent per se under Alabama law in part because it violated its statutory duty to prevent racially motivated conspiracy from depriving freedom riders of equal protection. 42 U.S.C.A. § 1986.

9. Civil Rights ⚿13.17(5, 6)
Damages ⚿130(1)

In Federal Tort Claims Act suit for negligence in protecting civil rights demonstrator from being beaten while on "freedom ride," demonstrator was entitled to damages of $15,000 for his physical pain and suffering, $20,000 for emotional injury and deprivation of constitutional rights. 28 U.S.C.A. §§ 1346, 2671 et seq.

OPINION ON DAMAGES

ENSLEN, District Judge.

Plaintiffs in this action under the Federal Tort Claims Act (FTCA) are Dr. Walter Bergman and the personal representative of the estate of his late wife, Frances Bergman. Both Walter and Frances Bergman were among the "freedom riders" who traveled by bus into the South in May, 1961 to test a recent pronouncement by the United States Supreme Court that the Constitution required racial equality in interstate transportation facilities. Their encounter with a conspiracy of violent racism in Alabama was described in detail by this Court in an earlier opinion. *Bergman v. United States,* 565 F.Supp. 1353 (W.D.MI. 1983). That decision followed upon trial of the United States' liability for the injuries plaintiffs suffered during their journey into Alabama.[1] I held that the federal Government was negligent in failing to take steps available to it to avoid the violence, and concluded that,

Topic

As we have just seen, topics are the main classifications for cases. In a library, you would look at a West digest volume for the topic that you need. On WESTLAW, the topic is in the topic field and in the digest field.

Attorneys

The names of counsel are found preceding the opinion in a decision. If you need the briefs for a case at some time during your legal career, you may want to contact one of the attorneys. Since WESTLAW adds the city and state where the attorney practices, it is very easy to contact the attorney. When you begin your legal career, you may also want to use the attorney (AT) field in WESTLAW to prepare for an interview by searching for the attorney with whom you will be interviewing.

Figure 1.15 Headnote Numbers (continued)

(b) Headnote Reference in Text of Opinion

Text Related to Headnote 8

guish which can be compensated under Alabama law, the Court is not limited to direct testimony relating feelings of indignity, mental suffering and fright. Mental anguish may properly be inferred as a natural and usual consequence from all of the circumstances in a case such as this. *Standard Oil Co. v. Humphries, supra,* 96 So. at 631; *Harrison v. Mitchell, supra,* 391 So.2d at 1040. Dr. Bergman's description of the atmosphere of violence and the apprehension of the group, and the evidence of Frances Bergman's expressions of fear during the beatings, provide some direct indication of the emotional impact of the circumstances. I find that in light of these facts, and given the threat of violence on the bus and in Birmingham, the beatings of Bergman and the others, and the knowledge that the police could not be counted on to protect them, the fright and mental anguish the Bergmans suffered must have been profound.

[8] In addition to these injuries, the Bergmans were clearly deprived of their constitutional rights to equal protection of the law and to travel freely interstate. If this were an action to redress violations of civil rights under federal law, the deprivation of the substantive rights involved here would play some role in determining the scope of the intangible injury sustained. *Brandon v. Allen,* 719 F.2d 151 (CA 6 1983); *Green v. Francis,* 705 F.2d 846 (CA 6 1983); *Baskin v. Parker,* 602 F.2d 1205 (CA 5 1979); *Lenard v. Argento,* 699 F.2d 874 (CA 7), *cert. den.* — U.S. —, 104 S.Ct. 69, 78 L.Ed.2d 84 (1983); *Herrera v. Valentine,* 653 F.2d 1220 (CA 8 1981); *Corriz v. Naranjo,* 667 F.2d 892 (CA 10, 1981), *appeal dismissed per stipulation,* 458 U.S. 1123, 103 S.Ct. 5, 73 L.Ed.2d 1394 (1982). *Carey v. Piphus,* 435 U.S. 247, 98 S.Ct. 1042, 55 L.Ed.2d 252 (1978), is not to the contrary. In that case, the Supreme Court held that in the absence of proof of actual damages, plaintiffs whose procedural due process rights were violated were entitled to only nominal damages. Similarly, in *Nekolny v. Painter,* 653 F.2d 1164 (CA 7 1981), *cert. den.* 455 U.S. 1021, 102 S.Ct. 1719, 72 L.Ed.2d 139 (1982), the Seventh Circuit denied a substantial recovery to the plaintiffs, where they had failed to show any actual emotional injury.[23] Here, the Bergmans were not only deprived of important substantive rights, but Dr. Bergman was brutally beaten, and both he and his wife were subjected to extreme emotional stress.

The United States argues that in this negligence action under the FTCA, it would be inappropriate to take into account the constitutional aspect of the injury the Bergmans sustained, and that the Court may only consider whatever physical and emotional impact the assaults may have had on the Bergmans. It is true that a plaintiff may not sue the United States directly under the FTCA for violations of the federal constitution. *Birnbaum v. United States,* 588 F.2d 319 (CA 2 1978); *Diminnie v. United States,* 522 F.Supp. 1192 (E.D.MI. 1981). But this case presents a unique situation, where state negligence law incorporates a federal duty. This Court has found that the United States was negligent *per se* under Alabama law in part because it violated its statutory duty under 42 U.S.C. § 1986 to prevent the racially motivated conspiracy from depriving the freedom riders of the equal protection of the laws.

One of the elements encompassed in the finding of negligence *per se* is that the injuries suffered by the Plaintiffs were of the type contemplated by the statute violated. Clearly, the deprivation of the right to equal protection and to travel freely interstate falls within the category of injuries contemplated by § 1986. *See, Bergman v. United States, supra,* 565 F.Supp. at 1394–

Figure 1.16 Variations in Headnotes

(a) United States Reports

112 OCTOBER TERM, 1987

Syllabus 485 U. S.

CITY OF ST. LOUIS *v.* PRAPROTNIK

CERTIORARI TO THE UNITED STATES COURT OF APPEALS FOR THE EIGHTH CIRCUIT

No. 86–772. Argued October 7, 1987—Decided March 2, 1988

Two years after respondent, a management-level employee in one of petitioner city's agencies, successfully appealed a temporary suspension to petitioner's Civil Service Commission (Commission), he was transferred

1. Petitioner's failure to timely object under Federal Rule of Civil Procedure 51 to a jury instruction on municipalities' § 1983 liability for their employees' unconstitutional acts does not deprive this Court of jurisdiction to determine the proper legal standard for imposing such liability. The same legal issue was raised by petitioner's motions for summary judgment and a directed verdict, was considered and decided by the Court of Appeals, and is likely to recur in § 1983 litigation against municipalities. Review in this Court will not undermine the policy of judicial efficiency that underlies Rule 51. Pp. 118–121.

2. The Court of Appeals applied an incorrect legal standard for determining when isolated decisions by municipal officials or employees may expose the municipality to § 1983 liability. The identification of officials having "final policymaking authority" is a question of state (including local) law, rather than a question of fact for the jury. Here, it appears that petitioner's City Charter gives the authority to set employment policy to the Mayor and Aldermen, who are empowered to enact ordinances,

Opinion

We are now to the actual text of the judge's decision, which is called the opinion. An opinion is a court's written explanation of why it did what it did. The structure of an opinion includes the nature of the case, a general statement of the issues presented, the facts, the errors assigned, and a dispositional section.

Opinions may be unanimous. That used to be good form, but today it is less frequent. This means that you may find other opinions after the majority's statement. A dissenting opinion is written by a single judge or a minority of judges who disagree with the result. There may also be concurring opinions when a judge or judges agree with the result of the main opinion but not with

Figure 1.16 Variations in Headnotes (continued)

(b) Supreme Court Reporter

916 108 SUPREME COURT REPORTER

findings that decisions of supervisors were not individually reviewed for substantive priority by higher supervisory officials and that civil service commission decided appeals from such decisions in some circumscribed manner that gave substantial deference to original decision maker were insufficient to support conclusion that supervisors were authorized to establish employment policy for city with respect to transfers and layoffs.

Reversed and remanded.

Justice Brennan filed opinion concurring in judgment in which Justices Marshall and Blackmun joined.

Justice Stevens filed dissenting opinion.

Justice Kennedy took no part in the consideration or decision of the case.

1. Federal Courts ⚷461

City's failure to timely object to jury instruction on municipalities' liability for their employees' unconstitutional acts did not deprive Supreme Court of jurisdiction to determine proper legal standard for im-

curring in the judgment.) 42 U.S.C.A. § 1983.

3. Civil Rights ⚷13.7

Municipalities may be liable under § 1983 only for acts for which municipality itself is actually responsible, that is, acts which municipality had officially sanctioned or ordered. (Per Justice O'Connor with the Chief Justice and two Justices concurring and three Justices concurring in the judgment.) 42 U.S.C.A. § 1983.

4. Civil Rights ⚷13.7

Only those municipal officers who have final policymaking authority may by their actions subject municipal government to § 1983 liability. (Per Justice O'Connor with the Chief Justice and two Justices concurring and three Justices concurring in the judgment.) 42 U.S.C.A. § 1983.

5. Civil Rights ⚷13.7

Whether particular official has final policymaking authority for purposes of § 1983 liability is question of state law. (Per Justice O'Connor with the Chief Justice and two Justices concurring and three Justices concurring in the judgment.) 42 U.S.C.A. § 1983.

(c) United States Supreme Court Reports, Lawyers' Edition

ST. LOUIS v PRAPROTNIK

(1988) 485 US 112, 99 L Ed 2d 107, 108 S Ct 915

HEADNOTES

Classified to U.S. Supreme Court Digest, Lawyers' Edition

Appeal § 1677; Civil Rights § 27; Trial § 165 — reversal — liability of city — retaliatory employment actions — supervisors — jury question

1a-1c. The United States Supreme Court will reverse a Federal Court of Appeals decision, which affirmed a Federal District Court judgment finding a city liable under 42 USCS § 1983 for the violation of a city employee's federal constitutional rights through retaliatory employee transfer and layoff actions taken by city agency supervisors in response to the employee's appeal of his suspension to the city's grievance review board, where (1) four Justices are of the opinion that the Federal Court of Appeals applied an incorrect legal standard in concluding that the supervisors were city "policymakers" whose actions could subject the city to liability under § 1983, in that (a) the identification of officials with such final policymaking authority is a question of state and local law, rather than a question of the reasoning. Because of the doctrine of precedent, this policy is important. In complex cases, a judge may concur in part and dissent in part. Especially in U.S. Supreme Court cases, this can be very hard to sort out.

You may also encounter a few other kinds of opinions. A per curiam opinion is an opinion written anonymously that includes the reasoning of the entire court. Such opinions are generally short and are weak precedent. Memorandum decisions report routine decisions.

In reading *any* opinion, remember that only the issues of law that are resolved by the opinion are the "stuff" of the law. Much of the opinion will not be resolving such issues. Opinions may contain factual summaries, the judge's opinions on the state of civilization, or anything else. Judges can write what they like, but everything that does not resolve a legal issue is dictum. You will find that dicta, though not binding precedent, may be "persuasive." That is, the dicta may still be helpful to your case.

The last paragraph in a majority opinion is the mandate of the court. It states what action is being taken on appeal. For example, the court may indicate that the decision is affirmed, reversed, remanded, modified, or dismissed.

Conclusion

You should now feel familiar with cases. They are not really like the cryptic, heavily edited versions that lurk in your casebooks. In their fully reported form, they have lots of editorial enhancements and useful parts. In addition, they all follow a similar pattern, so you will find familiar aspects as you move from the state court system to the federal system.

This chapter has explained how to locate a case in a reporter from a legal citation and how to find and use parallel citations. At this point, you should also be able to recognize and understand the parts of a case in a reporter volume and the different fields of a case on WESTLAW. Now that you understand the basics of reporters in print and on WESTLAW, we will proceed to finding particular cases.

2 Finding Cases

Finding cases has been a challenge for lawyers for hundreds of years, and a variety of tools have been developed to help. In some ways every tool that you will encounter is designed to help you find cases. This chapter concentrates on print sources, called digests, and the on-line WESTLAW databases. Both the digests and WESTLAW try to be comprehensive. This means that they do not offer access to cases on just one topic, but instead provide access to *all* cases—a full-tilt blunderbuss approach. Given that some three million cases are already out there with perhaps another 130,000 being added each year, it is no surprise that these tools need some special instruction. This chapter will explain them.

Digests

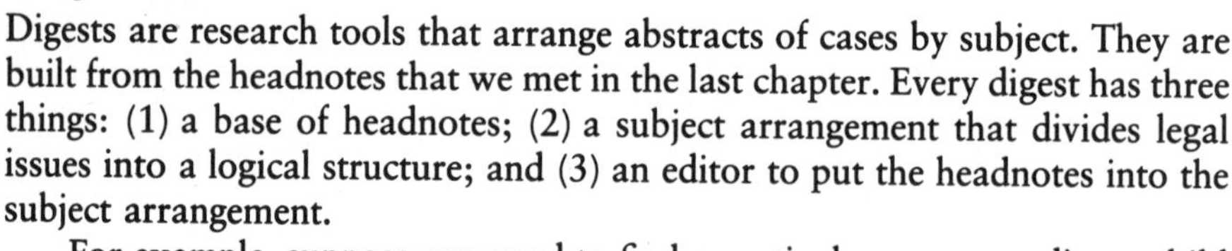

Digests are research tools that arrange abstracts of cases by subject. They are built from the headnotes that we met in the last chapter. Every digest has three things: (1) a base of headnotes; (2) a subject arrangement that divides legal issues into a logical structure; and (3) an editor to put the headnotes into the subject arrangement.

For example, suppose you need to find a particular case regarding a child that was injured by a pit bull because your client wants to file a claim against the local humane society for not enforcing the city's "leash law." The only clue you have is that you remember reading a "pit bull" case that took place in the state of Washington. How could you use your clue to find the case you need?

The traditional answer has been to use a digest. A digest is a comprehensive subject index to cases. The digest contains a comprehensive list of legal topics, including some personal favorites of the authors, such as "Dueling" and "Hawkers and Peddlers." Every conceivable legal issue appears in the subject list. Then, the headnotes from reported cases are dropped into their proper location in the subject list. As a result, the headnotes of decisions on the same point of law appear together.

Therefore, to find the case on pit bulls, you would use the state of Washington digest and begin searching for cases by using the Descriptive-Word Index (Figure 2.1). We will discuss this index later in the chapter.

Figure 2.1 The Descriptive-Word Index in the *Washington Digest*

A digest is *one* way of locating a case by a its subject. Digests are particularly useful for finding cases involving legal issues or concepts, such as ownership of property or various contract theories. Often, you will get maximum results by using digests in conjunction with WESTLAW, but for the time being, let's examine how to use a digest alone to find the information we need.

The digests that we will discuss are published by West, although other companies also publish digests. West has the largest system, the only one that covers *all* jurisdictions. West organizes its digests according to the West key number system that we discussed in Chapter 1. The paragraphs in the digests are basically the headnote paragraphs from the cases in the reporters rearranged according to subject (Figure 2.2).

Understanding the relationship between the headnotes and the digests is crucial to using the digests. Remember that the West editors create headnotes by isolating every issue of law that appears in the opinion. West then assigns topics and key numbers to every headnote. Each headnote is assigned at least one key number, and some headnotes are assigned several.

West developed the key number system to organize the digest paragraphs. In this system, the entire body of law has been broken down into general topics. Each topic has been further divided into a number of points of law. A separate number, the "key number" is assigned to each point of law.

Animals 🔑 54

Figure 2.2 Headnote Paragraph in the Reporter and in the Digest

(a) Headnote in Pacific Reporter

1280 Wash. **737 PACIFIC REPORTER, 2d SERIES**

5. Municipal Corporations 🔑723

Special relationship exception to public duty doctrine arises where relationship develops between individual and agents of entity performing governmental function, such that duty is created to perform mandated act for benefit of particular person or class of persons.

6. Municipal Corporations 🔑723

Before entity may be held liable under

[1888]John H. Loeffler, Olson, Loeffler & Landis, Spokane, for appellants.

Jonathan C. Rascoff, Spokane, for respondents.

MUNSON, Judge.

John and Roxie Champagne brought this action on behalf of their minor son, John, against the Spokane Humane Society for personal injuries resulting from the attack

9. Animals 🔑54

Although owner of pit bulls was negligent in allowing them to run loose, humane society, which had been contractually delegated authority to enforce animal regulations of city's ordinance, could be liable for its later negligence, if any, in failing to apprehend the pit bulls.

and to enforce the animal regulatory provisions of the Spokane city ordinances. Spokane city ordinance C13835 [1889]provides in pertinent part:

Section 1. Dogs at Large. It shall be unlawful for any person to cause, permit, or allow any dog or dogs, owned, harbored, controlled or kept by him, in the

1. Mr. Mason subsequently disappeared and is not a party to this action.

Figure 2.2 Headnote Paragraph in the Reporter and in the Digest (continued)

(b) Identical Headnote in Washington Digest

1 Wash D 2d—515 **ANIMALS** ⚷68

For references to other topics, see Descriptive-Word Index

value of use and occupation thereof. RCW 16.24.070.

MacKenzie-Richardson, Inc. v. Allert, 272 P.2d 146, 45 Wash.2d 1.

Wash. 1927. To recover for dog bite, it must be shown that dog was wrongfully on sidewalk.

Shelby v. Seung, 257 P. 838, 144 Wash. 317.

Recovery for injuries for dog bite held improperly allowed without showing dog was wrongfully on street.

Shelby v. Seung, 257 P. 838, 144 Wash. 317.

Wash. 1906. The owner of a steer who has knowledge of its dangerous character is liable for injuries inflicted by the steer while running at large, irrespective of whether the owner was negligent in securing the steer.

Harris v. Carstens Packing Co., 86 P. 1125, 43 Wash. 647, 6 L.R.A., N.S., 1164.

⚷54. —— Persons liable for injuries.

Wash.App. 1987. Although owner of pit bulls was negligent in allowing them to run loose, humane society, which had been contractually delegated authority to enforce animal regulations of city's ordinance, could be liable for its later negligence, if any, in failing to apprehend the pit bulls.

Champagne v. Spokane Humane Soc., 737 P.2d 1279, 47 Wash.App. 887, review denied.

Evidence that defendant was running in excess of 300 head of cattle on approximately 12,000 acres of leased pasture, that county road ran through the pasture for four miles, that there was no fence separating pasture from the road, that it was necessary for cattle to cross road to reach watering place, that cattle were frequently observed on the road with no herdsman tending them and that herdsman, who patrolled the entire tract, ordinarily made only one daily check of the road, warranted misdemeanor conviction of owner for permitting his cattle to run at large and not under the care of a herder. West's RCWA 16.13.010.

State v. Dear, 638 P.2d 85, 96 Wash.2d 652.

⚷58–66. ***For other cases see the Decennial Digests and WESTLAW.***

Library references

C.J.S. Animals.

⚷66. Personal injuries.

Library references

C.J.S. Animals §§ 170, 177.

⚷67. —— Domestic animals in general.

Wash. 1980. Negligence cause of action against animal owner arises when there is ineffective control of an animal in a situation where it would reasonably be expected that an injury could occur and injury does proximately result from the negligence; amount of control required is that which would be exercised by a reasonable person based on the total situation at the time, including the past behavior of the

You must have both parts, the topic and the key number, in order to use the digests.

In the digests, the paragraphs under each key number are arranged by jurisdiction, and under each jurisdiction, they are arranged by date of decision. The cases are listed in reverse chronological order with the most recent at the beginning (Figure 2.3).

The beauty of the key number system is that the key number assigned is uniform throughout all West's digests. As a result, when you find a relevant case on point in the *Georgia Digest,* you can look under the identical key number in all other jurisdictions and find relevant cases. A particularly regional or state digest may not list cases under every topic and key number. When you see the statement "For other cases see the Decennial Digests and WESTLAW" in a digest, you should follow those directions.

Table 2.1 lists the digests published by West. As you can see, there are different digests, each designed to fill specific needs. Logically, you would

Figure 2.3 Cases Arranged by Jurisdiction in Reverse Chronological Order in the *Federal Practice Digest*

13 F P D 4th—115 **CIVIL RIGHTS ⚷112**

For references to other topics, see Descriptive-Word Index

constitutional wrong, for § 1983 purposes. 42 U.S.C.A. § 1983; U.S.C.A. Const.Amend. 14.
Davis v. Bucher, 853 F.2d 718.

C.A.7 (Wis.) 1989. Deprivation of civil rights claim based on due process clause of Fourteenth Amendment does not translate every tort committed by state actor into a constitutional wrong. 42 U.S.C.A. § 1983; U.S.C.A. Const.Amend. 14.
Erwin v. County of Manitowoc, 872 F.2d 1292.

C.A.7 (Wis.) 1987. Fact that tort-feasor is municipal employee is not sufficient alone to make his or her tort "abuse of power" in violation of due process clause which is redressable in action brought under § 1983. 42 U.S.C.A. § 1983.
Archie v. City of Racine, 826 F.2d 480, rehearing granted, vacated 831 F.2d 152.

C.A.7 (Wis.) 1985. Section 1983 imposes liability for violations of rights protected by the Constitution, not for violations of duties of care arising out of tort law. U.S.C.A. Const. Amend. 14.
Gumz v. Morrissette, 772 F.2d 1395, certiorari denied 106 S.Ct. 1644, 475 U.S. 1123, 90 L.Ed.2d 189.

C.A.7 (Wis.) 1985. General principles of tort liability govern the liability imposed under 42 U.S.C.A. § 1983.
Hibma v. Odegaard, 769 F.2d 1147.

States so as to be actionable under 42 U.S.C.A. § 1983.
Metcalf v. Long, 615 F.Supp. 1108.

M.D.Ga. 1988. Under Georgia law, payment of a higher salary to male comanager of restaurant than to female comanager, removal of some of female comanager's supervisory duties, and her proposed demotion were not so terrifying or insulting as to cause female comanager the humiliation, embarrassment or fright necessary to justify recovery from employer for intentional infliction of emotional distress.
Thompson v. John L. Williams Co., Inc., 686 F.Supp. 315.

N.D.Ga. 1988. Defendant cannot be held liable under § 1983 merely for commission of common-law tort, instead, § 1983 plaintiff must show that defendant's conduct was constitutionally tortious and violated plaintiff's federal constitutional or legal right. 42 U.S.C.A. § 1983.
Terrell v. Shope, 687 F.Supp. 579.

D.C.Ga. 1985. A negligent deprivation of a constitutional right is actionable under 42 U.S.C.A. § 1983 if requirements of the statute are met.
Gravitt v. Graves, 609 F.Supp. 925, affirmed in part, reversed in part 797 F.2d 980.

retrieve federal cases (including Supreme Court cases) from one of the various federal digests, and you would use the Supreme Court digest to retrieve only Supreme Court cases. If you want all cases from all jurisdictions, use the American Digest System, which consists of the *Decennial Digests* and the *General Digests*. This system has enormous scope: it includes all reported American cases, state and federal, from 1658 to the present. To make this digest manageable, West has divided it into five- or ten-year periods. West updates the *Decennial Digests* with a series of bound volumes known as the *General Digest* (seventh series); a volume is published approximately every six weeks.

If you are researching state law, you should select a state digest since it will provide you with the quickest way to determine case law in one state. A regional digest would be useful when you need cases from neighboring jurisdictions. A good rule of thumb is to always use the smallest possible digest (Figure 2.4).

Now that you have the correct digest for your jurisdiction, you need to learn how to use it.

Table 2.1 West's Digests

State	All states except Delaware, Nevada, and Utah. For Delaware, use the *Atlantic Digest;* for Nevada and Utah, use the *Pacific Digest.*
Region	Only four current regional digests: *Atlantic, North Western, Pacific,* and *South Eastern.* Use the state digests for states not covered in the regional digests.
Federal (both lower federal courts and Supreme Court)	*Federal Digest,* red, all cases prior to 1939 *Modern Federal Practice Digest,* green, 1939–1960 *Federal Practice Digest 2d,* blue, 1961–1975 *Federal Practice Digest 3d,* red, 1976–date (until volumes are supplemented by the 4th series *Federal Practice Digest 4th,* blue, 1989– (volumes are in the process of being published)
Supreme Court only	*United States Supreme Court Digest,* 1790–date
American Digest System (all cases, both federal and state)	*Century Digest,* 1658–1896 *First—Ninth Decennial Digests,* 1897–1986 *General Digest 7th,* 1986–date

Figure 2.4
Always Use the Smallest Digest

Finding a Case in a Digest

If you are lucky enough to know one relevant case, perhaps obtained from a classmate or a textbook, for example, you should read the case and determine the key numbers that are relevant to your legal issue. Once you have relevant key numbers, you can go directly to the digest volume that indexes additional cases on point. For example, your client is charged with importing cocaine into the United States. He claims that the customs officer unlawfully searched his suitcase while it was in the baggage hold of the aircraft. Your colleague suggests that you read the case *United States v. Franchi-Forlando,* 838 F.2d 585 (1st Cir. 1988). From this one relevant case, you can determine the relevant topic and key numbers and head to the digest to retrieve other pertinent cases (Figure 2.5). Legal research skills revolve around the finding of one good case, and you will encounter many methods of doing so.

Descriptive-Word Index

If you do not have one great case by which to find other relevant cases, your gateway into the digest can be the Descriptive-Word Index (DWI). The DWI is a long list of everyday words, legal terms, and phrases. In a way, it is an index to the collected headnotes (this may sound odd, but don't worry—it is very useful). Under these DWI terms, you can find relevant topics and key numbers.

Figure 2.5 Key Numbers from One Relevant Case Can Lead to Others

(a) Key Numbers in a Case

586 838 FEDERAL REPORTER, 2d SERIES

1. Drugs and Narcotics ⚷74, 124

The Government did not have to prove that defendant knew that airplane en route from Colombia to Spain would stop in the United States in order for defendant to be convicted of unlawfully importing cocaine into the United States when airplane made scheduled stop in Puerto Rico and, in any event, evidence was sufficient for jury to find that defendant knew he would land in the United States. Comprehensive Drug Abuse Prevention and Control Act of 1970, § 1002(a), 21 U.S.C.A. § 952(a).

2. Customs Duties ⚷126(7)

Customs officer could lawfully search suitcase of passenger who was in transit from Colombia to Spain, while suitcase was in baggage hold during scheduled stop in Puerto Rico. Tariff Act of 1930, §§ 467, 496, 581(a), 19 U.S.C.A. §§ 1467, 1496, 1581(a).

3. Customs Duties ⚷126(7)

Customs regulation providing that customs officers are not to open baggage but are to detain it until owner opens or refuses to open it did not preclude search of suitcase which was not accompanying passenger through customs but which was in baggage hold of aircraft en route from Colombia to Spain, during scheduled stop in Puerto Rico.

6. Criminal Law ⚷200(1)

Convictions for both unlawfully importing cocaine into the United States and unlawfully possessing cocaine on an aircraft arriving in the United States without proper listing in the aircraft's documents did not violate double jeopardy, in that the applicable statutory provisions each required proof of a fact which the other did not, in that the undocumented importation offense applied to approved as well as unapproved controlled substances. Comprehensive Drug Abuse Prevention and Control Act of 1970, §§ 1002(a), 1005, 21 U.S.C.A. §§ 952(a), 955; U.S.C.A. Const. Amend. 5.

Rafael F. Castro–Lang, San Juan, P.R., by Appointment of the Court, for defendant, appellant.

Jose R. Gaztambide, Asst. U.S. Atty., with whom Daniel F. Lopez–Romo, U.S. Atty., Hato Rey, P.R., was on brief for appellee.

Before CAMPBELL, Chief Judge, TIMBERS,* Senior Circuit Judge, and BREYER, Circuit Judge.

BREYER, Circuit Judge.

The appellant, Orlando Franchi–Forlando, is an Italian citizen, living in Colombia. He was flying on Iberia Airlines from Co-

Before you use the DWI, analyze your fact situation thoroughly in order to generate sufficient words to look up in the DWI. You cannot use the DWI effectively if you do not fully understand your fact situation; you may overlook important terms.

Let's return to our problem involving the pit bull. West suggests that before consulting a Descriptive-Word Index, you should analyze your problem and determine very specific words or phrases to be searched by breaking the problem down into the following elements common to every case:

1. The *parties* involved: In our case, the owner of the pit bull; the injured child; and the humane society.

Figure 2.5 Key Numbers from One Relevant Case Can Lead to Others (continued)

(b) Digest Entries Under a Key Number

36 F P D 4th—385 **CUSTOMS DUTIES** ⚷126(7)

For references to other topics, see Descriptive-Word Index

"Reasonable suspicion" standard for justifying an "extended border search" was not applicable to search of package at Pittsburgh airport, where package was searched while still under customs bond and prior to its delivery to addressee, even though package had stopped in New York and Chicago before reaching Pittsburgh.
U.S. v. Caminos, 770 F.2d 361.

C.A.1 (Puerto Rico) 1990. Search conducted by customs officials of baggage of aircraft passengers proceeding from Columbia to Europe was a "border search" irrespective of passengers' in-transit status or their lack of knowledge that stop would be made in the United States.
U.S. v. Garcia, 905 F.2d 557.

C.A.1 (Puerto Rico) 1988. Customs officer could lawfully search suitcase of passenger who was in transit from Colombia to Spain, while suitcase was in baggage hold during scheduled stop in Puerto Rico. Tariff Act of 1930, §§ 467, 496, 581(a), 19 U.S.C.A. §§ 1467, 1496, 1581(a).
U.S. v. Franchi–Forlando, 838 F.2d 585.

Customs regulation providing that customs officers are not to open baggage but are to detain it until owner opens or refuses to open it did not preclude search of suitcase which was not accompanying passenger through customs but which was in baggage hold of aircraft en route from Colombia to Spain, during scheduled stop in Puerto Rico.
U.S. v. Franchi–Forlando, 838 F.2d 585.

intent to unlade and also includes planned stops of commercial airplanes whatever their passengers' final destinations. Tariff Act of 1930, § 496, 19 U.S.C.A. § 1496.
U.S. v. McKenzie, 818 F.2d 115.

C.A.6 (Tenn.) 1986. Customs officials have authority to conduct border-type search of aircraft pursuant to Anti-Smuggling Act where they are reasonably certain that aircraft entered from foreign country. Anti-Smuggling Act, § 3(a), 19 U.S.C.A. § 1703(a).
U.S. v. One (1) 1966 Beechcraft Baron, No. N242BS, 788 F.2d 384.

Customs officials had authority to conduct border-type search of abandoned aircraft, even though unidentified aircraft that crossed border while operating without navigation lights, which officials had been tracking on radar, evaded surveillance and disappeared and there was one-hour time lapse between disappearance of monitored aircraft and discovery of abandoned aircraft. Anti-Smuggling Act, § 3(a, c), 19 U.S.C.A. § 1703(a, c).
U.S. v. One (1) 1966 Beechcraft Baron, No. N242BS, 788 F.2d 384.

C.A.5 (Tex.) 1988. Border patrol agents' detention of defendant's suitcase for approximately an hour and a half after seizure of suitcase when agents could have employed more diligent, less intrusive investigatory techniques and when there was an absence of probable cause was unreasonable. U.S.C.A. Const.Amend. 4.
U.S. v. Cagle, 849 F.2d 924.

2. The *places* where the facts arose and the *objects* or *things* involved: The facts took place in the city; the pit bull or the vicious dog was involved.
3. The *acts* or *omissions* that form the *basis of action* or *issue:* The owner of the pit bull was negligent in allowing the dog to run loose, and the humane society was negligent in failing to apprehend the loose pit bull.
4. The *defense* to the action or issue: The defendant, the humane society, claims that it never saw the pit bull running loose.
5. The *relief* sought: The humane society is liable for personal injuries.

Therefore, you would begin with the Descriptive-Word Index in the *Washington Digest* and might look under the term "Pit Bulls." You would find that "Pit Bulls" is not listed; therefore, this term is too restrictive and you must think of alternative terms. You should broaden your search term to "Animals." When you look under "Animals," you will find the subtopic "Injuries—Running at Large." This entry will lead you to Animals Key Numbers 52–55. Next you will pull the digest volume marked "Animals" off the shelf and turn to Key Numbers 52–55. You will then note that Key Number 54 is applicable (Figure 2.6).

Topic Method

The digests can also be used in other ways. If, for example, you had analyzed your legal problem in terms of subject areas, such as animals, you could then go directly to the volume of the digest entitled "Animals." Next you would read through the summary of contents or analysis that appears at the beginning of the text of each topic until you find the appropriate entry. The topic approach is only useful for someone who knows the legal topics involved in the problem, however. As a beginning researcher, if you use the topic method, you probably will not select the proper topic and key numbers because you are not yet well acquainted with all of the subject possibilities (Figure 2.7).

Finding a Case by Case Name

If you know the name of the case that you want to read, you have only to look in the Table of Cases in any digest. This table is easy to use and will lead you to the correct reporter and page number (Figure 2.8).

When you know the jurisdiction, use the Table of Cases volumes at the end of the digest for that jurisdiction. Every digest has its own Table of Cases. If you do not know the jurisdiction, but do know the approximate year, use the Table of Cases in West's American Digest System, which consists of the *Decennial Digests* and the *General Digests*.

Figure 2.6 Using the Descriptive-Word Index to Find Key Numbers

(a) Listings in Descriptive Word Index

37 Wash D 2d—79 **ANIMALS**

References are to Digest Topics and Key Numbers

ANIMALS—Cont'd
DESTRUCTION of diseased animals. **Anim 32**
DETINUE, killing or injuring animals. **Anim 44**
DISEASES. **Anim 28–37**
Lessee's liability for destruction of barn used for glandered horses. **Land & Ten 134**
Vaccination by stockyards company. **Wareh 8**
DISTRAINING trespassing animals. **Anim 95, 100(5)**
DRIVING from range of pasture. **Anim 14**
DRIVING off trespassing animals. **Anim 94**
DUTIES of owners, stock laws. **Anim 50(3)**
ELECTIONS, stock law election. **Anim 50(2)**
ESTRAYS, see this index **Estrays**
EVIDENCE—
Actions for—
Damages caused by trespassing animals. **Anim 100(4)**
Personal injuries caused by animals. **Anim 74(3–5)**
Condition of animal. **Evid 477(5)**
Damages for loss or injury. **Damag 174(2)**
Judicial notice of—
Phenomena of animal life. **Evid 13**
Ownership. **Anim 3, 10**
Value or market price. **Evid 113(22)**

ANIMALS—Cont'd
INJURIES by or to animals—Cont'd
Railroads injuring animals, see this index **Railroads**
Running at large. **Anim 52–55**
Evidence, similar transactions. **Evid 141**
Statutory regulations. **Anim 79**
Street railroad injuring animals, see this index **Street Railroads**
Trespassing animals. **Anim 96**
INSPECTION—
Officers. **Inspect 4**
INSTRUCTIONS to jury—
Personal injuries. **Anim 74(7)**
INSURANCE of livestock. **Insurance 426**
JUDGMENT in actions for injuries caused by trespassing animals. **Anim 100(9)**
JUDICIAL notice—
Phenomena of animal life. **Evid 13**
KEEPING and use, municipal regulations. **Mun Corp 604, 631(3)**
KILLING. **Anim 43–45**
Animals running at large. **Anim 52**
Trespassing animals. **Anim 96**
Vicious animals. **Anim 73, 84**

Figure 2.6 Using the Descriptive-Word Index to Find Key Numbers (continued)

(b) Digest Entries Under a Key Number

1 Wash D 2d—515 **ANIMALS ⚷68**

For references to other topics, see Descriptive-Word Index

value of use and occupation thereof. RCW 16.24.070.
MacKenzie-Richardson, Inc. v. Allert, 272 P.2d 146, 45 Wash.2d 1.

Wash. 1927. To recover for dog bite, it must be shown that dog was wrongfully on sidewalk.
Shelby v. Seung, 257 P. 838, 144 Wash. 317.

Recovery for injuries for dog bite held improperly allowed without showing dog was wrongfully on street.
Shelby v. Seung, 257 P. 838, 144 Wash. 317.

Wash. 1906. The owner of a steer who has knowledge of its dangerous character is liable for injuries inflicted by the steer while running at large, irrespective of whether the owner was negligent in securing the steer.
Harris v. Carstens Packing Co., 86 P. 1125, 43 Wash. 647, 6 L.R.A., N.S., 1164.

⚷54. —— Persons liable for injuries.

Wash.App. 1987. Although owner of pit bulls was negligent in allowing them to run loose, humane society, which had been contractually delegated authority to enforce animal regulations of city's ordinance, could be liable for its later negligence, if any, in failing to apprehend the pit bulls.
Champagne v. Spokane Humane Soc., 737 P.2d 1279, 47 Wash.App. 887, review denied.

Evidence that defendant was running in excess of 300 head of cattle on approximately 12,000 acres of leased pasture, that county road ran through the pasture for four miles, that there was no fence separating pasture from the road, that it was necessary for cattle to cross road to reach watering place, that cattle were frequently observed on the road with no herdsman tending them and that herdsman, who patrolled the entire tract, ordinarily made only one daily check of the road, warranted misdemeanor conviction of owner for permitting his cattle to run at large and not under the care of a herder. West's RCWA 16.13.010.
State v. Dear, 638 P.2d 85, 96 Wash.2d 652.

⚷58–66. ***For other cases see the Decennial Digests and WESTLAW.***

Library references
C.J.S. Animals.

⚷66. Personal injuries.

Library references
C.J.S. Animals §§ 170, 177.

⚷67. —— Domestic animals in general.

Wash. 1980. Negligence cause of action against animal owner arises when there is ineffective control of an animal in a situation where it would reasonably be expected that an injury could occur and injury does proximately result from the negligence; amount of control required is that which would be exercised by a reasonable person based on the total situation at the time, including the past behavior of the animal and the injuries that could have been

In addition to providing you with the correct citation to the case, the Table of Cases also lists all key numbers under which that case has been digested. Note that the entry for *Champagne v. Spokane Humane Society* in the Table of Cases in Figure 2.9 lists Animals Key Number 54. Therefore, from the entry in the Table of Cases, you can go to the digest and find related cases under the appropriate topic and key number.

If the case was decided during the previous year, you may find the citation through the pocket parts to the Table of Cases in the digests, or you may have to check the Cases Reported tables in the advance sheets to the reporter in which you expect the case to appear (Figure 2.9).

What if you only know the defendant's name in a case? Check the Defendant-Plaintiff Table in the state and federal digests (Figure 2.10). The regional digests do not contain Defendant-Plaintiff Tables.

Figure 2.7 Using the Topic Method to Find Key Numbers

ANIMALS 1 Wash D 2d—504

20. —— Right to offspring.
21. Agistment, keeping, and care.
22. —— Rights and duties in general.
23. —— Loss of or injuries to animals.
    (1). In general.
    (2). Actions.
24. —— Injuries by animals.
25. —— Compensation.
26. —— Lien.
    (1). Existence, nature and incidents.
    (2). Persons entitled to lien.
    (3). Persons liable and property subject to lien.
    (4). Waiver and extinguishment.
    (5). Enforcement.

51. —— Impounding animals at large.
52. —— Killing or injuring animals at large.
53. —— Injuries by animals at large.
54. —— Persons liable for injuries.
55. —— Actions.
56. —— Penalties for violations of regulations.
57. —— Criminal prosecutions.
58. Estrays.

Finding a Case on WESTLAW

Now that you understand how to find a case in a digest, let's look at different ways of finding cases using WESTLAW.

Finding a Case on WESTLAW by Subject

To find a case in the digest, we started with the clue that you remember reading a "pit bull" case that took place in the state of Washington. With that same clue, you can search WESTLAW for relevant cases. Actually, with one specific piece of information about a case, you can easily retrieve cases by telling the computer to look for that unique term. To find the Washington pit bull case, you simply access the Washington cases database **WA-CS** and type

```
pit +5 bull
```

Figure 2.11 shows the results of your search.

Figure 2.8 Finding a Case in the Table of Cases

References are to Digest Topics and Key Numbers

Chamberlain v. Cobb, Wash, 225 P 414, 129 Wash 549.—Bills & N 398.
Chamberlain v. Geer, Wash, 237 P 719, 135 Wash 340.—Bills & N 342, 378.
Chamberlain v. Piercy, Wash, 143 P 977, 82 Wash 157.—Bankr 3066(1), 3066(5); Corp 228, 259(7).
Chamberlain v. Winn, Wash, 24 P 446, 1 Wash 259.—Replev 91.
Chamberlain & Co. v. French, Wash, 230 P 837, 131 Wash 394. See Northern Cedar Co v. French.
Chamberlain & Co v. Gloyd 46 SCt 204, 270 US 625, 70 LEd 767. Mem.
Chamberlin v. Chamberlin, Wash, 270 P2d 464, 44 Wash2d 689, 68 ALR2d 457.—Divorce 145, 146, 151, 184(5); Pretrial Proc 713, 722, 724.
Chamberlin v. Winn, Wash, 24 P 446, 1 Wash 259. See Chamberlain v. Winn.
Chamberlin v. Winn, Wash, 20 P 780, 1 Wash 501, aff Chamberlain v. Winn, 24 P 446, 1 Wash 259.—Replev 69(4); Sales 147.
Chambers v. Calvin Philips & Co., Wash, 312 P2d 659, 50 Wash2d 413.—Corp 1.6(3); Trusts 167, 262.
Chambers v. Carlyon, Wash, 62 P2d 726, 188 Wash 352.—Corp 123(24); Plgs 56(4).
Chambers v. City of Mount Vernon, WashApp, 522 P2d 1184, 11 WashApp 357.—Health & E 25.15(10); Mun Corp 722; Nuis 85.
Chamness v. Marquis, Wash, 383 P2d 886, 62 Wash2d 509.—App & E 717, 1071.1(1); Brok 56(3), 84(1), 85(2), 86(4).
Chamness Realty v. Marquis 62 Wash2d 509, 383 P2d 886. See Chamness v. Marquis.
Champa v. Washington Compressed Gas Co., Wash, 262 P 228, 146 Wash 190.—Damag 62(1); Nuis 3(6), 4, 50(5), 54.
Champagne v. Birnot, Wash, 254 P 829, 143 Wash 187.—App & E 415; Chat Mtg 138(2).
Champagne v. Department of Labor and Industries, Wash, 156 P2d 422, 22 Wash2d 412.—Trial 182, 260(1); Work Comp 1853, 1911, 1929.
Champagne v. Hygrade Food Products, Inc., DCWash, 79 FRD 671.—Fed Civ Proc 1372.
Champagne v. McDonald, Wash, 251 P 874, 141 Wash 617.—Accord 8(1).
Champagne v. Spokane Humane Soc., WashApp, 737 P2d 1279, 47 WashApp 887, review den.—Anim 54; Judgm 181(33); Mun Corp 723, 751(1); Neglig 61(1).
Champ Arcade v. City of Seattle 86 Wash2d 395, 544 P2d 1242. See Bitts, Inc v. City of Seattle.
Champion v. Shoreline School Dist. No. 412 of King County, Wash, 504 P2d 304, 81 Wash2d 672.—Schools 63(1), 130, 147.34(1); Statut 181(1), 208, 223.-2(1).
Contracts 176(1); Damag 76, 78(1); Evid 80(1); Frds St of 130(1), 130(2); Impl & C C 81; Motions 51; Plead 34(1), 53(2), 214(2), 214(4), 354.
Chandler v. Gallemore, Wash, 43 P2d 968, 181 Wash 345.—Corp 80(12), 261, 263(2).
Chandler v. Humphrey, Wash, 31 P2d 1012, 177 Wash 402.—Corp 217; Lim of Act 2(1).
Chandler v. Miller, Wash, 19 P2d 1108, 172 Wash 252.—Corp 80(12), 247, 262(1), 262(2), 269(2); Plead 147.
Chandler v. Miller, Wash, 13 P2d 22, 168 Wash 563.—Corp 262(1), 563(2); Judgm 822(3).
Chandler v. Otto, Wash, 693 P2d 71, 103 Wash2d 268.—Mun Corp 159(5); Offic 70½.
Chandler v. Washington Toll Bridge Authority, Wash, 137 P2d 97, 17 Wash2d 591.—Bridges 5, 20(1), 20(2), 20(4), 20(5), 20(6); Contracts 4, 5, 187(1); Impl & C C 1, 2, 3, 4.
Chaney v. Chaney, Wash, 105 P 229, 56 Wash 145.—App & E 655(1), 1074(3); Divorce 161, 167.
Chantler v. Hubbell, Wash, 75 P 802, 34 Wash 211.—Fraud Conv 176(2); Trusts 96.
Chantry, In re, Wash, 524 P2d 909, 84 Wash2d 153.—Atty & C 61.
Chantry, In re, Wash, 407 P2d 160, 67 Wash2d 190.—Atty & C 32(2), 58.
Chaoussis' Estate, In re, Wash, 247 P 732, 139 Wash 479.—Ex & Ad 24.

Figure 2.9 A Table of Cases Reported in an Advance Sheet

CUMULATIVE CASES REPORTED

793 P.2d

(Cases in bold type appear in this issue)

ALASKA

(Cases in this issue, pp. 1025–1085)

	Page
A., In re—Alaska	1033
Alam v. State—Alaska App.	1081
Alascom, Inc. v. Alaska Public Utilities Com'n—Alaska	1028
Alaska Consumer Advocacy Program v. Alaska Public Utilities Com'n—Alaska	1028
Caucus Distributors, Inc. v. State, Dept. of Commerce and Economic Development, Div. of Banking, Securities and Corporations—Alaska	1048
City of Valdez v. State, Dept. of Community & Regional Affairs—Alaska	532
Davis v. State—Alaska App.	1064
D.J.A., In re—Alaska	1033
F/V Chicamin—Alaska	69
Gutierres v. State—Alaska App.	1078
McCormick v. Smith—Alaska	1042
Murat v. F/V Shelikof Strait—Alaska	69
Napayonak v. State—Alaska App.	1059
Russell v. State—Alaska App.	1085
Shapiro v. State—Alaska App.	535
State v. Chryst—Alaska App.	538
State v. Echols—Alaska App.	1066
State, Dept. of Revenue v. Gazaway—Alaska	1025
Taylor v. State—Alaska App.	1078
Valdez, City of, v. State, Dept. of Community & Regional Affairs—Alaska	532

Figure 2.10 A Defendant-Plaintiff Table

SPOKANE 41 Wash D 2d—404

References are to Digest Topics and Key Numbers

AND FOR—State, Wash, 177 P 654, 105 Wash 49.

SPOKANE COUNTY, SUPERIOR COURT OF WASHINGTON IN AND FOR—State, Wash, 174 P 646, 103 Wash 402.

SPOKANE COUNTY, SUPERIOR COURT OF WASHINGTON IN AND FOR—State, Wash, 147 P 436, 85 Wash 72.

SPOKANE COUNTY, SUPREME COURT OF—State, Wash, 34 P 930, 7 Wash 234.

SPOKANE COUNTY, TAXPAYERS OF—Spokane County, 85 Wash2d 216, 533 P2d 128.

SPOKANE COUNTY, TAXPAYERS OF—Spokane County, 84 Wash2d 475, 527 P2d 263.

SPOKANE COUNTY, TAXPAYERS OF, AND WITHIN, SCHOOL DIST. NO. 81 OF—School Dist. No. 81 of Spokane County, Wash, 225 P2d 1063, 37 Wash2d 669.

SPOKANE COUNTY, WASH.—Dodd, CAWash, 393 F2d 330.

SPOKANE CULVERT & FABRICATING CO.—Novenson, Wash, 588 P2d 1174, 91 Wash2d 550.

SPOKANE CYCLE & AUTO SUPPLY CO.—Maskell, Wash, 170 P 350, 100 Wash 16.

SPOKANE DAIRY PRODUCTS CO.—Royal Dairy Products Co., Wash, 225 P 412, 129 Wash 424.

SPOKANE DRUG CO.—Adams, CCWash, 57 F 888.

SPOKANE DRY GOODS CO.—Spokane Merchants' Ass'n, Wash, 299 P 371, 162 Wash 577.

SPOKANE DRY GOODS CO.—U.S., DCWash, 264 F 209.

SPOKANE, EACH AND EVERY LOT IN CITY OF—Spokane County, Wash, 13 P2d 1084, 169 Wash 355.

SPOKANE FALLS & N. RY.—Williams, Wash, 87 P 491, 44 Wash 363.

SPOKANE FALLS & N. RY. CO.—Fleutsch, Wash, 6 Wash 623, 34 P 150.

SPOKANE FALLS & N. RY. CO.—Flutsch, Wash, 6 Wash 623, 34 P 150.

SPOKANE FALLS & N. RY. CO.—Allend, Wash, 58 P 244, 21 Wash 324.

SPOKANE FALLS & N. RY. CO.—Dunkle, Wash, 55 P 51, 20 Wash 254.

SPOKANE FALLS & NORTHERN RY. CO.—Taylor, Wash, 73 P 499, 32 Wash 450.

SPOKANE FALLS & N. RY. CO.—Williams, Wash, 84 P 1129, 42 Wash 597.

SPOKANE FALLS & N. RY. CO.—Williams, Wash, 80 P 1100, 39 Wash 77.

SPOKANE FALLS, CITY OF—Curry, Wash, 27 P 477, 2 Wash 541.

SPOKANE FALLS, CITY OF—Spokane St. Ry. Co., CCWash, 46 F 322.

SPOKANE FALLS, CITY OF—Spokane Street Railway Co., Wash, 33 P 1072, 6 Wash 521.

SPOKANE FALLS, CITY OF—State, Wash, 25 P 903, 2 Wash 40.

SPOKANE FALLS, CITY OF—Town of Denver, Wash, 34 P 926, 7 Wash 226.

SPOKANE FALLS GASLIGHT CO.—Theis, Wash, 95 P 1074, 49 Wash 477.

SPOKANE FALLS GASLIGHT CO.—Theis, Wash, 74 P 1004, 34 Wash 23.

SPOKANE FUEL DEALERS CREDIT ASS'N—U.S., DCWash, 55 FSupp 387.

SPOKANE GAS & FUEL CO.—City of Spokane, Wash, 47 P2d 671, 182 Wash 475.

SPOKANE GAS & FUEL CO.—City of Spokane, Wash, 26 P2d 1034, 175 Wash 103.

SPOKANE GAS & FUEL CO.—Cole, Wash, 119 P 831, 66 Wash 393.

SPOKANE GAS & FUEL CO.—Jobe, Wash, 131 P 235, 73 Wash 1, 48 LRANS 931.

SPOKANE GRAIN CO.—Frederick & Nelson, Wash, 91 P 570, 47 Wash 85.

SPOKANE HARDWARE CO.—Conlan, Wash, 201 P 26, 117 Wash 378.

SPOKANE, HOME TEL. & TEL. CO. OF—Cavers, Wash, 201 P 20, 117 Wash 299.

SPOKANE, HOME TEL. & TEL. CO. OF—State, Wash, 172 P 899, 102 Wash 196.

SPOKANE HUMANE SOC.—Champagne, WashApp, 737 P2d 1279, 47 WashApp 887.

SPOKANE HYDRAULIC CO.—Cunningham, Wash, 52 P 235, 18 Wash 524.

SPOKANE INTERN. RY. CO.—Neitzel, Wash, 141 P 186, 80 Wash 30.

SPOKANE INTERN. RY. CO.—Neitzel, Wash, 117 P 864, 65 Wash 100, 36 LRA,NS, 522.

SPOKANE INTERN. RY. CO.—Pierce, Wash, 131 P2d 139, 15 Wash2d 431.

SPOKANE-INTERNATIONAL RY. CO.—Schaefer, Wash, 188 P 530, 110 Wash 316.

SPOKANE INTERN. RY. CO.—Walters, Wash, 108 P 593, 58 Wash 293, 42 LRA,NS, 917.

SPOKANE INTERN. R. CO.—McEwen, CAWash, 325 F2d 491.

SPOKANE INTERSTATE FAIR—Polk, Wash, 132 P 401, 73 Wash 610.

SPOKANE INTERSTATE FAIR ASS'N—Fidelity & Deposit Co. of Md., CCAWash, 8 F2d 224, 44 ALR 468.

SPOKANE JOBBERS' ASS'N—Hoffman, Wash, 102 P 1045, 54 Wash 179.

SPOKANE KNITTING MILLS—Jantzen Knitting Mills, DCWash, 44 F2d 656.

SPOKANE, LOCAL NO. 400 OF COOKS AND HELPERS, WAITERS AND WAITRESSES OF—Adams, Wash, 215 P 19, 124 Wash 564.

SPOKANE LODGE NO. 228, BENEV. AND PROTECTIVE ORDER OF ELKS—Local Joint Executive Bd. of Spokane, CAWash, 443 F2d 403.

SPOKANE MERCANTILE CO.—Burnham, Wash, 51 P 363, 18 Wash 207.

SPOKANE MERCHANTS' ASS'N—Fidelity & Deposit Co. of Maryland, Wash, 157 P 464, 91 Wash 170.

SPOKANE MERCHANTS' ASS'N—Kasper, Wash, 151 P 800, 87 Wash 447.

SPOKANE MERCHANT'S ASS'N—Kriegler, Wash, 189 P 1004, 111 Wash 179.

SPOKANE MILL CO.—U. S., DCWash, 206 F 999.

SPOKANE MORTG. CO.—Ellingson, WashApp, 573 P2d 389, 19 WashApp 48.

SPOKANE NAT. BANK—Grant, CCWash, 47 F 673.

SPOKANE NAT. BANK—Weber, CCAWash, 64 F 208, 12 CCA 93.

SPOKANE NAT. BANK—Weber, CCAWash, 50 F 735.

When using WESTLAW, it is not necessary to translate specific fact situations into legal concepts. This is a very important point that can be illustrated by an example. Assume that your friend is distributing political literature on a private college campus. The college president has ordered her to stop these activities, and she refuses. To locate cases in the **NJ-CS** database, type

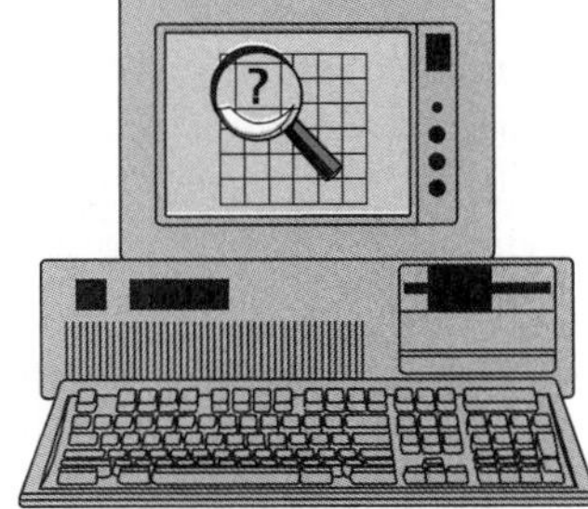

```
politic! /s literature flyer pamphlet /s campus
university! school
```

As you can see from the results of this search in Figure 2.12, it is not necessary to translate the specific fact situation of distributing political literature into the legal concept of the First Amendment right to free speech that you would use in searching a digest. In other words, when you are using the digests, you must elevate your thinking into abstract terms, whereas when you are searching on-line, you can simply type in the words that need to appear in the document.

Figure 2.11 Finding a Case on WESTLAW

```
                          COPR. (C) WEST 1990 NO CLAIM TO ORIG. U.S. GOVT. WORKS
Citation                       Rank(R)          Page(P)          Database   Mode
737 P.2d 1279                  R 1 OF 1         P 1 OF 24        WA-CS      T
 47 Wash.App. 887
(CITE AS: 737 P.2D 1279)
      John CHAMPAGNE and Roxie Champagne, husband and wife, as Parents and
 Guardians of John Douglas Champagne, a Minor;  and Roger A. Felice, as Guardian
                Ad Litem of John Douglas Champagne, Appellants,
                                        v.
 SPOKANE HUMANE SOCIETY and Society for the Prevention of Cruelty to Animals, a
                    Non-Profit Corporation, Respondents.
                                No. 7709-8-III.
                    Court of Appeals of Washington, Division 3.
                                May 28, 1987.
                          Review Denied Sept. 1, 1987.
 Parents brought suit on behalf of their son against humane society for
 personal INJURIES resulting from attack on their child by a PIT BULL.  The
 Superior Court, Spokane County, Thomas Merryman, J., dismissed claim on summary
 judgment holding that action was barred by public duty doctrine, and parents
 appealed.  The Court of Appeals, Munson, J., held that there was issue of
 material fact as to each element of special relationship exception to public
 duty doctrine, and as to society's duty of care and whether such duty was met,
 precluding summary judgment.
 Reversed and remanded.
```

Figure 2.12 Finding a Case from a Specific Fact Situation on WESTLAW

```
                          COPR. (C) WEST 1990 NO CLAIM TO ORIG. U.S. GOVT. WORKS
Citation                       Rank(R)          Page(P)          Database   Mode
423 A.2d 615                   R 4 OF 4         P 1 OF 90        NJ-CS      T
 84 N.J. 535
(CITE AS: 423 A.2D 615)
                    STATE of New Jersey, Plaintiff-Respondent,
                                        v.
                        Chris SCHMID, Defendant-Appellant.
                            Supreme Court of New Jersey.
                                Argued Feb. 4, 1980.
                                Decided Nov. 25, 1980.
 Defendant was found guilty in the Superior Court, Law Division, of trespass.
 Following certification of the case while defendant's appeal was pending in the
 Appellate Division, the Supreme Court, Handler, J., held that: (1) UNIVERSITY,
 which was predominantly private, unregulated and autonomous in its character
 and functioning as institution of higher education, was not subject to First
 Amendment obligations by virtue of joint relationship with or direct regulation
 by State, but (2) private UNIVERSITY'S regulations which were devoid of
 reasonable standards designed to protect both legitimate interest of the
 UNIVERSITY as institution of higher education and individual exercise of
 expressional freedom, could not constitutionally be invoked to prohibit
 otherwise noninjurious and reasonable exercise of such freedom, and thus the
 UNIVERSITY violated state constitutional rights of defendant by evicting him
 and securing his arrest for DISTRIBUTING POLITICAL LITERATURE upon its CAMPUS.
```

Rather than a specific piece of information, you may have an issue. Begin your search by stating your issue in one or two sentences. Next, translate your issue into the components of your query: terms, alternatives, root expanders, and connectors (check the appendix for help in formulating your query). Spend time off-line writing your query; it will prove to be time well spent in getting results. Issue-based searching can become very complicated very quickly. Use care when searching on-line for legal concepts, such as "free speech," that would have a multitude of "hits" on an on-line service. The experts are still arguing over how effective such searching can be because of the ambiguities in the English language. So proceed with care.

Fields on WESTLAW

At this point, it is important to discuss the most cost-efficient way of searching on WESTLAW; that is, by using field restrictions. In Chapter 1, we walked through the parts of a printed case and compared those elements with the fields of a case on WESTLAW. Almost all WESTLAW documents are divided into several parts called fields. For example, the title, citation, synopsis, court, judge, attorney, topic, headnote, opinion, and digest are each considered a separate field in a case. To find out which fields are available for a specific database, type **f** while you are in that database (Figure 2.13). By using a field restriction, you can narrow your search to look for terms in a specific field instead of in an entire case. We will illustrate the different field restrictions throughout the rest of this chapter.

Choosing a Database

We are now ready to use WESTLAW. After signing on to WESTLAW, usually the first thing you will do is choose a database. Use the WESTLAW Directory and the SCOPE command to choose the best database for your search. The Directory provides the identifier for the databases in which you are interested. Use SCOPE to retrieve a detailed description of the database. You may choose the **ALLSTATES** database for all fifty states or **ALLFEDS** for the U.S. Supreme Court, courts of appeals, district courts, and other federal courts. Many databases contain cases from one court, such as the U.S. Supreme Court cases database **SCT**. Other databases may include several courts; for example, the district court database **DCT** contains cases from all the district courts as well as the U.S. Court of International Trade and the former U.S. Court of Claims.

For this reason, limiting a search by using the court field will produce just the cases you are interested in. For example, if you type **co(tx fl)** while in the **DCT** database, you would retrieve federal district court cases from Texas and Florida. You can also use the court field restriction in a state database to designate cases from only the state's highest court. For example, if you type

Figure 2.13 A Fields Screen for Cases on WESTLAW

```
                COPR. (C) WEST 1990 NO CLAIM TO ORIG. U.S. GOVT. WORKS
                                    FIELDS

    TI  TITLE          CO  COURT        TO  TOPIC        DI   DIGEST
    CI  CITATION       JU  JUDGE        HE  HEADNOTE
    SY  SYNOPSIS       AT  ATTORNEY     OP  OPINION

To display a field, enter the field name or its abbreviation. To display
multiple fields, enter the names or abbreviations separated by commas
(no spaces between comma and fields).  To display the entire document,
press ENTER
```

in the Arizona cases database (**AZ-CS**), you would retrieve Arizona Supreme Court opinions concerning age discrimination.

Finding a Case by Its Name

It is extremely easy to search for the text of a case by its case name on WESTLAW. Searching WESTLAW for recent cases is particularly efficient because the pocket part to the Table of Cases in the digests can be a year out of date depending on the time of year. When you wish to retrieve a case on WESTLAW, you can search in the title field **TI** to retrieve a case name. Since the title field includes the complete title, including first names and extra parties, you should select significant or unique names from the title and combine them with the "&" connector. For example, type

```
ti(brown & education)
```

If you do not use a title field restriction in your search, you will probably retrieve your case, but you will also retrieve any case where your case was cited, plus many totally irrelevant documents.

Searching for a Case by Its Citation

If you have a citation of a case in a reporter or a WESTLAW cite and you want to find the case on WESTLAW, it is easily retrievable by the FIND service. FIND allows you to retrieve a document from anywhere in WESTLAW by simply entering its citation. There is no need to access a database; just type FIND. For example, to FIND 347 U.S. 483, type

```
fi 347 us 483
```

Synopsis Field Searching

West's editors write a synopsis for each case published in the West reporters. This information appears in the synopsis field on WESTLAW. Generally, a synopsis includes a review of the facts presented in the case; the name and holding of the lower court judge; the holding of the court in the case; and the names of the dissenting or concurring judges. Since the synopsis summarizes the procedural issues of a case, use the synopsis field restriction when a procedural issue is important. For example, to retrieve cases where federal district judge Merhige's opinions have been affirmed by the federal court of appeals, access the **CTA** database and type

```
sy(merhige & affirmed)
```

Slip opinions, unreported cases, and cases not published by West generally do not have synopses. The synopses are added to cases published by West within a few weeks. Therefore, if you wish to retrieve very recent opinions, do not use the synopsis field restriction—simply search in the database without using any field restrictions.

Topic Field Searching

Cases published by West are classified by West editors through individual headnotes under as many topics or legal issues as apply. These topics appear with their appropriate key numbers in the headnotes. When searching on WESTLAW, you can retrieve cases under a West digest topic by using a topic field restriction. West digest topics on WESTLAW are numbered; you can use either the topic name "criminal" or the topic number "110" in a topic field restriction, e.g., **to(110)**. A list of the digest topics and their WESTLAW numerical equivalents is located in Appendix A of the *WESTLAW Reference Manual* and in the **TOPIC** database. These numerical equivalents are peculiar to WESTLAW and do not appear in the print versions of the West reporters.

Topic searches are effective since you may not be certain which specific key number is relevant. With the topic field restriction, you can limit your search to a specific legal concept combined with a fact or specific term. For example, access the database for cases from U.S. Court of Appeals for the Fourth Circuit ((**CTA4**) and type

```
to(110) /p guilty /p plea
```

You will retrieve Fourth Circuit cases with headnotes classified under West digest topic number 110, the number for "criminal law," where the headnote paragraphs also contain the terms "guilty" and "plea."

Searching by Topic and Key Number

If you know a topic and key number, using WESTLAW in your search is a snap. These topic and key number searches let you quickly retrieve cases dealing with specific legal areas. With a key number search, you can be sure of retrieving some cases that relate to your issue. Remember that the West digests are indexes of case law organized around topics and key numbers. A key number is a permanent number given to a specific point of case law.

You will need some special instruction on how to search WESTLAW by topic and key number. Unlike the search techniques described under field searches, the topic and key number search is not a field search. This means you do not include a field name as part of the query.

First, you have to use a digest volume, some other background materials, or a known case to obtain a relevant topic and key number. You then may choose to locate cases on WESTLAW by topic and key number. The computer will not understand that you are looking for a topic and key number if you just type in the topic, so you must convert the topic into a number. The West digest topics have been assigned numbers for WESTLAW use only. To find the numerical equivalent of a West digest topic, you must first check Appendix A of your *WESTLAW Reference Manual* or the **TOPIC** database. For example, 28 is the number for "Animals." The **"k"** in your search stands for "key number." It is used on-line instead of the familiar key symbol in the digest. The last portion of the number is the same key number that appeared in the digest; for example, 54 stands for "Person liable for injuries." Thus, you would type **28k54** to retrieve cases relevant to the pit bull problem. You will find that by using topic and key numbers, you will retrieve cases that deal with very specific areas of law that will prove very useful. They can be used to effectively supplement word searches on WESTLAW.

Digest Field Searching

You may also want to narrow your search to the most important of the editorial fields, the digest field. The digest field contains the text of the headnote, the name of the West digest topic to which the headnote has been classified, and the court, title, and citation fields. A digest field is also particularly useful when your search contains common words, such as "contracts" or "wills." This also avoids the problem of judges who use idiosyncratic words or phrases. Since you use the computer to search for particular words, an unusual usage can really confuse you. The editors at West use a standard vocabulary, which can be a big help. For searching purposes, all the information contained in a digest paragraph is considered to be in the same paragraph. By using the digest field search, you do not have to rely on the cases being indexed under the key numbers by the editors. If the most important information of the case is included in the headnotes, you will find relevant cases in an efficient way.

Searching in the digest field at the same time that you search with the synopsis field can be very effective because these two fields contain summaries of the useful issues of a case. For example, if you are searching for cases involving the legal theory of assumption of risk in regard to automobile accidents, you should search in the digest field and the synopsis field by typing

```
sy,di(assum! /p risk /p automobile car vehicle)
```

Finding Cases by a Particular Judge

On WESTLAW, you can search for cases authored by a particular judge by using the judge field **ju(posner)**. The only catch is that the judge has to author the majority opinion. A judge field search does not retrieve an opinion where a judge dissented or concurred. To retrieve the name of a dissenting or concurring judge, you have to search in the synopsis field. To retrieve a concurring opinion by a judge, type

```
sy(powell /s concur!)
```

and to retrieve dissenting opinions written by a judge, type

```
sy(powell /s dissent!)
```

Opinion Field

Although it is possible to limit your search to the opinion field on WESTLAW, you will rarely want to do so. The opinion field is so broad that it does not add to the precision of your search.

Searching for a Docket Number

Decisions that have not been published but are available in slip opinion form are usually filed and cited by docket number. Simply type the docket number 86-1234 in the correct database.

Searching for Counsel

If you are searching for cases that involved a particular attorney, you should search the attorney field. For example, to search for district court cases in which Griffin Bell represented a party, access the **DCT** database and enter

```
at(griffin +3 bell)
```

Searching for a Case by Date

By using WESTLAW, you can restrict your search in a variety of ways: to a specific day, month, or year; before or after a specific date; or between a range of dates.

To formulate a date restriction, type **da** followed by the date or date range in parentheses. Many date formats are acceptable; for example:

`da(6-11-88)`	cases decided on June 11, 1988
`da(aft aug 11, 1965)`	cases decided after August 11, 1965
`da(bef 1982)`	cases decided before January 1982

Connect the date restriction to the rest of your query with the ampersand "&" connector. To retrieve the 1974 Supreme Court decision concerning former President Nixon's authority to withhold incriminating tape recordings, access the **SCT** database and type

```
ti(nixon) & executive president! /s privilege &
                    da(1974)
```

Combining Fields

To search the same terms in more than one field, separate the field abbreviations with a comma but no space, e.g., **sy,di**. Use the "&" connector to add a second field search or descriptive words to your query (as described above with date restrictions). Thus, to retrieve state cases that were decided after 1970 and have the words comatose and incompetent in the synopsis field and the digest field, access the **ALLSTATES** database and type

```
sy,di(comatose & incompetent) & da(aft 1970)
```

Browsing Cases on WESTLAW

Once you retrieve cases on WESTLAW, you must determine if they are relevant to your issue. You can browse cases on-line in various ways. The easiest way to search for relevant materials is to browse in the term mode (Figure 2.14).

When you run your query, your search result will automatically be displayed in term mode. When you are in term mode, each time you press **ENTER,** the next page containing your search terms in the required relationships is displayed. The first page of each case is always displayed, whether it contains your search terms or not. To move from one document to another, type **r** followed by the document rank number. The LOCATE (**loc**) command allows you to browse your result for a particular term, whether or not the term appeared in your original query.

After viewing your search result, you may wish to edit your query. To do this, type **q.** This will display your query so you can edit it. To begin a completely new search, type **s.** Rather than viewing the text of the documents, you may want to print a list of the document citations. To do this, type **L.** Since your library will more than likely contain the reporters and other legal materials that you retrieve on WESTLAW, sign off the computer and turn to the books. It is very expensive to read the full text of the materials on-line.

You should be aware of a feature known as star paging. You may need to cite the exact page of the official *United States Reports,* even though you are using the unofficial *Supreme Court Reporter.* The device of "star paging" is used to indicate the precise word or letter with which the next page begins. In the printed *Supreme Court Reporter,* the number of the page in the official *United States Reports* is in the margin, and an upside down "T" symbol

Figure 2.14 The Term Mode

Term Mode

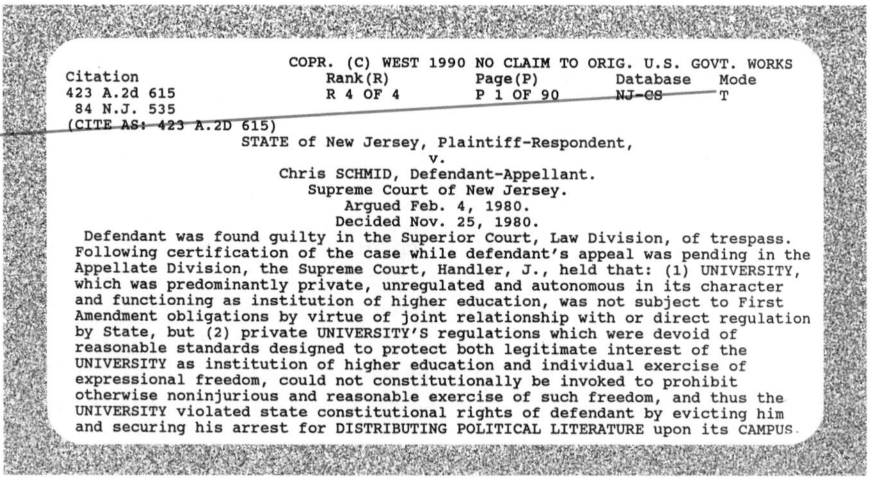

```
                    COPR. (C) WEST 1990 NO CLAIM TO ORIG. U.S. GOVT. WORKS
Citation                 Rank(R)          Page(P)        Database   Mode
423 A.2d 615             R 4 OF 4         P 1 OF 90      NJ-CS      T
 84 N.J. 535
(CITE AS: 423 A.2D 615)
              STATE of New Jersey, Plaintiff-Respondent,
                                 v.
                   Chris SCHMID, Defendant-Appellant.
                      Supreme Court of New Jersey.
                          Argued Feb. 4, 1980.
                          Decided Nov. 25, 1980.
 Defendant was found guilty in the Superior Court, Law Division, of trespass.
Following certification of the case while defendant's appeal was pending in the
Appellate Division, the Supreme Court, Handler, J., held that: (1) UNIVERSITY,
which was predominantly private, unregulated and autonomous in its character
and functioning as institution of higher education, was not subject to First
Amendment obligations by virtue of joint relationship with or direct regulation
by State, but (2) private UNIVERSITY'S regulations which were devoid of
reasonable standards designed to protect both legitimate interest of the
UNIVERSITY as institution of higher education and individual exercise of
expressional freedom, could not constitutionally be invoked to prohibit
otherwise noninjurious and reasonable exercise of such freedom, and thus the
UNIVERSITY violated state constitutional rights of defendant by evicting him
and securing his arrest for DISTRIBUTING POLITICAL LITERATURE upon its CAMPUS.
```

appears in the text at the point where the page break occurs in the official reporter (Figure 2.15).

Star paging is also available on WESTLAW where it allows you to view page numbers of cases as they appear in the bound volumes or the advance sheets of West's National Reporter System and the *United States Reports* or official reports from many states. Page numbers will appear highlighted within the text exactly where page breaks occur in the printed volumes (Figure 2.16).

Conclusion

You have just learned how to find cases using digests and on WESTLAW. We discussed how digests are put together and how to use them. We also introduced West topic and key numbers. The same topic and key numbers that appear in cases are the subject access points in the digests. We noted that West has individual sets of digests for almost all of the states in addition to several regional and federal digests and the mammoth *Decennial* and *General Digests.* You also learned how to search on WESTLAW by identifying words or phrases that are pertinent to your issue without having to deal with specific key num-

Figure 2.15 Star Paging in the *Supreme Court Reporter*

1022 **105 SUPREME COURT REPORTER** **469 U.S. 559**

eral labor regulation as applied to state railroad employees, 426 U.S., at 854, n. 18 [96 S.Ct., at 2475, n. 18], *National League of Cities* acknowledged that not all aspects of a State's sovereign authority are immune from federal control." 456 U.S., at 764, n. 28, 102 S.Ct., at 2153, n. 28.

tution itself. A unique feature of the United States is the *federal* system of government guaranteed by the Constitution and implicit in the very name of our country. Despite some genuflecting in the Court's opinion to the concept of federalism, today's decision effectively reduces the Tenth Amendment to meaningless rhetoric when

these cases.[3]

Whatever effect the Court's decision may have in weakening the application of *stare decisis,* it is likely to be less ⊥560 important than what the Court has done to the Constitution—

the Court that *it*—an unelected majority of five Justices—today rejects almost 200 years of the understanding of the constitutional status of federalism. In doing so, there is only a single passing reference to

2. Justice O'CONNOR, the only new member of the Court since our decision in *National League of Cities,* has joined the Court in reaffirming its principles. See *Transportation Union v. Long Island R. Co.,* 455 U.S. 678, 102 S.Ct. 1349, 71 L.Ed.2d 547 (1982), and *FERC v. Mississippi,* 456 U.S. 742, 775, 102 S.Ct. 2126, 2145, 72 L.Ed.2d 532 (1982) (O'CONNOR, J., dissenting in part).

3. As one commentator noted, *stare decisis* represents "a natural evolution from the very nature of our institutions." Lile, Some Views on the Rule of *Stare Decisis,* 4 Va.L.Rev. 95, 97 (1916).

Figure 2.16 Star Paging on WESTLAW

Star Paging on WESTLAW

```
                              COPR. (C) WEST 1990 NO CLAIM TO ORIG. U.S. GOVT. WORKS
105 S.Ct. 1005                      FOUND DOCUMENT P 54 OF 100     SCT          P
(CITE AS: 469 U.S. 528, *559,  105 S.CT. 1005, **1022)
 today participated in National League of Cities and the cases reaffirming it.
 [FN2]  The stability of judicial decision, and with it respect for the
 authority of this Court, are not served by the precipitate overruling of
 multiple precedents that we witness in these cases. [FN3]

     FN2. Justice O'CONNOR, the only new member of the Court since our decision
    in National League of Cities, has joined the Court in reaffirming its
    principles.  See Transportation Union v. Long Island R. Co., 455 U.S. 678,
    102 S.Ct. 1349, 71 L.Ed.2d 547 (1982), and FERC v. Mississippi, 456 U.S.
    742, 775, 102 S.Ct. 2126, 2145, 72 L.Ed.2d 532 (1982) (O'CONNOR, J.,
    dissenting in part).

     FN3. As one commentator noted, stare decisis represents "a natural
    evolution from the very nature of our institutions."  Lile, Some Views on
    the Rule of Stare Decisis, 4 Va.L.Rev. 95, 97 (1916).

  Whatever effect the Court's decision may have in weakening the application of
 stare decisis, it is likely to be less *560 important than what the Court
 has done to the Constitution itself.  A unique feature of the United States is
 the federal system of government guaranteed by the Constitution and implicit in
 the very name of our country.  Despite some genuflecting in the Court's opinion
```

bers. On the other hand, you can also search by topic and key number. Restricting your searching to specific fields—that is, the title, citation, synopsis, court, judge, topic, headnote, opinion, and digest—helps you focus your research and retrieve relevant cases. WESTLAW gives you enormous flexibility in getting the best results.

3 Updating Case Law Research

Finding the law is only half of the legal research battle. Updating it is the second, and equally important, half. Because of the constant possibility of change in the law, systems have been created that help you determine the current status of any legal authority. The four methods that will be discussed in this chapter are *Shepard's Citations, Shepard's PreView,* Insta-Cite, and using WESTLAW as a citator.

Shepard's Citations

Case law is very dependent on precedent. Courts give deference to legal principles that have been established by prior decisions. Because of this respect for accumulated judicial wisdom, Frank Shepard developed a citation service more than one hundred years ago. It provides a method of historically tracking all references to a specific case in succeeding cases.

His service, *Shepard's Citations,* lists, in tabular form, all authority citing a specific authority. For case authority, it lists all cases (known as the *citing* cases) that have cited a specific case (known as the *cited* case). Figure 3.1 shows part of the table listing all cases that have cited the Supreme Court decision at 411 U.S. 1. For reasons given below, using Shepard's citators, a process called "Shepardizing," is an essential part of legal practice. An eminent legal historian described the evolving dependence of the profession on *Shepard's Citations* thusly: "These red books, thick and thin, useful but unloved, became as familiar to lawyers as West's little keys."

Why *Shepard's Citations* Are Used

The first reason to use *Shepard's Citations* is to determine whether an authority—a U.S. Supreme Court decision, for example—on which you might be relying is still valid. Though the law is conservative, it does change at times; some of what was once "good law" is now "bad law." Thousands of cases in the two-hundred year history of American jurisprudence have been reversed or overruled by subsequent adjudications. These "bad" cases are still found in law books, and they are still in the on-line services.

Figure 3.1 A Portion of *Shepard's Citations* for *U.S. Reports*

Cited Case

Citing Cases

Vol. 410 UNITED STATES SUPREME COURT REPORTS

501FS[1]564
Cir. 6
473FS[2]338
504FS474
Cir. 7
h566F2d[1]37
603F2d[1]1269
419FS1310
Cir. 9
559F2d[1]1144
d613F2d[1]183
613F2d[2]185
j613F2d187
643F2d653
f403FS[4]356
Cir. 11
719F2d1087
Ala
294Ala577
319So2d704
Ariz
135Az151
25AzA146
541P2d937
659P2d1296
Calif
32CA3d64
40CA3d659
51CA3d678
54CA3d801
17C3d666
17C3d670
32C3d800
107CaR850
115CaR311
124CaR655
127CaR44
131CaR658
131CaR660
187CaR412
552P2d442
552P2d444
654P2d182
Colo
193Col474
568P2d41
Del
314A2d212
327A2d752
Idaho
99Ida503
584P2d648
Ill
37IlA940
117IlA566
75Il2d582
347NE44
389NE1167
453NE943
Kan
231Kan642
648P2d715
Mo
574SW361
NJ
70NJ572
74NJ353
129Su244
145Su375
152Su499
322A2d844
362A2d24
367A2d1195
378A2d67

378A2d222
NM
96NM536
632P2d1174
NY
41Ap2d294
41Ap2d297
83Ap2d92
83Ap2d95
78Msc2d318
116Msc2d990
32NY240
56NY310
56NY315
298NE71
437NE1092
437NE1095
342S2d582
342S2d585
356S2d993
444S2d963
444S2d965
452S2d335
452S2d338
456S2d935
RI
433A2d174
SD
260NW641
287NW484
Tex
636SW489
Utah
614P2d1239
Wash
87W2d547
554P2d1067

– 743 –
(35LE675)
(93SC1237)
Wyo
s490P2d1069
cc500FS1323
439US[1]69
451US[1]364
j451US377
Cir. 2
497F2d728
f503F2d1189
j503F2d1191
d520F2d[1]802
379FS[1]1165
382FS[1]1233
385FS[1]225
427FS[1]1191
Cir. 3
493FS[1]88
Cir. 4
d456FS[1]1155
Cir. 5
485F2d[1]1304
496F2d[1]111
498F2d[1]1235
538F2d[1]1083
396FS[1]813
Cir. 7
h566F2d[1]37
Cir. 9
559F2d1149
613F2d[1]183
j613F2d187
Calif
40CA3d660

54CA3d801
115CaR311
127CaR44
Colo
193Col474
568P2d41
Del
314A2d212
327A2d752
Mo
574SW361
NJ
74NJ353
378A2d222
NY
41Ap2d297
78Msc2d318
32NY240
56NY311
298NE71
437NE1093
342S2d585
344S2d890
356S2d993
452S2d336
SD
260NW641
287NW484
Wyo
575P2d1112
656P2d1145

– 752 –
(36LE1)
(93SC1245)
US reh den
in411US959
s406US957
s458F2d649
413US[1]567
d414US[1]59
j414US[1]62
j414US[1]65
414US530
j414US535
j414US[1]537
415US715
e415US[1]731
j415US760
415US770
415US[1]786
416US[1]126
j418US[1]68
419US[1]401
d421US[1]300
j421US[1]304
424US30
431US403
435US775
442US300
450US115
450US[1]122
j450US131
Cir. D.C.
378FS[1]1235
Cir. 1
f482F2d98
f482F2d[1]100
519F2d1366
358FS1198
373FS[1]631
417FS448
437FS443
460FS1044

495FS[1]734
e497FS[1]400
Cir. 2
477F2d1115
j498F2d807
508F2d986
f532F2d[1]873
575F2d382
365FS[1]52
366FS793
374FS248
379FS77
382FS984
382FS[1]985
388FS253
394FS[1]590
d402FS[1]184
f417FS845
417FS[1]846
e443FS323
457FS[1]299
f497FS[1]423
e550FS[1]1034
Cir. 3
502F2d[1]1128
552F2d538
365FS363
382FS[1]387
d393FS123
j393FS[1]126
399FS[1]1262
501FS782
501FS[1]783
83FRD[1]477
Cir. 4
513F2d242
710F2d[1]181
477FS[1]323
Cir. 5
e498F2d[1]247
506F2d819
508F2d[1]777
526F2d288
541F2d1154
580F2d752
717F2d[1]1493
d377FS[1]1020
d382FS[1]807
382FS[1]816
d396FS[1]812
e402FS[1]927
531FS764
546FS[1]454
Cir. 6
519F2d404
664F2d561
666F2d[1]1027
362FS[1]32
387FS[1]1128
f419FS[1]1007
e424FS[1]592
496FS209
499FS134
d499FS[1]137
Cir. 7
542F2d1280
370FS68
73FRD112
Cir. 8
637F2d1162
385FS[1]705
387FS[1]402
404FS[1]646
424FS[1]954

493FS1327
546FS[1]486
Cir. 9
540F2d1365
591F2d[1]1261
706F2d1527
358FS355
390FS[1]62
88FRD[1]542
Cir. 10
f631F2d[1]711
Cir. 11
435FS1094
Ariz
132Az163
132Az167
644P2d899
644P2d903
Calif
131CA3d104
182CaR234
Colo
184Col76
186Col63
518P2d810
525P2d466
Conn
175Ct561
400A2d720
DC
324A2d189
Fla
295So2d292
351So2d46
Haw
60H289
588P2d920
Idaho
97Ida202
541P2d626
Ill
57Il2d84
309NE591
Ind
422NE716
Iowa
211NW341
Mass
368Mas823
385Mas1206
388Mas192
389Mas937
333NE382
434NE963
446NE46
452NE1142
Mich
412Mch382
317NW4
Mo
504SW88
Mont
177Mt78
580P2d448
NJ
81NJ70
81NJ78
149Su490
374A2d63
405A2d353
405A2d357
NY
54Ap2d266
64Ap2d878

113Msc2d713
35NY185
35NY191
45NY808
316NE862
316NE866
381NE337
359S2d543
359S2d549
388S2d472
408S2d772
409S2d130
453S2d598
Ohio
53OA217
373NE1278
Pa
255PaS365
387A2d92
PR
110DPR261
Tenn
633SW307
Wash
93W2d703
611P2d1258
Wis
93Wis2d504
287NW532
W Va
233SE423
270SE645

Vol. 411

– 1 –
(36LE16)
(93SC1278)
US reh den
in411US959
s406US966
s411US980
s337FS280
411US208
j411US928
412US458
j412US461
413US462
j414US[2]432
414US656
415US[2]271
j415US[1]278
415US375
415US[1]539
415US713
417US[1]612
d418US[2]742
j418US[1]760
j419US[2]420
j419US[1]586
420US[1]538
426US324
426US[1]602
426US[2]814
427US[1]312
j427US[1]318
427US506
j429US[1]216
429US[1]259
j430US515
431US[1]503
j432US15
j432US459
f432US[1]470
433US291

433US295
433US410
434US[1]381
434US391
435US221
436US[1]378
436US[1]663
d438US[1]290
j438US357
j438US[1]357
439US[2]70
j439US1053
440US[2]97
j440US114
440US[1]199
j440US597
441US[1]77
j441US398
442US[1]272
446US[1]76
j446US113
447US[1]462
448US[1]323
j448US341
448US[1]518
448US[1]588
448US[1]1329
449US[1]174
j449US188
450US[1]230
j450US243
450US[2]478
j451US35
457US9
457US[1]217
457US230
457US232
e457US[1]235
e457US[1]239
j457US245
457US[1]963
457US[2]969
458US[1]200
j458US214
458US[1]486
51USLW
[4170
j51USLW
[4322
51USLW
[4585
j51USLW
[4779
4MJ802
12MJ910
77TC872
97FRD614
Cir. D.C.
477F2d1182
483F2d[1]1317
525F2d561
593F2d[1]1125
665F2d1233
674F2d10
676F2d730
j676F2d753
686F2d[2]980
d386FS1326
430FS[2]822
436FS[2]136
468FS[2]690
488FS[1]133
Cir. 1
482F2d[1]99

508F2d[2]498
d519F2d
[[1]1367
537F2d564
554F2d[1]497
578F2d[1]450
614F2d2
638F2d[1]268
641F2d1012
649F2d[2]77
659F2d[1]282
671F2d4
699F2d[2]6
e373FS635
373FS[1]648
377FS621
d377FS[1]622
379FS[2]49
385FS[1]400
388FS[2]393
388FS[2]1035
390FS1316
390FS[1]1317
392FS[1]302
e392FS[1]1141
395FS[2]627
396FS[1]1296
396FS[2]1298
406FS[1]855
415FS[2]495
j415FS[1]505
j415FS[2]506
f423FS[1]1265
435FS[1]262
439FS1128
465FS[2]660
522FS206
536FS[1]1388
561FS[1]1057
Cir. 2
476F2d[1]405
j476F2d[1]826
j476F2d[1]828
d482F2d
[[1]1336
489F2d[1]1091
489F2d[2]1091
e507F2d[1]1068
j507F2d[1]1073
f508F2d[1]1028
554F2d[1]538
562F2d843
562F2d[2]844
j562F2d[1]865
576F2d462
j579F2d181
584F2d[2]604
601F2d[1]1234
601F2d[2]1238
696F2d[1]223
715F2d[1]783
717F2d[1]41
357FS[1]763
357FS[2]763
359FS[2]971
360FS232
f361FS[1]440
361FS[1]1053
f361FS[2]1327
362FS[2]660
363FS669
365FS[2]78
365FS[2]1167
366FS[2]739

Continued

36

You can find, for example, the 1942 Supreme Court case of *Betts v. Brady* in any of the reporters for U.S. Supreme Court cases or in the **SCT-OLD** database on WESTLAW. The case held that the Sixth Amendment did not apply to the states and that there is no absolute right to counsel in a state criminal trial. Nothing in those reports says *"This case has been overruled and is no longer good law."* If you found *Betts* in the court reports and stopped researching at this point, you would be convinced that a state has no obligation to provide an attorney for an indigent defendant in a criminal trial. If you Shepardize *Betts v. Brady,* however, you will find that the case was overruled twenty years later by the Supreme Court in *Gideon v. Wainwright* (Figure 3.2).

Nothing is more damaging to your client's interests or your own professional reputation than to rest your arguments firmly on bad law. The first reason to Shepardize is to avoid such damage.

The second reason to Shepardize is to determine how a case has been *treated* by other cases. Aside from the question of being "good law" or "bad law," the value of a case may be strengthened or weakened by the interpretation subsequently given it by the same court and/or other courts. It may be that every court that has confronted a situation similar to the one in the cited case has chosen to construe that case narrowly. Although the case is still "good law," subsequent interpretations of it may make it less compelling authority. The precedential value of a case greatly depends on the treatment it has received by later cases.

A third, and final, reason to Shepardize is simply to find more cases. Citators are not comprehensive case-finding tools in the same way that West digests are, but because cases tend to cite the seminal case in a particular area of law, if you find the seminal case and Shepardize it, you are likely to discover numerous cases on the same issue.

Figure 3.2 Shepardizing *Betts v. Brady*

(a) Shepardizing on WESTLAW

```
                                   SHEPARD'S  (Rank 1 of 1)          Page 5 of 35
CITATIONS TO: 62 S.Ct. 1252
CITATOR: UNITED STATES CITATIONS
Retrieval                                                  Headnote
   No.     -----Analysis----- -------Citation------          No.
    1      Q  Questioned        82 S.Ct. 884, 892             6
    2                           82 S.Ct. at 1259
    3                           83 S.Ct. 768, 770             7
    4                           83 S.Ct. 792, 793             7
    5      O  Overruled         83 S.Ct. 792, 794
    6                           83 S.Ct. 792, 799             7
    7      E  Explained         83 S.Ct. 792, 799             7
    8      J  Dissenting Opin   84 S.Ct. 80, 81               7
    9      Q  Questioned        84 S.Ct. 1489, 1492           7
   10      J  Dissenting Opin   84 S.Ct. 1489, 1503           6
   11      J  Dissenting Opin   84 S.Ct. 1774, 1797
   12      Q  Questioned        85 S.Ct. 209, 218             4
   13      Q  Questioned        85 S.Ct. 1065, 1073
   14                           85 S.Ct. 1628, 1663
   15      J  Dissenting Opin   85 S.Ct. 1628, 1677
   16      J  Dissenting Opin   85 S.Ct. 1678, 1697           6

Copyright (C) 1990 McGraw-Hill, Inc.; Copyright (C) 1990 West Publishing Co.
```

Figure 3.2 Shepardizing *Betts v. Brady* (continued)

(b) Shepardizing in the Hard Copy Volume

Citing Case—*Gideon v. Wainwright*

"o" indicates overruling.

Cited Case—*Betts v. Brady*

Vol. 316 UNITED STATES SUPREME COURT REPORTS

– 450 –
(86LE1591)
(62SC1144)
s315US793
s41FS537
s94CCL699
4TCt216
18TCt12
24TCt637
29TCt271
36TCt282
58TCt911
59TCt74
66TCt356
77TCt63
Cir. D.C.
707F2d[2]561
Cir. 1
61FS[1]1016
Cir. 2
158F2d[2]161
306F2d[1]827
199FS458
199FS[2]466
Cir. 3
181F2d[2]405
Cir. 4
205F2d[1]342
Cir. 5
562F2d978
Cir. 6
151F2d[1]1000
229F2d[2]698
400F2d[1]823
270FS[1]939
Cir. 7
160FS[1]328
Cir. 8
266F2d69
Cir. 9
172FS[2]938
Cir. 10
80FS[2]344
CCPA
j359F2d[2]885
CtCl
f97CCL262
99CCL570
99CCL571
101CCL743
104CCL122
179CCL610
208CCL579
223CCL430
375F2d[1]838
530F2d869
620F2d855
f47FS[1]119
e48FS[1]358
55FS[1]624
60FS[2]469
Mass
378Mas273
391NE263
PR
74PRR922
So C
233SoC48
103SE427
– 455 –
(86LE1595)
(62SC1252)
s315US791
317US[1]24
317US[7]276

321US[7]115
j322US[4]495
322US[4]602
324US[7]46
324US[7]764
324US[1]768
325US[4]95
325US[7]97
326US[3]326
327US[1]85
329US[6]665
j332US[7]83
332US[7]137
j332US[7]140
j332US[7]141
333US[7]281
333US[6]656
333US[4]659
333US[5]660
333US[3]666
333US[7]676
j333US[3]677
j333US[5]677
j333US[6]677
j333US[7]677
j333US[4]679
334US[7]684
j334US[7]685
334US[7]730
334US[7]739
335US[7]441
337US[6]780
c337US782
339US661
339US[4]666
342US[6]64
342US[6]179
d348US[7]9
348US[3]108
349US[4]391
350US[6]118
j351US[3]36
354US[4]77
355US[6]159
j356US[6]83
d357US[6]441
j357US[7]442
358US[7]636
361US[4]246
j361US[7]255
j363US[3]704
j364US[5]275
365US[3]117
q365US[3]119
j365US[3]208
j366US[3]158
368US[6]459
369US[4]517
q369US[4]519
q369US[4]520
370US908
372US[6]337
o372US339
372US[6]348
e372US[6]349
372US[6]478
j375US[6]3
q378US[6]6
j378US[4]26
j378US[3]407
q379US[2]80
q380US[3]414
j381US[4]512
381US[3]590
j381US[3]616
384US[4]469

e385US399
385US[4]564
q386US[7]43
j388US[6]172
q389US[6]134
395US[4]794
q395US[4]795
c405US[7]484
j405US[7]485
q407US[7]31
q407US[4]65
408US287
q411US[4]788
j419US255
422US[6]807
j422US[6]844
q440US[7]371
j440US378
q452US[7]25
j452US35
9MJ305
15MJ116
Cir. D.C.
139F2d[7]367
148F2d[7]875
j177F2d[4]87
259F2d[5]790
j419F2d[6]1174
421F2d1160
485F2d[1]957
584F2d488
624F2d[3]201
624F2d[3]218
146FS[4]882
Cir. 1
181F2d[3]602
d191F2d[6]965
203F2d[7]935
204F2d[7]362
96FS[4]707
f101FS[4]165
f105FS[6]529
111FS[3]418
123FS[3]443
124FS[3]37
141FS[4]606
332FS[6]834
377FS1341
432FS[4]115
Cir. 2
e137F2d[1]1010
190F2d[6]253
221F2d[4]629
d250F2d[7]354
263F2d[3]943
292F2d[4]323
303F2d[4]885
d313F2d460
315F2d[4]866
j319F2d[3]318
330F2d[4]304
q330F2d[4]310
j330F2d[4]315
332F2d[4]891
q333F2d[7]610
398F2d[4]985
q465F2d[7]121
j611F2d421
694F2d[5]22
e709F2d[6]168
113FS[3]920
171FS[6]561
177FS[1]507
184FS[4]282

184FS[6]542
200FS[4]907
205FS[6]514
209FS[7]530
210FS[3]277
f210FS[3]279
212FS[5]880
212FS[7]928
214FS[4]646
219FS[4]153
e219FS[4]266
q219FS[6]268
261FS[5]400
q327FS[6]546
24FRD79
39FRD284
Cir. 3
130F2d[4]657
175F2d[2]254
203F2d[5]426
203F2d[7]806
224F2d[4]508
224F2d[5]512
f310F2d[4]724
j310F2d[4]735
329F2d[4]858
e329F2d[5]858
q334F2d[3]529
355F2d[7]313
j359F2d[7]947
j430F2d[5]469
74FS[1]848
74FS[3]848
74FS[5]848
81FS[3]870
81FS[6]871
84FS[3]940
85FS[3]787
88FS[3]780
97FS[7]939
148FS[6]684
187FS[3]715
196FS[3]53
208FS[6]639
226FS[3]420
q226FS[6]582
243FS[7]700
271FS[4]409
33FRD424
33FRD438
33FRD454
38FRD463
Cir. 4
128F2d[7]1013
129F2d[7]110
130F2d[7]881
133F2d[2]477
155F2d[7]5
280F2d[4]539
280F2d[6]539
280F2d[3]541
294F2d[6]396
294F2d[3]609
297F2d853
d299F2d[7]173
j310F2d[3]917
315F2d[4]644
315F2d[5]644
q319F2d[6]2
q319F2d[6]4
q319F2d[5]772
c368F2d298
375F2d628
375F2d[6]628

c381F2d[4]641
c415F2d1325
f443F2d[5]1095
f443F2d[6]1095
j443F2d[5]1100
447F2d[5]57
447F2d[6]57
483F2d[3]655
q561F2d[4]542
47FS[1]366
165FS[3]24
176FS[7]954
201FS[6]447
206FS[6]302
q216FS[5]290
227FS[5]2
q227FS[5]3
251FS[4]665
e257FS[7]808
q307FS[4]206
j310FS[4]563
q312FS[4]310
324FS[5]697
355FS[6]344
Cir. 5
158F2d[7]617
194F2d[7]865
205F2d[3]668
j205F2d[4]675
224F2d[4]905
228F2d[6]659
228F2d[7]664
250F2d[3]647
258F2d[6]941
j258F2d[7]944
261F2d[7]233
j263F2d[4]44
j263F2d[6]46
330F2d[4]525
341F2d[4]98
c341F2d[6]776
341F2d[5]780
e353F2d[3]107
366F2d[4]27
q400F2d[3]596
q400F2d[5]596
410F2d335
j416F2d[5]1027
422F2d[3]301
430F2d[5]1117
430F2d[6]1117
496F2d[4]1058
j505F2d[3]1344
j505F2d[6]1344
525F2d933
c618F2d[4]384
j618F2d388
j640F2d608
126FS[3]546
139FS[6]901
140FS[7]726
185FS[5]936
q217FS[7]172
236FS[7]240
238FS[5]595
261FS[4]265
q270FS[6]51
272FS[4]511
q298FS298
331FS[5]433
345FS[6]1030
385FS[4]1047
Cir. 6
163F2d[1]823

256F2d[4]378
256F2d[6]382
j256F2d[6]386
q317F2d[5]783
q371F2d[3]667
q558F2d[6]337
666F2d[4]1054
137FS[6]536
q313FS[3]1060
q357FS[3]81
522FS[6]763
9FRD348
Cir. 7
146F2d[4]247
155F2d[6]912
157F2d[6]808
158F2d[4]350
166F2d[7]980
167F2d[3]803
172F2d[7]696
173F2d[3]670
189F2d[6]768
238F2d[7]312
241F2d[3]108
281F2d[7]786
q329F2d[6]358
q402F2d309
q403F2d701
j440F2d839
719F2d[6]904
52FS[7]270
54FS[7]925
54FS[4]980
54FS[7]1000
60FS[2]657
60FS[3]821
60FS[6]821
74FS[1]993
77FS[4]21
86FS[4]384
Cir. 8
144F2d[1]918
161F2d[3]304
308F2d[4]72
q407F2d[5]128
435F2d[6]371
e55FS[6]961
103FS[7]149
119FS[4]784
241FS[5]1013
281FS[5]797
313FS[4]205
q313FS[4]206
q421FS[7]673
Cir. 9
198F2d[7]471
j253F2d[3]847
258F2d[4]306
259F2d[6]280
280F2d[4]735
310F2d[4]37
q321F2d[7]712
q372F2d[6]370
403F2d860
j425F2d617
e490F2d366
q551F2d1166
586F2d1328
j586F2d1335
647F2d[4]880
j678F2d799
60FS[3]853
88FS[5]949
88FS[6]949

88FS[4]950
112FS[3]443
154FS[5]238
154FS[7]238
177FS[7]390
230FS[3]178
268FS[4]1008
553FS[4]1318
Cir. 10
156F2d[6]941
170F2d[7]741
269F2d[3]487
315F2d[6]617
j315F2d[6]620
508F2d[4]149
77FS[1]555
126FS[5]568
171FS[7]390
195FS[4]196
202FS[3]78
223FS[6]596
q224FS[7]866
Cir. 11
46FS[4]421
79FS[3]916
209FS[5]302
h209FS[4]303
222FS872
222FS[6]872
234FS[3]1010
237FS[3]274
239FS[4]142
q273FS[5]843
357FS[3]1081
q442FS[5]264
q442FS[7]264
Ala
254Ala541
277Ala156
34A1A196
41A1A494
41A1A558
41A1A656
42A1A425
42A1A453
42A1A505
42A1A551
44A1A104
38So2d288
49So2d290
136So2d576
141So2d208
148So2d253
167So2d179
167So2d914
167So2d915
169So2d313
203So2d286
342So2d956
409So2d897
Alk
438P2d230
487P2d840
604P2d1108
Ariz
96Az126
392P2d786
Ark
227Ark50
243Ark354
256Ark429
296SW207
420SW536
508SW56

Calif
114CA2d844
154CA2d236
174CA2d826
200CA2d24
242CA2d728
260CA2d526
12CA3d763
17CA3d20
80CA3d439
82CA3d204
112CA3d116
132CA3d99
22C2d575
24C2d338
28C2d851
28C2d863
47C2d359
51C2d795
57C2d166
64C2d17
65C2d205
66C2d625
28C3d345
18CaR59
19CaR459
48CaR699
51CaR742
53CaR289
58CaR591
67CaR249
90CaR834
92CaR513
94CaR914
113CaR746
135CaR855
145CaR734
147CaR43
168CaR636
169CaR84
182CaR891
133P2d462
133P2d466
140P2d28
149P2d701
172P2d689
172P2d696
250P2d371
303P2d761
316P2d15
336P2d950
345P2d538
367P2d699
409P2d923
417P2d873
427P2d191
618P2d182
Colo
120Col5
131Col360
206P2d339
281P2d810
Conn
1Cir358
1Cir423
1Cir554
1Cir560
2Cir573
24CS17
24CS96
24CS271
24CS276
25CS67
135Ct273

Continued

54

How *Shepard's Citations* Work

Thus far we have talked about Shepardizing cases. This is probably the first and most frequent way you will use the citators. But, in fact, it is possible to Shepardize nearly any legal authority, primary or secondary. You can Shepardize cases, statutes, administrative regulations and decisions, law review articles, and other types of legal authority. The sheer abundance of citators creates the first problem in the mechanics of Shepardizing (Figure 3.3).

The initial step in Shepardizing is to make sure that you have the appropriate set of volumes to find the authority that you wish to Shepardize. A library collection of Shepard's citators contains literally hundreds of different volumes. They all have the same dark red bindings. You must read the titles carefully to find the correct set. This sounds simple, but novice users frequently start with the wrong set by accident. If you have a case from the *North Eastern Reporter,* you need to find *Shepard's North Eastern Reporter Citations;* even though *Shepard's North Western Reporter Citations* looks similar, it won't do the job.

It is also possible to Shepardize the same case in more than one citator set, and the citing authority that you find will be different depending on the set that you use. For example, a state supreme court case can be Shepardized in either a state citator or a regional reporter citator. In the state citator, the citing authority will include (1) federal cases, (2) state cases from that state, and (3) selected law review articles. The regional reporter citator has as citing authority (1) federal cases, (2) state cases *from all states,* but (3) *no* law review articles. The title page of every Shepard's lists the sources of citing authority for that set (Figure 3.4).

The second step in the process is getting all the volumes in the appropriate set of citators. Some sets of citators, such as *Shepard's United States Reports Citations,* may have more than five volumes, beginning with the initial hard-

Figure 3.3 A Wide Variety of Citators

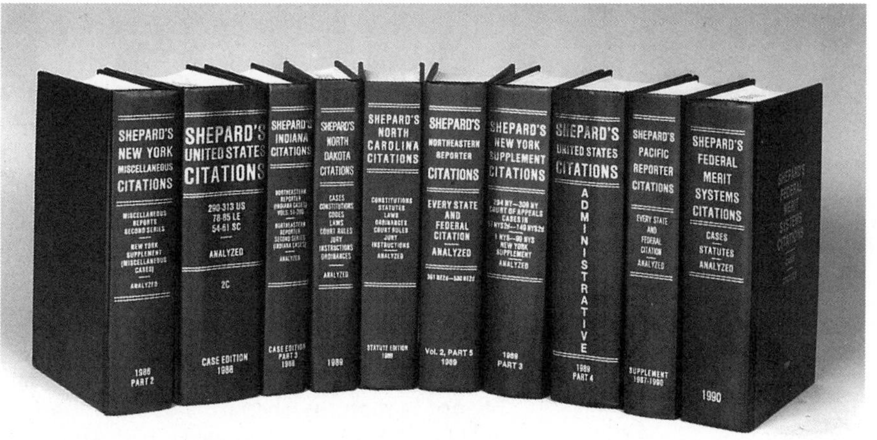

Figure 3.4 Titles Pages from a State Citator and a Regional Reporter Citator

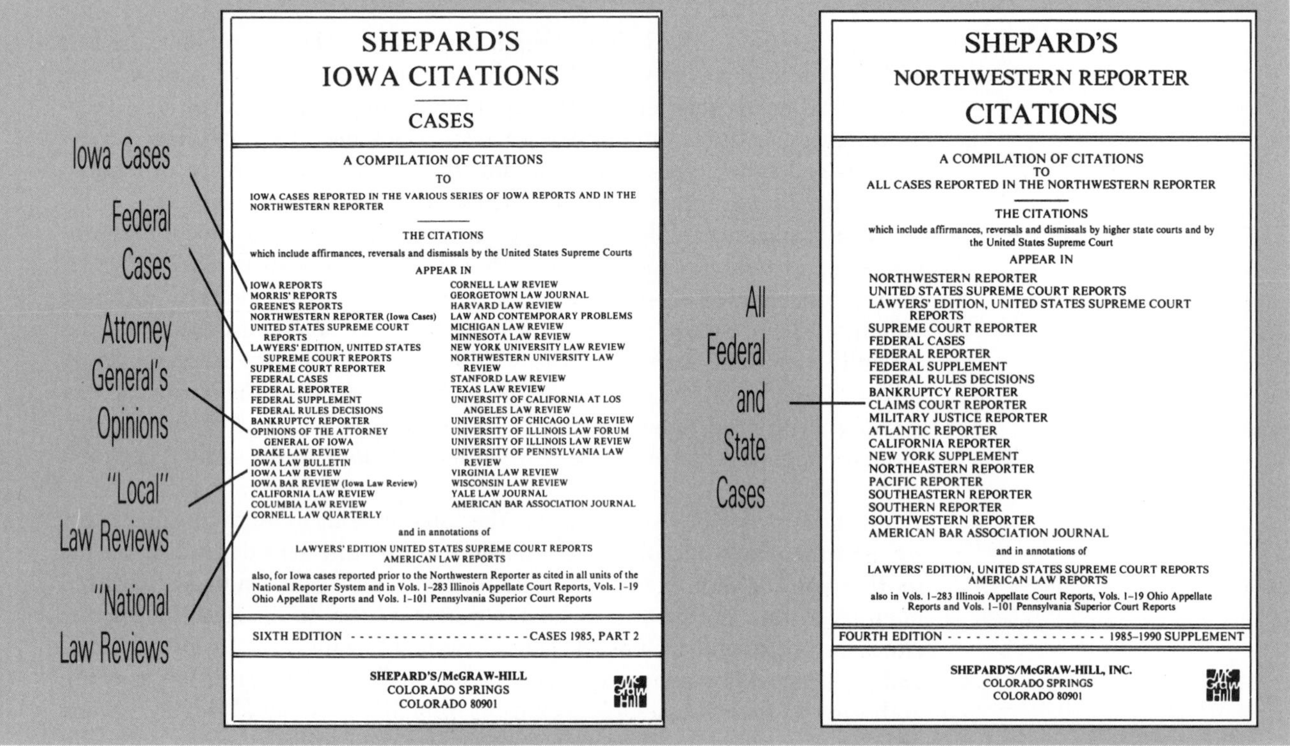

SHEPARD'S
IOWA CITATIONS

CASES

A COMPILATION OF CITATIONS
TO
IOWA CASES REPORTED IN THE VARIOUS SERIES OF IOWA REPORTS AND IN THE NORTHWESTERN REPORTER

THE CITATIONS
which include affirmances, reversals and dismissals by the United States Supreme Courts
APPEAR IN

IOWA REPORTS
MORRIS' REPORTS
GREENE'S REPORTS
NORTHWESTERN REPORTER (Iowa Cases)
UNITED STATES SUPREME COURT REPORTS
LAWYERS' EDITION, UNITED STATES SUPREME COURT REPORTS
SUPREME COURT REPORTER
FEDERAL CASES
FEDERAL REPORTER
FEDERAL SUPPLEMENT
FEDERAL RULES DECISIONS
BANKRUPTCY REPORTER
OPINIONS OF THE ATTORNEY GENERAL OF IOWA
DRAKE LAW REVIEW
IOWA LAW BULLETIN
IOWA LAW REVIEW
IOWA BAR REVIEW (Iowa Law Review)
CALIFORNIA LAW REVIEW
COLUMBIA LAW REVIEW
CORNELL LAW QUARTERLY
CORNELL LAW REVIEW
GEORGETOWN LAW JOURNAL
HARVARD LAW REVIEW
LAW AND CONTEMPORARY PROBLEMS
MICHIGAN LAW REVIEW
MINNESOTA LAW REVIEW
NEW YORK UNIVERSITY LAW REVIEW
NORTHWESTERN UNIVERSITY LAW REVIEW
STANFORD LAW REVIEW
TEXAS LAW REVIEW
UNIVERSITY OF CALIFORNIA AT LOS ANGELES LAW REVIEW
UNIVERSITY OF CHICAGO LAW REVIEW
UNIVERSITY OF ILLINOIS LAW FORUM
UNIVERSITY OF ILLINOIS LAW REVIEW
UNIVERSITY OF PENNSYLVANIA LAW REVIEW
VIRGINIA LAW REVIEW
WISCONSIN LAW REVIEW
YALE LAW JOURNAL
AMERICAN BAR ASSOCIATION JOURNAL

and in annotations of

LAWYERS' EDITION UNITED STATES SUPREME COURT REPORTS
AMERICAN LAW REPORTS

also, for Iowa cases reported prior to the Northwestern Reporter as cited in all units of the National Reporter System and in Vols. 1–283 Illinois Appellate Court Reports, Vols. 1–19 Ohio Appellate Reports and Vols. 1–101 Pennsylvania Superior Court Reports

SIXTH EDITION - CASES 1985, PART 2

SHEPARD'S/McGRAW-HILL
COLORADO SPRINGS
COLORADO 80901

SHEPARD'S
NORTHWESTERN REPORTER
CITATIONS

A COMPILATION OF CITATIONS
TO
ALL CASES REPORTED IN THE NORTHWESTERN REPORTER

THE CITATIONS
which include affirmances, reversals and dismissals by higher state courts and by the United States Supreme Court
APPEAR IN

NORTHWESTERN REPORTER
UNITED STATES SUPREME COURT REPORTS
LAWYERS' EDITION, UNITED STATES SUPREME COURT REPORTS
SUPREME COURT REPORTER
FEDERAL CASES
FEDERAL REPORTER
FEDERAL SUPPLEMENT
FEDERAL RULES DECISIONS
BANKRUPTCY REPORTER
CLAIMS COURT REPORTER
MILITARY JUSTICE REPORTER
ATLANTIC REPORTER
CALIFORNIA REPORTER
NEW YORK SUPPLEMENT
NORTHEASTERN REPORTER
PACIFIC REPORTER
SOUTHEASTERN REPORTER
SOUTHERN REPORTER
SOUTHWESTERN REPORTER
AMERICAN BAR ASSOCIATION JOURNAL

and in annotations of

LAWYERS' EDITION, UNITED STATES SUPREME COURT REPORTS
AMERICAN LAW REPORTS

also in Vols. 1–283 Illinois Appellate Court Reports, Vols. 1–19 Ohio Appellate Reports and Vols. 1–101 Pennsylvania Superior Court Reports

FOURTH EDITION - - - - - - - - - - - - - - - - - - 1985–1990 SUPPLEMENT

SHEPARD'S/McGRAW-HILL, INC.
COLORADO SPRINGS
COLORADO 80901

Source: Copyright © 1985 by McGraw-Hill, Inc. Reprinted with permission by Shepard's/McGraw-Hill, Inc. Further reproduction is strictly prohibited.

copy volumes, followed by several supplements, and ending with a current advance sheet. To be comprehensive in your Shepardizing and to be as up-to-date as possible, you must have *all* the volumes of a particular Shepard's set.

The easiest way to make sure that you have all volumes in a citator set is to begin with the most recent advance sheet in the set. Normally (though not always), this will be a monthly *red* pamphlet, and it will have a current date (Figure 3.5). On the cover of this pamphlet will be an instructional guide of "WHAT YOUR LIBRARY SHOULD CONTAIN." Make sure that you have all the volumes that you need. (A corollary to Murphy's Law says that if you are missing one volume, it will be the one that includes a citing case that has overruled the case that you are Shepardizing.)

Assume that you now have the right set of citators and all the volumes in the set. Next you must learn the very concise language of Shepard's.

First, you must become familiar with Shepard's abbreviations (Figure 3.6). Shepard's uses its own citation form; it does not use the Bluebook. For example, FS, not F.Supp., is Shepard's designation for the *Federal Supplement*. A table of these abbreviations appears at the beginning of every volume of Shepard's. Note also that the page numbers in a Shepard's list are to the page of the

Figure 3.5 An Advance Sheet for *Shepard's United States Citations*

VOL. 89 NOVEMBER, 1990 NO. 6

Shepard's United States Citations

CUMULATIVE SUPPLEMENT (IN TWO PARTS) PART 2
STATUTES AND COURT RULES

(USPS 605470)

IMPORTANT NOTICE

A 1988-1990 hardbound supplement for Shepard's United States Citations, Case Edition will be published in December, 1990 and delivered by January 31, 1991.

Do not destroy the July, 1990 gold paper-covered Semiannual Cumulative Supplement (Parts 1A, 1B, 1C, 1D and 2) for Shepard's United States Citations, Cases and Statutes.

WHAT YOUR LIBRARY SHOULD CONTAIN:
PART 1, CASES

- (6) 1988 Bound Volumes* (Vols. 1A, 1B, 1C, 2A, 2B, 2C)
- (4) 1984 Bound Volumes* (Vols. 3, 4, 5, 6)
- (2) 1984-1986 Bound Volumes* (Vols. 7A and 7B)
- (5) 1986-1988 Bound Volumes* (Vols. 8, 9, 10, 11, 12)

PART 2, STATUTES

- (5) 1986 Bound Volumes (Parts 1–5)*
- (2) 1986-1990 Bound Volumes (Parts 1 and 2)*

**Supplemented with July, 1990 Semiannual Cumulative Supplement Vol. 89 No. 2 (Parts 1A, 1B, 1C, 1D and 2), Sept., 1990 Cumulative Supplement Vol. 89 No. 4 (Part 1) and Nov., 1990 Cumulative Supplement Vol. 89 No. 6 (Parts 1 and 2)*

DESTROY ALL OTHER ISSUES

SEE TABLE OF CONTENTS ON PAGE III

RECYCLE YOUR OUTDATED SUPPLEMENTS

When you receive new supplements and are instructed to destroy the outdated versions, please consider taking these paper products to a local recycling center to help conserve our nation's natural resources. Thank you.

citing case where the citation occurs, not to the starting page of the case (Figure 3.7).

Shepard's also uses a second type of abbreviations, known as "history" and "treatment" abbreviations. The Shepard's editors read the citing cases to

Figure 3.6 *Shepard's* Abbreviations of Reporters

ABBREVIATIONS—REPORTS

AA–Antitrust Adviser, Second Edition (Shepard's, 1978)
AABA–Atwood & Brewster, Antitrust and American Business Abroad (Shepard's, 1958)
A2d–Atlantic Reporter, Second Series
Ab–Abstracts
AB–American Bankruptcy Reports
ABA–American Bar Association Journal
ABA(2)–American Bar Association Journal, Part 2
AbD–Abbott's Court of Appeals Decisions (N.Y.)
AbN–Abstracts, New Series
ABn–American Bankruptcy Reports, New Series
Ark–Arkansas Reports
AS–American State Reports
At–Atlantic Reporter
Az–Arizona Reports
AzA–Arizona Court of Appeals Reports
Bar–Barbour's Supreme Court Reports (N.Y.)
BCh–Barbour's Chancery Reports (N.Y.)
Binn–Binney's Reports (Pa.)
Blackf–Blackford's Reports (Ind.)
Bland–Bland's Chancery Reports (Md.)
Bos–Bosworth's Reports (N.Y.)
Boy–Boyce's Reports (Del.)
BP–Drake & Mullins, Bankruptcy Practice (Shepard's, 1980)
Bradb–Bradbury's Pleading & Practice

Allen–Allen's Reports (Mass.)
AR–American Law Reports
ARF–American Law Reports, Federal
AN–Abbott's New Cases (N.Y.)
AntNP–Anthon's Nisi Prius Cases (N.Y.)
Ap–New York Appellate Division Reports
Ap2d–New York Appellate Division Reports, Second Series
AR–American Reports
ARD–Application for Review Decisions
Appeals Reports (Customs)
Cai–Caines' Reports (N.Y.)
CaiCs–Caines' Cases (N.Y.)
Cal–California Supreme Court Reports
CaR–California Reporter
CaU–California Unreported Cases
CCL–Court of Claims Reports (U.S.)
CCLM–Acret, California Construction Law Manual (Shepard's, 1975)
CD–Decisions of the Commissioner of Patents

(Continued)

determine their relationship to the cited case and assign analytical abbreviations that describe the relationship. The *history* of the case is its direct procedural history. For example, on appeal the case may have been "affirmed" or "reversed" by a higher court. The *treatment* of the case is the way other cases (those not within the direct procedural history) have treated it. The Shepard's editors may, in their editorial judgment, find a citing case to have "explained" or "followed" or "distinguished" the cited case. A list of history and treatment abbreviations is also found at the beginning of each volume (Figure 3.8).

Another potentially confusing aspect of Shepard's language is the use of small, superscript numbers that refer to the *headnote of the cited case.* In the

Figure 3.7 Page Numbers in *Shepard's*

Page Where Citation Occurs Not Initial Page of the Case

Vol. 410 UNITED STATES SUPREME COURT REPORTS

501FS[1]564
Cir. 6
473FS[2]338
504FS474
Cir. 7
h566F2d[1]37
603F2d[1]1269
419FS1310
Cir. 9
559F2d[1]1144
d613F2d[1]183
613F2d[2]185
j613F2d187
643F2d653
f403FS[4]356
Cir. 11
719F2d1087
Ala
294Ala577
319So2d704
Ariz
135Az151
25AzA146
541P2d937
659P2d1296
Calif
32CA3d64
40CA3d659
51CA3d678
54CA3d801
17C3d666
17C3d670
32C3d800
107CaR850
115CaR311
124CaR655
127CaR44
131CaR658
131CaR660
187CaR412
552P2d442
552P2d444
654P2d182
Colo
193Col474
568P2d41
Del
314A2d212
327A2d752
Idaho
99Ida503
584P2d648
Ill
37IlA940
117IlA566
75Il2d582
347NE44
389NE1167
453NE943
Kan
231Kan642
648P2d715
Mo
574SW361
NJ
70NJ572
74NJ353
129Su244
145Su375
152Su499
322A2d844
362A2d24
367A2d1195
378A2d67

378A2d222
NM
96NM536
632P2d1174
NY
41Ap2d294
41Ap2d297
83Ap2d92
83Ap2d95
78Msc2d318
116Msc2d990
32NY240
56NY310
56NY315
298NE71
437NE1092
437NE1095
342S2d582
342S2d585
356S2d993
444S2d963
444S2d965
452S2d335
452S2d338
456S2d935
RI
433A2d174
SD
260NW641
287NW484
Tex
636SW489
Utah
614P2d1239
Wash
87W2d547
554P2d1067

– 743 –
(35LE675)
(93SC1237)
Wyo
s490P2d1069
cc500FS1323
439US[1]69
451US[1]364
j451US377
Cir. 2
497F2d728
f503F2d1189
j503F2d1191
d520F2d[1]802
379FS[1]1165
382FS[1]1233
385FS[1]225
427FS[1]1191
Cir. 3
493FS[1]88
Cir. 4
d456FS[1]1155
Cir. 5
485F2d[1]1304
496F2d[1]111
498F2d[1]1235
538F2d[1]1083
396FS[1]813
Cir. 7
h566F2d[1]37
Cir. 9
559F2d1149
613F2d[1]183
j613F2d187
Calif
40CA3d660

54CA3d801
115CaR311
127CaR44
Colo
193Col474
568P2d41
Del
314A2d212
327A2d752
Mo
574SW361
NJ
74NJ353
378A2d222
NY
41Ap2d297
78Msc2d318
32NY240
56NY311
298NE71
437NE1093
342S2d585
344S2d890
356S2d993
452S2d336
SD
260NW641
287NW484
Wyo
575P2d1112
656P2d1145

– 752 –
(36LE1)
(93SC1245)
US reh den
in411US959
s406US957
s458F2d649
413US[1]567
d414US[1]59
j414US[1]62
j414US[1]65
414US530
j414US535
j414US[1]537
415US715
e415US[1]731
j415US760
415US770
415US[1]786
416US[1]126
j418US[1]68
419US[1]401
d421US[1]300
j421US[1]304
424US30
431US403
435US775
442US300
450US115
450US[1]122
j450US131
Cir. D.C.
378FS[1]1235
Cir. 1
f482F2d98
f482F2d[1]100
519F2d1366
358FS1198
373FS[1]631
417FS448
437FS443
460FS1044

495FS[1]734
e497FS[1]400
Cir. 2
477F2d1115
j498F2d807
508F2d986
f532F2d[1]873
575F2d382
365FS[1]52
366FS793
374FS248
379FS77
382FS984
382FS[1]985
388FS253
394FS[1]590
d402FS[1]184
f417FS845
417FS[1]846
e443FS323
457FS[1]299
f497FS[1]423
e550FS[1]1034
Cir. 3
502F2d[1]1128
552F2d538
365FS363
382FS[1]387
d393FS123
j393FS[1]126
399FS[1]1262
501FS782
501FS[1]783
83FRD[1]477
Cir. 4
513F2d242
710F2d[1]181
477FS[1]323
Cir. 5
e498F2d[1]247
506F2d819
508F2d[1]777
526F2d288
541F2d1154
580F2d752
717F2d[1]1493
d377FS[1]1020
d382FS[1]807
382FS[1]816
d396FS[1]812
e402FS[1]927
531FS764
546FS[1]454
Cir. 6
519F2d404
664F2d561
666F2d[1]1027
362FS[1]32
387FS[1]1128
f419FS[1]1007
e424FS[1]592
496FS209
499FS134
d499FS[1]137
Cir. 7
542F2d1280
370FS68
73FRD112
Cir. 8
637F2d1162
385FS[1]705
387FS[1]402
404FS[1]646
424FS[1]954

493FS1327
546FS[1]486
Cir. 9
540F2d1365
591F2d[1]1261
706F2d1527
358FS355
390FS[1]62
88FRD[1]542
Cir. 10
f631F2d[1]711
Cir. 11
435FS1094
Ariz
132Az163
132Az167
644P2d899
644P2d903
Calif
131CA3d104
182CaR234
Colo
184Col76
186Col63
518P2d810
525P2d466
Conn
175Ct561
400A2d720
DC
324A2d189
Fla
295So2d292
351So2d46
Haw
60H289
588P2d920
Idaho
97Ida202
541P2d626
Ill
57Il2d84
309NE591
Ind
422NE716
Iowa
211NW341
Mass
368Mas823
385Mas1206
388Mas192
389Mas937
333NE382
434NE963
446NE46
452NE1142
Mich
412Mch582
317NW4
Mo
504SW88
Mont
177Mt78
580P2d448
NJ
81NJ70
81NJ78
149Su490
374A2d63
405A2d353
405A2d357
NY
54Ap2d266
64Ap2d878

113Msc2d713
35NY185
35NY191
45NY808
316NE862
316NE866
381NE337
359S2d543
359S2d549
388S2d472
408S2d772
409S2d130
453S2d598
Ohio
53OA217
373NE1278
Pa
255PaS365
387A2d92
PR
110DPR261
Tenn
633SW307
Wash
93W2d703
611P2d1258
Wis
93Wis2d504
287NW532
W Va
233SE423
270SE645

Vol. 411

– 1 –
(36LE16)
(93SC1278)
US reh den
in411US959
s406US966
s411US980
s337FS280
411US208
j411US928
412US458
j412US461
413US462
j414US[2]432
414US656
415US[2]271
j415US[1]278
415US375
415US[1]539
415US713
417US[1]612
d418US[2]742
j418US[1]760
j419US[2]420
j419US[1]586
420US[1]538
426US324
426US[1]602
426US[2]814
427US[1]312
j427US[1]318
427US506
j429US[1]216
429US[1]259
j430US515
431US[1]503
j432US15
j432US459
f432US[1]470
433US291

433US295
433US410
434US[1]381
434US391
435US221
436US[1]378
436US[1]663
d438US[1]290
j438US357
j438US[1]357
439US[2]70
j439US1053
440US[2]97
j440US114
440US[1]199
j440US597
441US[1]77
j441US398
442US[1]272
446US[1]76
j446US113
447US[1]462
448US[1]323
j448US341
448US[1]518
448US[1]588
448US[1]1329
449US[1]174
j449US188
450US[1]230
j450US243
450US[2]478
j451US35
457US9
457US[1]217
457US230
457US232
e457US[1]235
e457US[1]239
j457US245
457US[1]963
457US[2]969
458US[1]200
j458US214
458US[1]486
51USLW [4170
j51USLW [4322
51USLW [4585
j51USLW [4779
4MJ802
12MJ910
77TCt872
97FRD614
Cir. D.C.
477F2d1182
483F2d[1]1317
525F2d561
593F2d[1]1125
665F2d1233
674F2d10
676F2d730
j676F2d753
686F2d[2]980
d386FS1326
430FS[2]822
436FS[2]136
468FS[2]690
488FS[1]133
Cir. 1
482F2d[1]99

508F2d[2]498
d519F2d [[1]1367
537F2d564
554F2d[1]497
578F2d[1]450
614F2d2
638F2d[1]268
641F2d1012
649F2d[2]77
659F2d[1]282
671F2d4
699F2d[2]6
e373FS635
373FS[1]648
377FS621
d377FS[1]622
379FS[2]49
385FS[1]400
388FS[2]393
388FS[2]1035
390FS1316
390FS[1]1317
392FS[1]302
e392FS[1]1141
395FS[2]627
396FS[1]1296
396FS[2]1298
406FS[1]855
415FS[2]495
j415FS[1]505
j415FS[2]506
f423FS[1]1265
435FS[1]262
439FS1128
465FS[2]660
522FS206
536FS[1]1388
561FS[1]1057
Cir. 2
476F2d[1]405
j476F2d[1]826
j476F2d[1]828
d482F2d [[1]1336
489F2d[1]1091
489F2d[2]1091
e507F2d[1]1068
j507F2d[1]1073
f508F2d[1]1028
554F2d[1]538
562F2d843
562F2d[2]844
j562F2d[1]865
576F2d462
j579F2d181
584F2d[2]604
601F2d[1]1234
601F2d[2]1238
696F2d[1]223
715F2d[1]783
717F2d[1]41
357FS[1]763
357FS[2]763
359FS[2]971
360FS232
f361FS[1]440
361FS[1]1053
f361FS[2]1327
362FS[2]660
363FS669
365FS[2]78
365FS[2]1167
366FS[2]739

Continued

36

Figure 3.8 *Shepard's* History and Treatment Abbreviations

ABBREVIATIONS—ANALYSIS

History of Case	
a (affirmed)	Same case affirmed on rehearing.
cc (connected case)	Different case from case cited but arising out of same subject matter or intimately connected therewith.
m (modified)	Same case modified on rehearing.
r (reversed)	Same case reversed on rehearing.
s (same case)	Same case as case cited.
S (superseded)	Substitution for former opinion.
v (vacated)	Same case vacated.
US reh den	Rehearing denied by U. S. Supreme Court.
US reh dis	Rehearing dismissed by U. S. Supreme Court.

Treatment of Case	
c (criticised)	Soundness of decision or reasoning in cited case criticised for reasons given.
d (distinguished)	Case at bar different either in law or fact from case cited for reasons given.
e (explained)	Statement of import of decision in cited case. Not merely a restatement of the facts.
f (followed)	Cited as controlling.
h (harmonized)	Apparent inconsistency explained and shown not to exist.
j (dissenting opinion)	Citation in dissenting opinion.
L (limited)	Refusal to extend decision of cited case beyond precise issues involved.
o (overruled)	Ruling in cited case expressly overruled.
p (parallel)	Citing case substantially alike or on all fours with cited case in its law or facts.
q (questioned)	Soundness of decision or reasoning in cited case questioned.

example in Figure 3.9, the small "2" means that the citing case has cited that portion of the cited case summarized by its second headnote. (You might want to re-read that sibilant sentence slowly. It does make sense—really.) As puzzling as this sounds, once you understand the function of these little numbers, you will find they are very time-saving. If you are Shepardizing a famous case that has been very frequently cited, such as *Miranda v. Arizona* for example, and you are interested in only one aspect of the case, using the headnote numbers is an excellent way to winnow a very long list of citing cases into a much shorter one. If you are just interested in cases citing *Miranda* for the legal issue summarized in its second headnote, you only need to read the cases that have that particular headnote reference number in the Shepard's display. Remember, however, that the same case is often published in more than one reporter and by more than one publisher. Different publishers write different

Figure 3.9 Headnote Numbers in *Shepard's*

Vol. 410 — UNITED STATES SUPREME COURT REPORTS

501FS[1]564
Cir. 6
473FS[2]338
504FS474
Cir. 7
h566F2d[1]37
603F2d[1]1269
419FS1310
Cir. 9
559F2d[1]1144
d613F2d[1]183
613F2d[2]185
j613F2d187
643F2d653
f403FS[4]356
Cir. 11
719F2d1087
Ala
294Ala577
319So2d704
Ariz
135Az151
25AzA146
541P2d937
659P2d1296
Calif
32CA3d64
40CA3d659
51CA3d678
54CA3d801
17C3d666
17C3d670
32C3d800
107CaR850
115CaR311
124CaR655
127CaR44
131CaR658
131CaR660
187CaR412
552P2d442
552P2d444
654P2d182
Colo
193Col474
568P2d41
Del
314A2d212
327A2d752
Idaho
99Ida503
584P2d648
Ill
37IlA940
117IlA566
75Il2d582
347NE44
389NE1167
453NE943
Kan
231Kan642
648P2d715
Mo
574SW361
NJ
70NJ572
74NJ353
129Su244
145Su375
152Su499
322A2d844
362A2d24
367A2d1195
378A2d67

378A2d222
NM
96NM536
632P2d1174
NY
41Ap2d294
41Ap2d297
83Ap2d92
83Ap2d95
78Msc2d318
116Msc2d990
32NY240
56NY310
56NY315
298NE71
437NE1092
437NE1095
342S2d582
342S2d585
356S2d993
444S2d963
444S2d965
452S2d335
452S2d338
456S2d935
RI
433A2d174
SD
260NW641
287NW484
Tex
636SW489
Utah
614P2d1239
Wash
87W2d547
554P2d1067

– 743 –
(35LE675)
(93SC1237)
Wyo
s490P2d1069
cc500FS1323
439US[1]69
451US[1]364
j451US377
Cir. 2
497F2d728
f503F2d1189
j503F2d1191
d520F2d[1]802
379FS[1]1165
382FS[1]1233
385FS[1]225
427FS[1]1191
Cir. 3
493FS[1]88
Cir. 4
d456FS[1]1155
Cir. 5
485F2d[1]1304
496F2d[1]111
498F2d[1]1235
538F2d[1]1083
396FS[1]813
Cir. 7
h566F2d[1]37
Cir. 9
559F2d1149
613F2d[1]183
j613F2d187
Calif
40CA3d660

54CA3d801
115CaR311
127CaR44
Colo
193Col474
568P2d41
Del
314A2d212
327A2d752
Mo
574SW361
NJ
74NJ353
378A2d222
NY
41Ap2d297
78Msc2d318
32NY240
56NY311
298NE71
437NE1093
342S2d585
344S2d890
356S2d993
452S2d336
SD
260NW641
287NW484
Wyo
575P2d1112
656P2d1145

– 752 –
(36LE1)
(93SC1245)
US reh den
in411US959
s406US957
s458F2d649
413US[1]567
d414US[1]59
j414US[1]62
j414US[1]65
414US530
j414US535
j414US[1]537
415US715
e415US[1]731
j415US760
415US770
415US[1]786
416US[1]126
j418US[1]68
419US[1]401
d421US[1]300
j421US[1]304
424US30
431US403
435US775
442US300
450US115
450US[1]122
j450US131
Cir. D.C.
378FS[1]1235
Cir. 1
f482F2d98
f482F2d[1]100
519F2d1366
358FS1198
373FS[1]631
417FS448
437FS443
460FS1044

495FS[1]734
e497FS[1]400
Cir. 2
477F2d1115
j498F2d807
508F2d986
f532F2d[1]873
575F2d382
365FS[1]52
366FS793
374FS248
379FS77
382FS984
382FS[1]985
388FS253
394FS[1]590
d402FS[1]184
f417FS845
417FS[1]846
e443FS323
457FS[1]299
f497FS[1]423
e550FS[1]1034
Cir. 3
502F2d[1]1128
552F2d538
365FS363
382FS[1]387
d393FS123
j393FS[1]126
399FS[1]1262
501FS782
501FS[1]783
83FRD[1]477
Cir. 4
513F2d242
710F2d[1]181
477FS[1]323
Cir. 5
e498F2d[1]247
506F2d819
508F2d[1]777
526F2d288
541F2d1154
580F2d752
717F2d[1]1493
d377FS[1]1020
d382FS[1]807
382FS[1]816
d396FS[1]812
e402FS[1]927
531FS764
546FS[1]454
Cir. 6
519F2d404
664F2d561
666F2d[1]1027
362FS[1]32
387FS[1]1128
f419FS[1]1007
e424FS[1]592
496FS209
499FS134
d499FS[1]137
Cir. 7
542F2d1280
370FS68
73FRD112
Cir. 8
637F2d1162
385FS[1]705
387FS[1]402
404FS[1]646
424FS[1]954

493FS1327
546FS[1]486
Cir. 9
540F2d1365
591F2d[1]1261
706F2d1527
358FS355
390FS[1]62
88FRD[1]542
Cir. 10
f631F2d[1]711
Cir. 11
435FS1094
Ariz
132Az163
132Az167
644P2d899
644P2d903
Calif
131CA3d104
182CaR234
Colo
184Col76
186Col63
518P2d810
525P2d466
Conn
175Ct561
400A2d720
DC
324A2d189
Fla
295So2d292
351So2d46
Haw
60H289
588P2d920
Idaho
97Ida202
541P2d626
Ill
57Il2d84
309NE591
Ind
422NE716
Iowa
211NW341
Mass
368Mas823
385Mas1206
388Mas192
389Mas937
333NE382
434NE963
446NE46
452NE1142
Mich
412Mch582
317NW4
Mo
504SW88
Mont
177Mt78
580P2d448
NJ
81NJ70
81NJ78
149Su490
374A2d63
405A2d353
405A2d357
NY
54Ap2d266
64Ap2d878

113Msc2d713
35NY185
35NY191
45NY808
316NE862
316NE866
381NE337
359S2d543
359S2d549
388S2d472
408S2d772
409S2d130
453S2d598
Ohio
53OA217
373NE1278
Pa
255PaS365
387A2d92
PR
110DPR261
Tenn
633SW307
Wash
93W2d703
611P2d1258
Wis
93Wis2d504
287NW532
W Va
233SE423
270SE645

Vol. 411

– 1 –
(36LE16)
(93SC1278)
US reh den
in411US959
s406US966
s411US980
s337FS280
411US208
j411US928
412US458
j412US461
413US462
j414US[2]432
414US656
415US[2]271
j415US[1]278
415US375
415US[1]539
415US713
417US[1]612
d418US[2]742
j418US[1]760
j419US[2]420
j419US[1]586
420US[1]538
426US324
426US[1]602
426US[2]814
427US[1]312
j427US[1]318
427US506
j429US[1]216
429US[1]259
j430US515
431US[1]503
j432US15
j432US459
f432US[1]470
433US291

433US295
433US410
434US[1]381
434US391
435US221
436US[1]378
436US[1]663
d438US[1]290
j438US357
j438US[1]357
439US[2]70
j439US1053
440US[2]97
j440US114
440US[1]199
j440US597
441US[1]77
j441US398
442US[1]272
446US[1]76
j446US113
447US[1]462
448US[1]323
j448US341
448US[1]518
448US[1]588
448US[1]1329
449US[1]174
j449US188
450US[1]230
j450US243
450US[2]478
j451US35
457US9
457US[1]217
457US230
457US232
e457US[1]235
e457US[1]239
j457US245
457US[1]963
457US[2]969
458US[1]200
j458US214
458US[1]486
51USLW[4170
j51USLW[4322
51USLW[4585
j51USLW[4779
4MJ802
12MJ910
77TCt872
97FRD614
Cir. D.C.
477F2d1182
483F2d[1]1317
525F2d561
593F2d[1]1125
665F2d1233
674F2d10
676F2d730
j676F2d753
686F2d[2]980
d386FS1326
430FS[2]822
436FS[2]136
468FS[2]690
488FS[1]133
Cir. 1
482F2d[1]99

508F2d[2]498
d519F2d[[1]1367
537F2d564
554F2d[1]497
578F2d[1]450
614F2d2
638F2d[1]268
641F2d1012
649F2d[2]77
659F2d[1]282
671F2d4
699F2d[2]6
e373FS635
373FS[1]648
377FS621
d377FS[1]622
379FS[2]49
385FS[1]400
388FS[2]393
388FS[2]1035
390FS1316
390FS[1]1317
392FS[1]302
e392FS[1]1141
395FS[2]627
396FS[1]1296
396FS[2]1298
406FS[1]855
415FS[2]495
j415FS[1]505
j415FS[2]506
f423FS[1]1265
435FS[1]262
439FS1128
465FS[2]660
522FS206
536FS[1]1388
561FS[1]1057
Cir. 2
476F2d[1]405
j476F2d[1]826
j476F2d[1]828
d482F2d[[1]1336
489F2d[1]1091
489F2d[2]1091
e507F2d[1]1068
j507F2d[1]1073
f508F2d[1]1028
554F2d[1]538
562F2d843
562F2d[2]844
j562F2d[1]865
576F2d462
j579F2d181
584F2d[2]604
601F2d[1]1234
601F2d[2]1238
696F2d[1]223
715F2d[1]783
717F2d[1]41
357FS[1]763
357FS[2]763
359FS[2]971
360FS232
f361FS[1]440
361FS[1]1053
f361FS[2]1327
362FS[2]660
363FS669
365FS[2]78
365FS[2]1167
366FS[2]739

Continued

36

Parallel Cites

Superscript Number

History/Treatment of Case

Court

headnotes. In order to use the Shepard's headnote numbers correctly, you must Shepardize with the citator that corresponds to the reporter volume you are reading. Thus, if you are Shepardizing a Supreme Court case as you read it in the *Supreme Court Reporter,* you must use the Shepard's table for S.Ct. cites.

In summary, Shepard's is a unique and essential research tool. Before you can use the citators effectively, however, you need to understand what they do, how they do it, and the language they use. Once you have accomplished that, Shepardizing is a relatively easy and very mechanical process.

Shepardizing Made Simple: WESTLAW Access to *Shepard's*

WESTLAW provides on-line access to most Shepard's case law citators. On-line Shepardizing offers several significant advantages over the manual version: First, when you Shepardize on WESTLAW, you retrieve a single, cumulative list of citing cases. You no longer need to worry about finding the right set of Shepard's or missing a volume in a Shepard's set. Second, as will be discussed later, you can manipulate the display to limit it to your research specifications. Third, and perhaps most important, Shepard's on WESTLAW is interactive with the rest of the WESTLAW databases. You can go back and forth from the cited case to Shepard's to citing cases. For all of these reasons, Shepard's on WESTLAW is a great time-saver.

There are two ways to enter Shepard's from WESTLAW. If you are viewing a case on WESTLAW and wish to Shepardize it, simply type **sh**. The second way is to type **sh** followed by the citation of the case you want to Shepardize.

A Shepard's display on WESTLAW is shown in Figure 3.10. Note that the top of the screen says "Rank 1 of 2." This means that your citation is found in two different citator sets; if you type **r**, you will see the display in the second set. In this example, r1 (rank 1) is a regional reporter citator, r2 is a state citator. "Only page" means that there is only one screen of citing cases.

Figure 3.10 A *Shepard's* Display on WESTLAW

```
                                SHEPARD'S  (Rank 1 of 2)           Only Page
CITATIONS TO: 250 N.W.2d 590
CITATOR: NORTHWESTERN REPORTER CITATIONS
COVERAGE: First Shepard's volume through Dec. 1990 Supplement
Retrieval                                             Headnote
   No.     ----Analysis---- -----Citation------        No.
              Same Text      (312 Minn. 1)
    1      SC Same Case      268 N.W.2d 705
    2                        267 N.W.2d 730, 732       6
    3      D  Distinguished  283 N.W.2d 897, 901       4
    4                        345 N.W.2d 723, 731
    5                        392 N.W.2d 679, 683       5
    6                        392 N.W.2d 679, 683       6
    7                        414 N.W.2d 227, 231       1
    8                        415 N.W.2d 341, 345       3

NOTE:  Check Shepard's PreView, Insta-Cite, and WESTLAW as a Citator
Copyright (C) 1990 McGraw-Hill, Inc.; Copyright (C) 1990 West Publishing Co.
```

Next, the screen tells you the citation you have entered, the citator series you have displayed, and the coverage of that series in WESTLAW. The WESTLAW coverage will always be as current as the hard-copy version of Shepard's—no more and no less.)

Next comes the Shepard's information itself. Everything that you would find in the manual version is in the on-line version, with two significant additions. The analytical abbreviations (and what they mean) are to the left of the citations; the numbers that refer to headnotes of the cited case are to the right. Additionally, the on-line version lists not only the page of the citing case where the reference to the cited case occurs, it also usually lists the *initial* page of the citing case. (The printed version of Shepard's only gives the internal—citing—page.) And, most important, on the far left of the display is a "retrieval number." If you wish to view a citing case, simply enter its number. WESTLAW first displays the initial page of the citing case (Figure 3.11) and then, if you press **ENTER** again, the first citing page (Figure 3.12). To return from a citing case to your Shepard's display, type **goback.**

Narrowing a *Shepard's* Search on WESTLAW

WESTLAW offers great flexibility in the display of citing authority; that is, the citing list can be limited to certain types of authority. WESTLAW allows limitation by abbreviation and headnote number. For example, you can use the LOCATE command to find only those cases that have "followed" the cited case (**loc f**) or those cases that have cited the Shepardized case for its second headnote (**loc 2**). You can also use the LOCATE command to find cases by reporter (**loc fs**) or jurisdiction (**loc cir9**). For a complete list, type **analysis** in Shepard's or see the *WESTLAW Reference Manual.*

It is also possible to use more than a single limit function at one time. For example, typing **loc fs, fed** will display any citing case from either the *Federal Supplement* or the *Federal Reporter, 2d.* Likewise, **loc e, f** will display citing

Figure 3.11 The Initial Page of the Citing Case on WESTLAW

```
                          COPR. (C) WEST 1990 NO CLAIM TO ORIG. U.S. GOVT. WORKS
Citation                                      Page(P)        Database   Mode
283 N.W.2d 897                   CITING CASE  P 1 OF 21      NW         T
(CITE AS: 283 N.W.2D 897)
                           STATE of Minnesota, Respondent,
                                         v.
                          David Allen ORSCANIN, Appellant.
                                 Nos. 47431, 49368.
                             Supreme Court of Minnesota.
                                   Aug. 17, 1979.
                          Certiorari Denied Nov. 26, 1979.
                                 See 100 S.Ct. 464
 Defendant appealed from an order of the District Court, Rice County, Urban J.
 Steimann, J., denying his request to have his judgment of conviction and
 sentence vacated and set aside. The District Court decision was made following
 a postconviction hearing held pursuant to remand of a prior appeal, 266 N.W.2d
 880. The Supreme Court, Rogosheske, J., held that: (1) evidence sustained trial
 court's finding that defendant's confession was voluntary and that its
 admission at trial did not deny defendant due process; (2) defendant was not
 promised leniency in exchange for a confession; and (3) defendant's confinement
 did not induce defendant to confess.
  Affirmed.
  Wahl, J., dissented and filed opinion in which Yetka, J., joined.
```

Figure 3.12 The Citing Page on WESTLAW

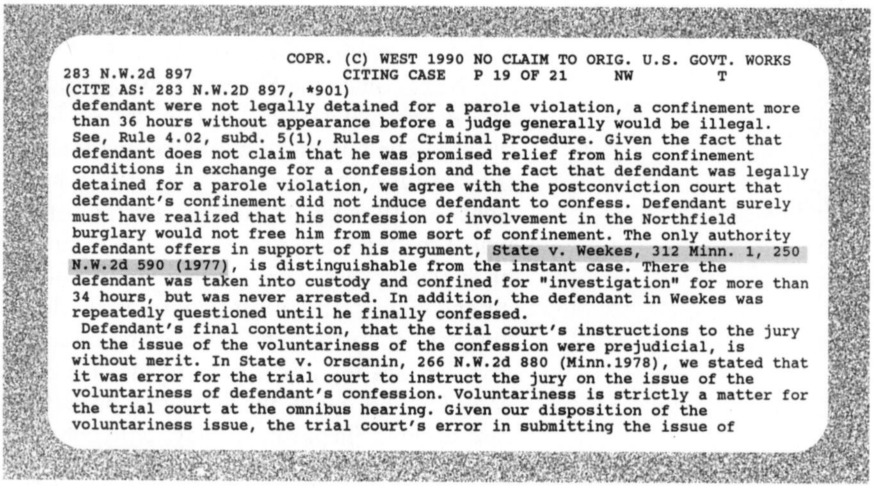

```
                           COPR. (C) WEST 1990 NO CLAIM TO ORIG. U.S. GOVT. WORKS
283 N.W.2d 897                  CITING CASE    P 19 OF 21      NW           T
(CITE AS: 283 N.W.2D 897, *901)
 defendant were not legally detained for a parole violation, a confinement more
 than 36 hours without appearance before a judge generally would be illegal.
 See, Rule 4.02, subd. 5(1), Rules of Criminal Procedure. Given the fact that
 defendant does not claim that he was promised relief from his confinement
 conditions in exchange for a confession and the fact that defendant was legally
 detained for a parole violation, we agree with the postconviction court that
 defendant's confinement did not induce defendant to confess. Defendant surely
 must have realized that his confession of involvement in the Northfield
 burglary would not free him from some sort of confinement. The only authority
 defendant offers in support of his argument, State v. Weekes, 312 Minn. 1, 250
 N.W.2d 590 (1977), is distinguishable from the instant case. There the
 defendant was taken into custody and confined for "investigation" for more than
 34 hours, but was never arrested. In addition, the defendant in Weekes was
 repeatedly questioned until he finally confessed.
  Defendant's final contention, that the trial court's instructions to the jury
 on the issue of the voluntariness of the confession were prejudicial, is
 without merit. In State v. Orscanin, 266 N.W.2d 880 (Minn.1978), we stated that
 it was error for the trial court to instruct the jury on the issue of the
 voluntariness of defendant's confession. Voluntariness is strictly a matter for
 the trial court at the omnibus hearing. Given our disposition of the
 voluntariness issue, the trial court's error in submitting the issue of
```

cases to which the Shepard's editors have assigned either an "explained" or a "followed" analytical abbreviation. Even more complicated and precise combinations are possible. For example, to find only *Federal Supplement* cases that have both been assigned an "explained" abbreviation and cite the case for its third headnote, type

```
loc fs, e, 3
```

The flexibility of the LOCATE commands permits you to "fine-tune" your Shepardizing. By limiting your Shepard's display, you can deal very efficiently with a cited case that might have several columns or even several pages of citing authority in the hard-copy version of Shepard's.

Shepard's PreView

The main problem with *Shepard's Citations,* whether in its hard-copy or its on-line format, is currentness. The editors at Shepard's work from published advance sheets, and their editorial work takes some time. Shepard's pamphlets may be from two to nine months out of date by the time they reach your library.

To make the citators more current, Shepard's and West Publishing have jointly created a new service called *Shepard's PreView. Shepard's PreView* exists solely as an on-line service and is exclusive to WESTLAW. *Shepard's PreView* is created from the printed West advance sheets; citing cases will be listed in it about five to six weeks after they are handed down (Figure 3.13).

Shepard's PreView contains *raw data,* offered to WESTLAW users before Shepard's has added its editorial enhancements. There is no "history" and "treatment" analysis or headnote numbers. *PreView* is simply a citation list. The absence of editorial additions is the cost of currentness.

Figure 3.13 An Introductory Screen on *Shepard's PreView*

```
                    WELCOME TO SHEPARD'S PREVIEW

Shepard's PreView is a citator service available exclusively on WESTLAW. The
service gives a preview of citing references that will appear in Shepard's
Citations.  Citing references are provided exclusively from West's National
Reporter System.  For comprehensive citator information use Insta-Cite,
Shepard's PreView, Shepard's and WESTLAW as a citator.

To view a Shepard's PreView result, type a CITATION (e.g., 107 SCT 3102)
   and press ENTER


Shepard's PreView is a trademark of Shepard's/McGraw-Hill, Inc.



If you wish to:
   View the list of Shepard's PreView commands, type CMDS and press ENTER
   Go back to the previously accessed service, type GB and press ENTER
   View the list of previously accessed services, type MAP and press ENTER

Copyright (C) 1990 Shepard's/McGraw-Hill, Inc. and West Publishing Company
```

The mechanics of *Shepard's PreView* are similar to those of the on-line version of *Shepard's Citations.* If you wish to see the *PreView* display for a case you are viewing on WESTLAW, type **sp.** Or, from anywhere in WESTLAW, type **sp** and a citation.

Insta-Cite

Insta-Cite is West Publishing's case history and citation verification system. Insta-Cite is *very current.* Case history information is added to the system as soon as it arrives at West. This means that if an appellate court reverses a federal district court case, that reversal will be noted in the Insta-Cite display of the district court case within one to five days of the receipt of the appellate decision by West. Thus, Insta-Cite has the most up-to-date information possible on the history of a case.

Insta-Cite is *not* the same as Shepard's. Shepard's contains *all* the reported cases that have cited a particular case. Insta-Cite will give you the direct procedural history of the case *plus* later cases that have had a substantial negative impact on the precedential validity of the case, but it is not a comprehensive citator. Thus, it will show overruling cases and questioning or limiting cases, but it will not show less consequential references. It will also give you *complete citation information,* including all parallel citations (Figure 3.14).

The statement at the bottom of the screen describes the "depth" of Insta-Cite. While the system has direct procedural history for federal cases as far back as 1754, it has indirect history only since 1972. To find indirect history before 1972, you must use Shepard's. Thus, the Insta-Cite display for *Betts v. Brady,* which was decided in 1942 and overruled in 1962, does not show the pre-1972 overruling case, *Gideon v. Wainwright,* but it does show two post-1972 cases that have noted its overruling (Figure 3.15a). The display for

Figure 3.14 Parallel Citations on Insta-Cite

```
                          INSTA-CITE                        Only Page
CITATION: 107 S.Ct. 1807
     1  Reed v. Lukhard, 578 F.Supp. 40 (W.D.Va., Jun 28, 1983)
          (NO. CIV. 83-0493-R)
        Related Reference
     2  Reed v. Lukhard, 591 F.Supp. 1247 (W.D.Va., Jul 26, 1984)
          (NO. CIV. 83-0493)
        Judgment Affirmed by
     3  Reed v. Health and Human Services, 774 F.2d 1270, 54 U.S.L.W. 2226,
          3 Fed.R.Serv.3d 178 (4th Cir.(Va.), Oct 10, 1985) (NO. 84-2167,
          84-2168, 84-2187)
        Certiorari Granted by
     4  Lukhard v. Reed, 477 U.S. 903, 106 S.Ct. 3271, 91 L.Ed.2d 561
          (U.S., Jun 23, 1986) (NO. 85-1358)
        AND Judgment Reversed by
=>   5  LUKHARD V. REED, 481 U.S. 368, 107 S.Ct. 1807, 95 L.Ed.2d 328,
          55 U.S.L.W. 4561 (U.S.Va., Apr 22, 1987) (NO. 85-1358)

Note: DIRECT HISTORY: Coverage begins - Federal 1754, State 1938.
      PRECEDENTIAL HISTORY: Coverage begins 1972.  For earlier history use
      Shepard's (SH).  Check Shepard's PreView (SP) and WESTLAW as a citator.
(C) Copyright West Publishing Company 1990
```

Roe v. Wade, which was decided in 1973, shows all direct case history plus the 1989 *Webster* case that "questioned" *Roe* (Figure 3.15b).

Like a Shepard's display, Insta-Cite displays are interactive with the WESTLAW databases. If, for example, you wished to view the *Webster* case in the above example, you would type **5**. Insta-Cite, *Shepard's Citations,* and *Shepard's PreView* are also interactive among themselves. You can move from one to another by typing **ic, sh,** or **sp** as appropriate.

WESTLAW as a Citator

You can also use WESTLAW itself as a citator simply by entering a query that will retrieve all occurrences of the name of a case. For example, to find all references to *Betts v. Brady,* type

```
betts /s brady
```

There are several applications where using WESTLAW as a citator may be the best (or only) way to find the needed documents:

1. Using WESTLAW to update Shepard's. With the introduction of *Shepard's PreView,* the need to update Shepard's by using WESTLAW as a citator has diminished, but there is still a modest difference in time—a little more than one month—between the loading of cases in WESTLAW and the creation of *Shepard's PreView,* which is done from the printed West advance sheets. On some occasions, you may find very recent cases in the case databases that do not yet appear in *Shepard's PreView.*
2. Using WESTLAW to update *statutes and regulations.* Shepard's has not licensed the statutory citators for accessibility on computer-assisted legal research services. If you wish to find cases that have cited a particular federal or state statute, court rule, or administrative regulation, you can

Figure 3.15 Precedential History on Insta-Cite

(a) Betts v. Brady

```
                              INSTA-CITE                          Only Page
CITATION: 62 S.Ct. 1252
 =>    1  BETTS V. BRADY, 316 U.S. 455, 62 S.Ct. 1252, 86 L.Ed. 1595
              (U.S.Md., Jun 01, 1942) (NO. 837)
            Overruling Recognized by
       2  Murray v. Giarratano, 109 S.Ct. 2765, 106 L.Ed.2d 1, 57 U.S.L.W. 4889
              (U.S.Va., Jun 23, 1989) (NO. 88-411)
            AND Overruling Recognized by
       3  Fletcher v. Armontrout, 725 F.Supp. 1075 (W.D.Mo., Nov 13, 1989)
              (NO. 89-0435-CV-W-JWO)
            Related Reference
       4  Fletcher v. Armontrout, 733 F.Supp. 1348 (W.D.Mo., Mar 07, 1990)
              (NO. 89-0435-CV-W-JWO)

                  CORPUS JURIS SECUNDUM (C.J.S.) REFERENCES
       22 C.J.S. Criminal Law Sec.277 Note 93

Note: DIRECT HISTORY: Coverage begins - Federal 1754, State 1938.
      PRECEDENTIAL HISTORY: Coverage begins 1972.  For earlier history use
      Shepard's (SH).  Check Shepard's PreView (SP) and WESTLAW as a citator.
(C) Copyright West Publishing Company 1990
```

(b) Roe v. Wade

```
                              INSTA-CITE                     Page   1 of   3
CITATION: 93 S.Ct. 705
       1  Roe v. Wade, 314 F.Supp. 1217 (N.D.Tex., Jun 17, 1970)
              (NO. CIV. 3-3690-B, CIV. 3-3691-C)
            Jurisdiction Postponed by
       2  Roe v. Wade, 402 U.S. 941, 91 S.Ct. 1610, 29 L.Ed.2d 108
              (U.S.Tex., May 03, 1971) (NO. 808)
            AND Judgment Affirmed in Part, Reversed in Part by
 =>    3  ROE V. WADE, 410 U.S. 113, 93 S.Ct. 705, 35 L.Ed.2d 147
              (U.S.Tex., Jan 22, 1973) (NO. 70-18)
            Rehearing Denied by
       4  Roe v. Wade, 410 U.S. 959, 93 S.Ct. 1409, 35 L.Ed.2d 694
              (U.S., Feb 26, 1973) (NO. 70-18)
            AND Holding Limited by
       5  Webster v. Reproductive Health Services, 109 S.Ct. 3040,
              106 L.Ed.2d 410, 57 U.S.L.W. 5023 (U.S.Mo., Jul 03, 1989)
              (NO. 88-605)

Note: DIRECT HISTORY: Coverage begins - Federal 1754, State 1938.
      PRECEDENTIAL HISTORY: Coverage begins 1972.  For earlier history use
      Shepard's (SH).  Check Shepard's PreView (SP) and WESTLAW as a citator.
(C) Copyright West Publishing Company 1990
```

do so by using WESTLAW as a citator. A typical search might involve typing **34.011** to retrieve cases that cite Fla. Stat. § 34.011.

3. Using WESTLAW to update *unreported cases. Shepard's Citations* lists as both *cited* and *citing* authority only those cases that have been *reported* (published in an official or unofficial print reporter). There are thousands of unreported cases that exist only in the on-line services and do not appear in print. Using WESTLAW as a citator is the only way to find citing material for those cases.
4. Using WESTLAW to find *unreported citing cases.* Just as you can only update an unreported case by using WESTLAW as a citator, you can only find unreported *citing* cases to either a reported or an unreported *cited* case by using the same procedure.
5. Using WESTLAW to update types of authority for which there is no Shepard's citator. Just as it is impossible to update an *unreported* case manually, some types of authority that you may wish to update do not appear in a citator set. For example, there is no citator for English cases cited by

American courts. *Overseas Tankship (U.K.) Ltd. v. Morts Dock & Engineering Co., Ltd.* (the first of the two so-called Wagon Mound cases found in every Torts casebook) changed the English rule on foreseeability in negligence actions. You can find American cases that have cited it simply by typing **"overseas tankship"** in the appropriate WESTLAW database. Likewise, there is no citator for legal treatises cited by the courts. If you wished to see whether John Hart Ely's *Democracy and Distrust* has received any judicial attention, you could use WESTLAW as a citator and type a query such as:

```
ely /s democracy /s distrust
```

6. Using WESTLAW to narrow a citation list. Finally, at times you may want to use WESTLAW as a citator, instead of *Shepard's Citations,* to narrow a search to citing cases involving particular fact situations. For example, you might wish to search for cases citing *Miranda v. Arizona* where the questioning of an accused has taken place in the accused's home. In *Shepard's Citations,* the list of cases that have cited *Miranda* is very long, and nothing in the list narrows it by fact pattern. But a search such as **miranda /p home residence** in WESTLAW will focus the search on your research problem.

Conclusion

There is no legal research tool that first-year law students find more confusing at first glance than *Shepard's Citations.* If you find yourself baffled by the endless pages of numbers and letter abbreviations, you are not alone—generations of students have initially been baffled by "these red books, thick and thin." But after some practice, you will find that Shepardizing is really quite simple. WESTLAW access to *Shepard's Citations* makes it even simpler. If, after you have worked with Shepard's, you still do not understand the procedure or the result, ask a reference librarian for help or read the pamphlet prepared by Shepard's called *How to Use Shepard's Citations* or the *WESTLAW Reference Manual.*

Insta-Cite is a case history and citation verification service. It is the most up-to-date way of determining whether a case is still good authority. Many attorneys routinely use Insta-Cite as both the first step and the last step in the research process or even as the final check before submitting a brief or memo. Updating your research with *Shepard's Citations, Shepard's PreView,* Insta-Cite, and WESTLAW as a citator is an essential part of every research assignment. It is a good practice to start in law school.

LEGISLATION

Introduction

If you suspect your issue involves a statute, you should begin your research with a check through the statutory codes. A practicing attorney is more likely to need a statute than a case, though this can vary from one legal specialty to another. Although you may become acquainted with the Uniform Commercial Code in Contracts and a few scattered constitutional provisions elsewhere, many first-year law students do not receive a systematic introduction to the legislative process and its resultant publications. This is changing as more courses concentrate on the legislative process, but case law still tends to receive more attention in law school. In this chapter, we will introduce you to the common forms of legislative publications, with a special focus on federal materials. Learn this and you will be ahead of the game.

Federal Laws

A federal law first appears in the information stream as a bill introduced in Congress by a representative or a senator. A bill is assigned its own unique number depending on the side of the legislature in which it originates and the order in which it is introduced. Then it is referred to the appropriate House or Senate Committee. For example, an amendment to the Truth in Lending Act passed in 1980 began life as H.R. 4986, which means that it came from the House of Representatives (H.R.) and was the 4986th bill introduced in the House during that Congress. Once a bill is introduced and sent to the appropriate committee, it can meet several fates. Most bills sink from sight never to be seen again. Others are passed by the House but die in the Senate. The same fate awaits many bills that are passed by the Senate and are then sent to the House. Sometimes both the House and Senate pass a bill, but in different versions due to the process of amendment; in that case, a Conference Committee, with members from each house, is appointed to try to hammer out a compromise that can then be passed by each house. If both the House and Senate pass the same version of the bill, this process can be skipped, but in either case, the final version is sent to the president who can sign it into law or veto it and send it back to the house where it started. The House and Senate can then try to override the president's veto by mustering a two-thirds vote in each house (Figure 4.1).

Figure 4.1 The Legislative Process and Accompanying Documents

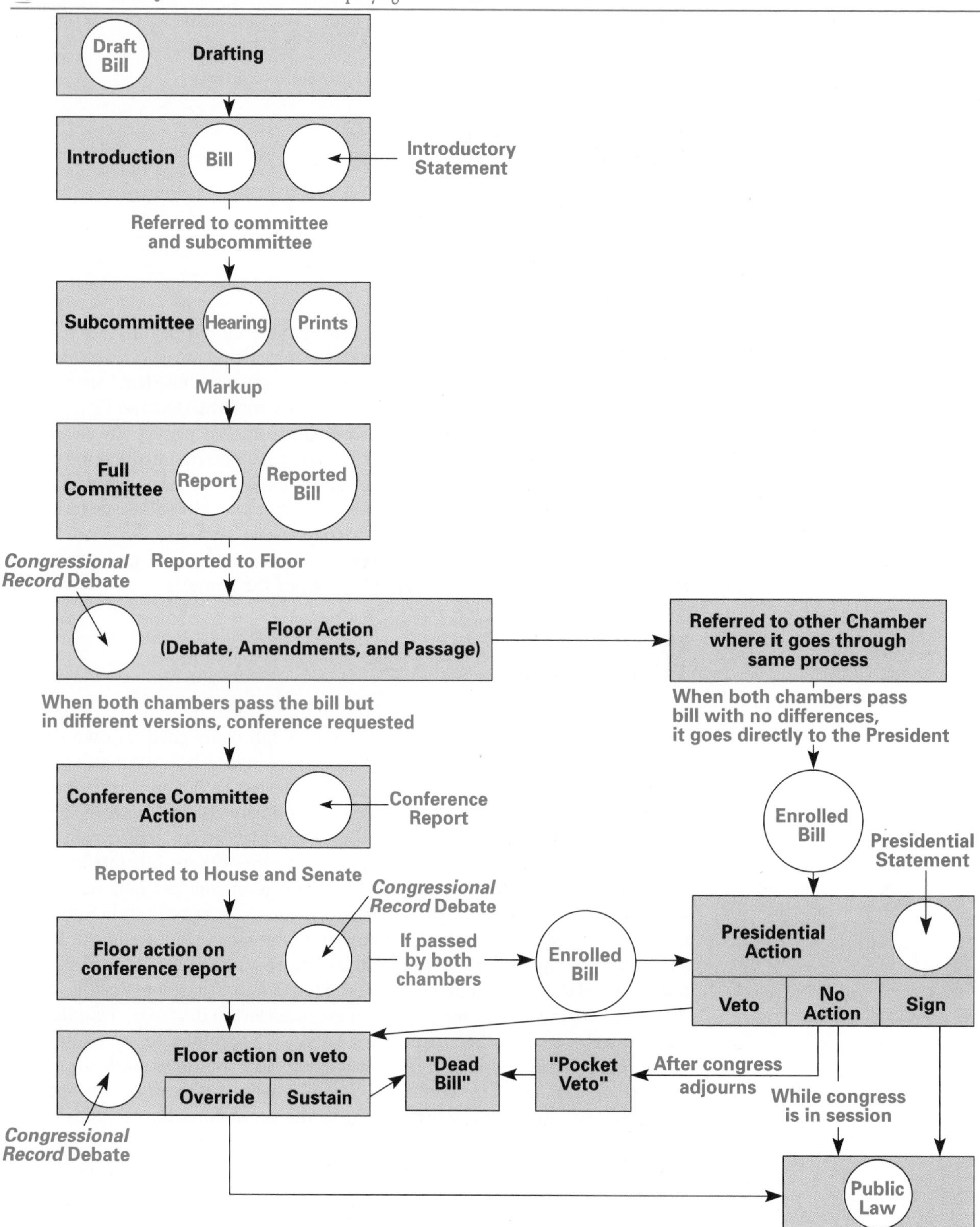

Each step in the process can be repeated, and when a controversial or high-profile issue is involved, there may be a host of bills on the same issue. Only a few hundred bills survive to become law. Later in life you may have to do a legislative history, a process that is as enjoyable as root canal work. Fortunately, using the laws themselves is relatively easy.

A law, also called a statute or an act, is identified by a public law number, which is comprised of the number of the Congress in which it passed, followed by a number that reflects the order in which the bill was enacted; for example, P.L. 101–12 refers to the 12th law passed in the 101st Congress. As soon as they are enacted, federal laws are published separately in pamphlet form as "slip laws." Slip laws include valuable information in the headings and margin notes (Figure 4.2). For example, you can learn when the law was approved, the number of the bill that was enacted into law, and the short title or popular name of the law. The reference to the *United States Code (U.S.C.)* will tell you where the provision will be codified in the *U.S.C.* The *U.S. Statutes at Large* citation will tell you the initial page of the law in the permanent bound volume. At the end of the slip law, you will find references to House and Senate Reports as well as citations to the congressional debates. These "legislative history" references will tell you where you can find congressional materials that may help you determine the intent of the language of the law.

Although slip laws sound rather useful, you will not find them in most libraries. They are messy and hard to keep organized. But fear not, the slip laws are compiled into several much more useful formats. You can access current public laws on WESTLAW in the United States Public Laws database (**US-PL**). Coverage in this database begins with laws passed in the second session of the 101st Congress (1989). To retrieve P.L. 101–165, the *National Affordable Housing Act,* type **ci(101–165)**. You can also retrieve the same act by searching for words in the heading, which is included in the caption field, **ca(affordable)**.

At the end of each session of Congress, all of the slip laws for that year are compiled in numerical order and published in bound volumes. These laws are generically called "session laws" because they are compiled for each session of Congress.

The law as it is passed by Congress and as it appears in the session laws is useful if you are looking for the original version of an act, before it has been codified by its subject areas or amended, or if you require the language of a particular amendment. You will also use the session laws if you need to find a law that has been repealed and deleted from the code. For example, assume that your client committed a crime for which she received a sentence and a fine. If the crime was committed in 1986 before the date on which a new law on the topic became effective, you would have to look for the language of the repealed law that has been deleted from the code. When new laws are printed in the session laws, they have a "preamble" that may explain what the law is designed to do. This preamble can be helpful in determining the legislative intent of the act.

Note: although session laws serve specific purposes, you cannot safely use the session law version of a statute to determine the *present* text of a law, since the original law may have been repealed or amended. You will find the present text of a law in a code, as explained later in this chapter.

Figure 4.2 A Slip Law: Headings, Margin Notes, and Legislative History References

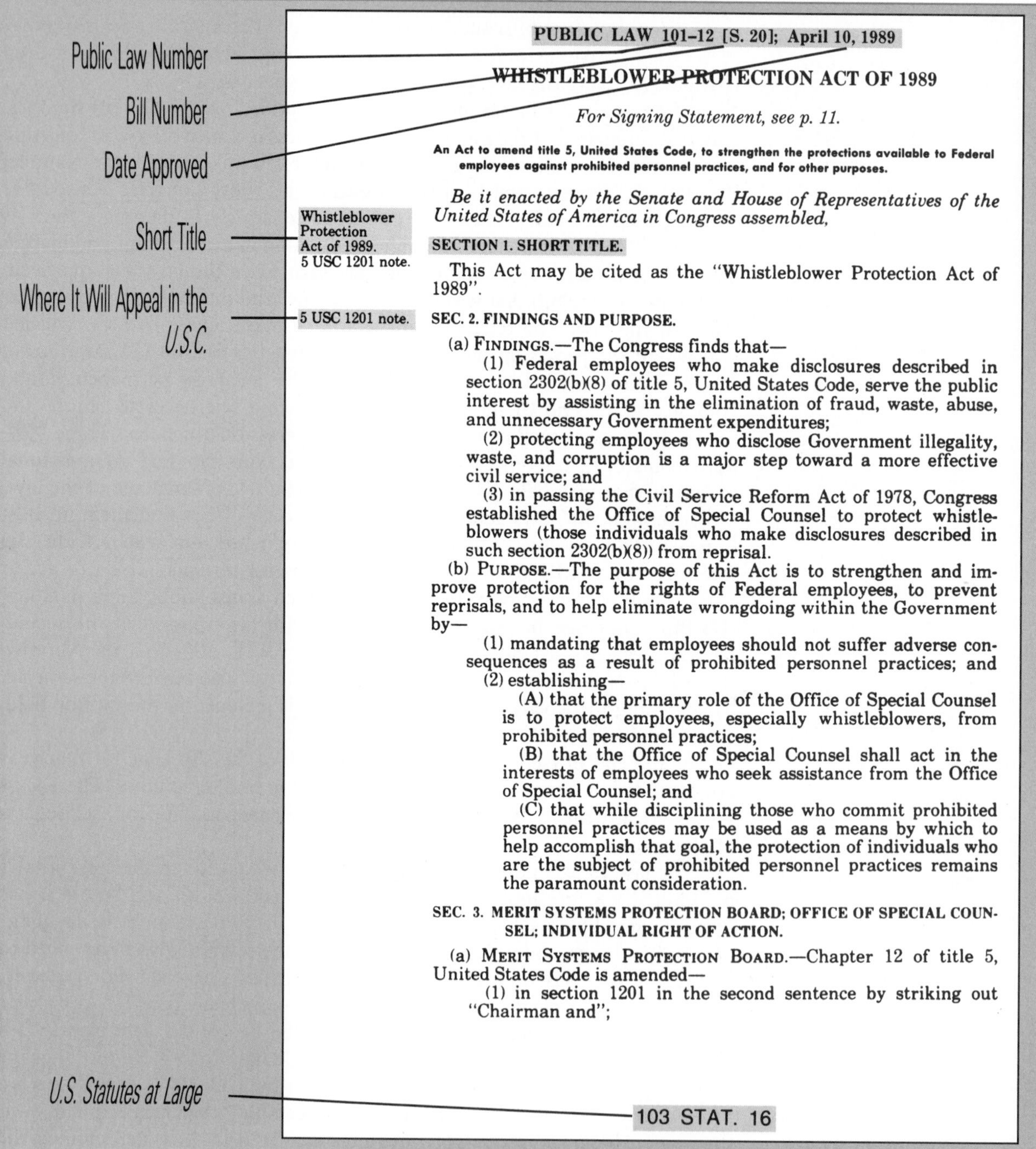

PUBLIC LAW 101–12 [S. 20]; April 10, 1989

WHISTLEBLOWER PROTECTION ACT OF 1989

For Signing Statement, see p. 11.

An Act to amend title 5, United States Code, to strengthen the protections available to Federal employees against prohibited personnel practices, and for other purposes.

Be it enacted by the Senate and House of Representatives of the United States of America in Congress assembled,

Whistleblower Protection Act of 1989. 5 USC 1201 note.

SECTION 1. SHORT TITLE.

This Act may be cited as the "Whistleblower Protection Act of 1989".

5 USC 1201 note.

SEC. 2. FINDINGS AND PURPOSE.

(a) FINDINGS.—The Congress finds that—

(1) Federal employees who make disclosures described in section 2302(b)(8) of title 5, United States Code, serve the public interest by assisting in the elimination of fraud, waste, abuse, and unnecessary Government expenditures;

(2) protecting employees who disclose Government illegality, waste, and corruption is a major step toward a more effective civil service; and

(3) in passing the Civil Service Reform Act of 1978, Congress established the Office of Special Counsel to protect whistleblowers (those individuals who make disclosures described in such section 2302(b)(8)) from reprisal.

(b) PURPOSE.—The purpose of this Act is to strengthen and improve protection for the rights of Federal employees, to prevent reprisals, and to help eliminate wrongdoing within the Government by—

(1) mandating that employees should not suffer adverse consequences as a result of prohibited personnel practices; and

(2) establishing—

(A) that the primary role of the Office of Special Counsel is to protect employees, especially whistleblowers, from prohibited personnel practices;

(B) that the Office of Special Counsel shall act in the interests of employees who seek assistance from the Office of Special Counsel; and

(C) that while disciplining those who commit prohibited personnel practices may be used as a means by which to help accomplish that goal, the protection of individuals who are the subject of prohibited personnel practices remains the paramount consideration.

SEC. 3. MERIT SYSTEMS PROTECTION BOARD; OFFICE OF SPECIAL COUNSEL; INDIVIDUAL RIGHT OF ACTION.

(a) MERIT SYSTEMS PROTECTION BOARD.—Chapter 12 of title 5, United States Code is amended—

(1) in section 1201 in the second sentence by striking out "Chairman and";

103 STAT. 16

Federal session laws can be located in three sources: *U.S. Statutes at Large* (Stat.) published by the U.S. Government Printing Office; *U.S. Code Congressional and Administrative News (U.S.C.C.A.N.)* published by West; and *Advance* pamphlets to *United States Code Service (U.S.C.S.)* published by Lawyers

Figure 4.2 A Slip Law: Headings, Margin Notes, and Legislative History References (continued)

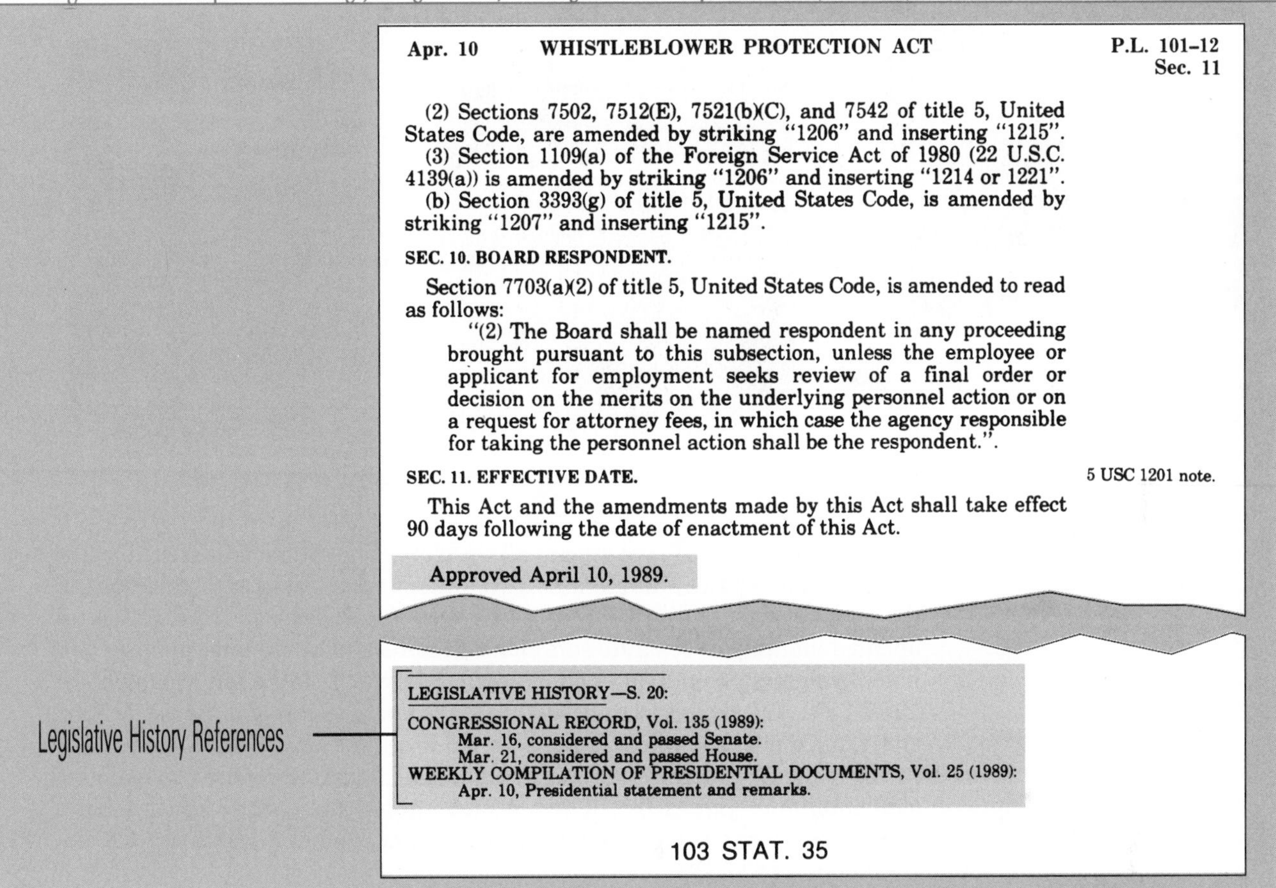

Apr. 10 WHISTLEBLOWER PROTECTION ACT P.L. 101–12
Sec. 11
(2) Sections 7502, 7512(E), 7521(b)(C), and 7542 of title 5, United States Code, are amended by striking "1206" and inserting "1215".
(3) Section 1109(a) of the Foreign Service Act of 1980 (22 U.S.C. 4139(a)) is amended by striking "1206" and inserting "1214 or 1221".
(b) Section 3393(g) of title 5, United States Code, is amended by striking "1207" and inserting "1215".
SEC. 10. BOARD RESPONDENT.
Section 7703(a)(2) of title 5, United States Code, is amended to read as follows:
"(2) The Board shall be named respondent in any proceeding brought pursuant to this subsection, unless the employee or applicant for employment seeks review of a final order or decision on the merits on the underlying personnel action or on a request for attorney fees, in which case the agency responsible for taking the personnel action shall be the respondent.".
SEC. 11. EFFECTIVE DATE.
5 USC 1201 note.
This Act and the amendments made by this Act shall take effect 90 days following the date of enactment of this Act.
Approved April 10, 1989.
LEGISLATIVE HISTORY—S. 20:
CONGRESSIONAL RECORD, Vol. 135 (1989):
Mar. 16, considered and passed Senate.
Mar. 21, considered and passed House.
WEEKLY COMPILATION OF PRESIDENTIAL DOCUMENTS, Vol. 25 (1989):
Apr. 10, Presidential statement and remarks.
103 STAT. 35
Legislative History References

Co-op (Figure 4.3). The *U.S. Statutes at Large* is the *official* session law publication produced by the U.S. Government Printing Office for federal laws. *Statutes at Large* is found in every law library, but, as is frequently true of government publications, it is very slow to arrive, lagging three to four years behind the end of the session covered.

One of the titles that publishes session laws also contains valuable information pertaining to the history of those laws. *U.S. Code Congressional and Administrative News (U.S.C.C.A.N.),* published by West, includes selective legislative history material. It lists the citations for the House, Senate, and Conference Reports and reprints the report or reports that it determines to be the most closely related to the public law. To determine the meaning of a statute, you may need to refer to these congressional committee reports. For example, assume that your client represents over 50 plaintiffs from the petroleum industry. The case revolves around the meaning of the term "well" in three statutory provisions. By reading the congressional reports for the various acts, you may be able to determine the exact meaning of the term. It is this type of information that is gleaned from the legislative history materials.

Figure 4.3 The Three Sources of Session Laws

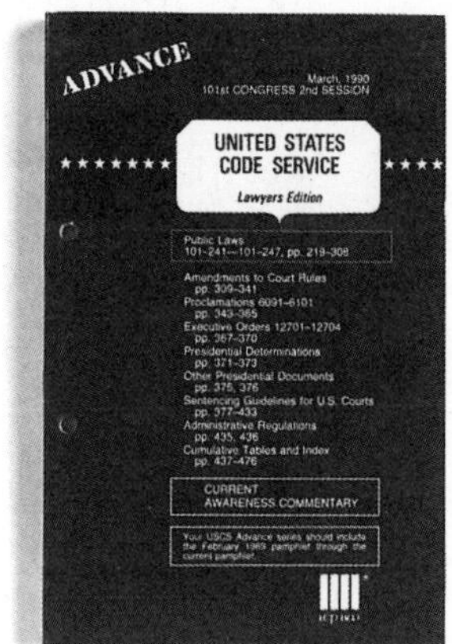

U.S.C.C.A.N. does not reprint all the congressional materials, such as the hearings and debates, but the legislative history table does list the citations to the bills, reports, and debates in the *Congressional Record. U.S.C.C.A.N.* is updated monthly in separate softbound pamphlets that are later published in bound volumes. To obtain the most current laws, check the latest pamphlets. On WESTLAW, the Legislative History (**LH**) database contains House, Senate, and Conference Committee reports as set forth in *U.S.C.C.A.N.* from 1978 to the present as well as all Congressional Committee reports on pending legislation after July, 1990. If you want to access the congressional debates as reported in the *Congressional Record* on-line, you can search the **CR** database on WESTLAW.

Codes

Laws are classified or "codified" by subject or topic in volumes called "codes." These Codes not only group the laws by subject, but also show all subsequent amendments. This makes life much simpler. Most often you will use one of the codes (actually, you will use an "annotated code," but that's in the next section) when you try to locate federal statutes with all of their amendments and deletions.

Codes are easy to use and are effective research tools if used correctly. To locate laws efficiently, you need a basic understanding of how the codes are organized. Federal laws are collected and organized by subject matter into fifty "titles" and compiled into a code. There is no magic to the number "50." Codes can be built around *any* subject arrangement. Some states use lots of topics, some only a few. The federal government decided on fifty topics in the 1920s and has retained the same arrangement ever since, even though a few of the topics are never used. For example, laws pertaining to age discrimination will be classified under Title 29, which is the title designated to laws concerning labor. Each title of the *U.S. Code* is further divided into subdivisions called

Figure 4.4 The Three Sources of Federal Codes

chapters and sections. For age discrimination, the chapter would be 14 "Age Discrimination in Employment," and the section would be 623 "Prohibition of Age Discrimination." The citation to the code would read 29 U.S.C. 623; you omit the chapter number in the citation and retain the section number. Recall that in addition to placing similar laws together under topics, codes also incorporate amendments and indicate repeals. Some laws may apply to more than one subject, so you may have to check more than one place in the code.

There are three federal codes: The *United States Code (U.S.C.)* is the official code for federal laws, while the *United States Code Annotated (U.S.C.A.)* and the *United States Code Service (U.S.C.S.)* are both unofficial annotated codes (Figure 4.4). Each of the codes is useful for certain purposes.

United States Code

The *United States Code (U.S.C.)* is published by the U.S. Government Printing Office. The whole set is recompiled every six years, using the same fifty subject categories or titles. Congress has deemed the *U.S.C.* prima facie evidence of the actual text, which means simply that the *U.S.C.* is sort of official. Ask your legal research instructor why we say "sort of."

The *U.S.C.* contains only the text of the law. It does not give citations to the cases that have interpreted the statutes; this information can only be found in one of the annotated codes. The *U.S.C.* is also very cumbersome to use. Although you can find material in the *U.S.C.* by checking the multivolume index, the material may not be as current as you need. As we noted, the *U.S.C.* is reissued every six years, with cumulative annual supplements between the new editions. In reality, the annual cumulative supplements do not appear in the library until eight months to two years have passed. Therefore, if you rely only on the *U.S.C.*, you will miss the current laws, amendments, and deletions.

The reason that you may need to use the *U.S.C.* at all is that the Bluebook says "to cite the *U.S.C.* if therein." Therefore, the *U.S.C.* has the advantage of being official, but the two unofficial codes are much more helpful research tools than the *U.S.C.*

Federal Codes on WESTLAW

You may prefer the convenience of accessing the codes on computer rather than searching in the printed materials. Fortunately, the federal statutes in codified form are available on-line in the WESTLAW USC database, and the *U.S.C.A.* is in the WESTLAW USCA database. To survey the coverage of the titles, use the SCOPE command to check the currentness of each title. Each title is updated through a specific public law number. You can retrieve the text of the code section by using the FIND service with the citation of the code section. For example, type **fi 20 usca 60** or, in the WESTLAW USCA file, use **ci(20 +5 60)**; the "+5" is an instruction to the computer to locate "60" within 5 characters of "20." If you are researching case law on-line and you see a citation to a code section, it is easy to jump to that section by using the FIND service, read the statutory language, and then resume reading your case.

The bound codes have print indexes, but you can also use the WESTLAW **USC** or **USCA** database when you are searching for the interpretation of a particular word or phrase or if you become frustrated by the indexing terms in the hard-copy codes. For example, if you are looking for the statutory definition of "displaced homemaker," the index to the *U.S.C.A.* has no entry for Displaced Homemaker, and the entry "Homemakers and Homemaking" refers you to "Vocational Education," which has no specific listing for displaced homemakers. However, if you run the query **"displaced homemaker"** in the WESTLAW **USC** or **USCA** database, you will retrieve the definition as it appears in 20 U.S.C. 1087vv(e) (Figure 4.5).

Annotated Codes

Annotated codes are more useful versions of the *U.S.C.* Not only do they contain the text of the *U.S.C.*, they also refer to the cases that have interpreted the federal laws. For any statutory research, you will want to use one of the annotated codes—they are universally accepted. Both of the annotated codes—West's *United States Code Annotated (U.S.C.A.)* and Lawyers Co-op's *United States Code Service (U.S.C.S.)*—contain basically the same text and title and section numbers as the official *U.S.C.* Both annotated codes contain references to cases that have construed the statutes, to administrative regulations, and to secondary sources. The annotated codes also contain cross-references to related sections within the code. Each annotated code refers to the research tools provided by its publisher; that is, *U.S.C.A.* cites to West's other publications, and *U.S.C.S.* cites to the publications of Lawyers Co-op. You may have a preference for one publisher's materials, or you may simply use whatever is available at the time that you need it.

Figure 4.5 Retrieving a Statutory Definition on WESTLAW

```
20 USCA s 1087vv              R 7 OF 18         P 7 OF 10        USC          P
  TEXT (D) (2) (G)

  determination of independence by reason of other unusual circumstances.
   (3) An individual may not be treated as an independent student pursuant to
  subparagraphs (C), (D), and (F) of paragraph (2) if the financial aid
  administrator determines that such individual was treated as an independent
  student during the preceding award year, but was claimed as a dependent by any
  other individual (other than a spouse) for income tax purposes for the first
  calendar year of such award year.
   (4) The financial aid administrator may certify an individual described in
  subparagraph (C), (D), or (F) of paragraph (2) on the basis of a demonstration
  made by the individual, but no disbursal of an award may be made without
  documentation.

   (e) DISPLACED HOMEMAKER

  The term "DISPLACED HOMEMAKER" means an individual who--
   (1) has not worked in the labor force for a substantial number of years but
  has, during those years, worked in the home providing unpaid services for
  family members;
   (2) (A) has been dependent on public assistance or on the income of another
  family member but is no longer supported by that income, or (B) is receiving
```

United States Code Annotated

The *United States Code Annotated (U.S.C.A.)* is an excellent example of West's publishing philosophy. West believes in providing as much information as possible, leaving it to the researcher to wade through the information and discard what is not relevant. Following this philosophy, *U.S.C.A.* occupies well over two hundred volumes and provides the researcher with citations to all the cases that it can locate and a wide variety of other references as well (Figure 4.6). If you like receiving as much information as possible, you will prefer using the *U.S.C.A.*

In essence, by enhancing the statutory text with notes and references to other research materials, West allows you to use the *U.S.C.A.* as an entryway to a statutory research system. In the *U.S.C.A.*, directly following the text of the statute, you will find the history of the statute. It indicates, in parentheses, when the law was originally passed and when it was amended or repealed. It will provide citations to the *U.S. Statutes at Large* origin of the text as well as to amendments. The historical notes provide detail on specific word changes.

Figure 4.6 Information Available in the *U.S.C.A.*

12 § 1702 **NATIONAL HOUSING Ch. 13**

SUBCHAPTER I—HOUSING RENOVATION AND MODERNIZATION

CROSS REFERENCES

Cross-References

Insurance of mortgages, see 12 USCA § 1743.
Maintenance of records and public disclosure, see 12 USCA § 2803.
State constitutional and legal limits upon interest chargeable on loans, mortgages, or other interim financing arrangements, see 12 USCA § 1709–1a.

§ 1702. Administrative provisions

The powers conferred by this chapter shall be exercised by the Secretary of Housing and Urban Development (hereinafter referred to as the "Secretary"). In order to carry out the provisions of this subchapter and subchapters II, III, V, VI, VII, VIII, IX–A, IX–B, and X of this chapter, the Secretary may establish such agencies, accept and utilize such voluntary and uncompensated services, utilize such Federal officers and employees, and, with the consent of the State, such State and local officers and employees, and appoint such other officers and employees as he may find necessary, and may prescribe their authorities, duties, responsibilities, and tenure and fix their compensation. The Secretary may delegate any of the functions and powers conferred upon him under this subchapter and

Figure 4.6 Information Available in the *U.S.C.A.* (continued)

U.S.C.C.A.N. References

HISTORICAL AND STATUTORY NOTES

Revision Notes and Legislative Reports

1941 Act. House Report No. 517, see 1941 U.S.Code Cong. Service, p. 570.

1948 Act. House Report No. 2389, see 1948 U.S.Code Cong. Service, p. 2351.

1949 Acts. House Report No. 854, see 1949 U.S.Code Cong. Service, p. 1757.

House Report No. 1396, see 1949 U.S. Code Cong. Service, p. 2216.

1950 Act. Senate Report No. 1286 and Conference Report No. 1893, see 1950 U.S.Code Cong. Service, p. 2021.

1951 Act. House Report No. 795 and Conference Report No. 901, see 1951 U.S.Code Cong. and Adm.Service, p. 1716.

1988 Act. House Report No. 100–122 (I & II) and House Conference Report No. 100–426, see 1987 U.S.Code Cong. and Adm.News, p. 3317.

References in Text

This chapter, referred to in text, was in the original "this Act", meaning Act June 27, 1934, c. 847, 48 Stat. 1246, as amended, known as the National Housing Act. For complete classification of this Act to the Code, see note under § 1701 of this title and Tables.

Codifications

Provisions of second sentence that authorized the Secretary to appoint officers and employees, prescribe their tenure, and fix their compensation "without re-

Figure 4.6 Information Available in the *U.S.C.A.* (continued)

Executive Orders

Cross-References

West Topic and Key Number

Library References

C.J.S. Reference

EXECUTIVE ORDERS

EXECUTIVE ORDER NO. 7058

Ex.Ord. No. 7058, May 29, 1935, authorized the former Federal Housing Administrator to adopt a seal for the former Federal Housing Administration; provided that copies of any books, records, papers, documents, agreements, orders, rules, or regulations of the Administration were admissible in evidence equally with the originals thereof; and empowered the Administrator or his designee to certify or exemplify copies of any books, records, papers, or documents of the Administration.

EXECUTIVE ORDER NO. 7280

Ex.Ord. No. 7280, Jan. 28, 1936, was issued as evidence of the creation of the former Federal Housing Administration and validated and confirmed the creation thereof.

CROSS REFERENCES

Construction of defense housing by private enterprise, see 42 USCA § 1591a.

LIBRARY REFERENCES

American Digest System

Disbursements for housing, see United States ⚿82(3 to 3.5, 7).

Instrumentalities of United States for housing, see United States ⚿53(9).

Encyclopedias

Federal loans, grants and insurance of loans for housing, see C.J.S. United States § 70.

191

Figure 4.6 Information Available in the *U.S.C.A.* (continued)

Text and Treatise Reference

WESTLAW Reference

Notes of Decisions

Subdivision Index

12 § 1702 **NATIONAL HOUSING Ch. 13**

Texts and Treatises

Actions against agencies and officers, see Wright, Miller & Cooper, Federal Practice and Procedure: Jurisdiction 2d § 3655.

WESTLAW ELECTRONIC RESEARCH

United States cases: 393k[add key number].
See, also, WESTLAW guide following the Explanation pages of this volume.

NOTES OF DECISIONS

I. GENERALLY 1–30
II. SOVEREIGN IMMUNITY 31–70
III. PRACTICE AND PROCEDURE—GENERALLY 71–100
IV. JURISDICTION 101–111

For Detailed Alphabetical Note Index, see the Various Subdivisions.

I. GENERALLY

Subdivision Index

Constitutionality 1
Construction
Generally 2
With other laws 3
Law governing 5
Nature of Department 8
Official capacity 9
Power of Congress 6
Purpose 4
Rules and regulations 7

1. Constitutionality

This subchapter is not unconstitutional, since aids to improve housing are within the ambit of governmental authority as conducive to the health and contentment of the community. U.S. v. Brooks, D.C.Wash.1939, 28 F.Supp. 712.

Manufacturers Nat. Bank of Detroit v. Brownstown Square Apartments, D.C. Mich.1980, 491 F.Supp. 206.

Waiver of immunity from suit by Secretary must be strictly construed. City of Philadelphia v. Page, D.C.Pa.1973, 363 F.Supp. 148, motion denied 373 F.Supp. 453.

3. Construction with other laws

Only the plainest inconsistency would warrant United States Supreme Court in finding an implied exception to § 191 of Title 31 giving priority to the United States in payment of claims against an insolvent debtor, and this subchapter is not inconsistent with § 191 and does not relinquish priority in favor of claims of the United States arising under this subchapter. U.S. v. Emory, Mo.1941, 62 S.Ct. 317, 314 U.S. 423, 86 L.Ed. 315, 48 Am.Bankr.Rep.N.S. 499.

This information can be extremely helpful when a law has gone through several revisions. Cross-references to related and qualifying laws are included to prevent oversights. Other references indicate where the legislative history can be located in the *U.S. Code Congressional and Administrative News (Figure 4.7 U.S.C.C.A.N.)*. You will also find citations to the *Code of Federal Regulations (C.F.R.)*, which contains administrative regulations (Figure 4.7).

The Library References section gives the applicable West topics and key numbers and citations to *Corpus Juris Secundum (C.J.S.)*, the West legal en-

Figure 4.7 References to the *Code of Federal Regulations* in the *U.S.C.A.*

42 § 7501 **PUBLIC HEALTH AND WELFARE**

§ 7501. Definitions

For the purpose of this part and section 7410(a)(2)(I) of this title—

(1) The term "reasonable further progress" means annual incremental reductions in emissions of the applicable air pollutant (including substantial reductions in the early years following approval or promulgation of plan provisions under this part and section 7410(a)(2)(I) of this title and regular reductions thereafter) which are sufficient in the judgment of the Administrator, to provide for attainment of the appli-

Code of Federal Regulations

Air pollution from motor vehicles, control of, see 40 CFR 86.078–3 et seq.
Air programs, see 40 CFR 81.1 et seq.
Implementation plans, requirements for preparation, adoption and submittal of, see 40 CFR 51.1 et seq.

586

Code of Federal Regulations References

cyclopedia. The West topics and key numbers give you access points into the West digests. The *U.S.C.A.* also contains references to other relevant materials published by West, such as West's *Federal Forms* and West's *Federal Practice Manual.*

As we observed earlier, the *U.S.C.A.* is known for its abundance of annotations of court and administrative decisions. Annotations are one-sentence summaries, written by West's editors, that indicate if, and how, courts or administrative bodies have interpreted a law. The case citation appears at the end of each annotation, so that you can find the case and read it yourself. At times, you will find an annotation to an opinion by the attorney general. Although these opinions are only persuasive, they could be useful and should be read. Some statutes have been interpreted by the courts so many times that West provides an index to the annotations so you can preselect cases involving your legal issue. Some statutes may not have been the subject of litigation and will not have any annotations.

To be absolutely sure that you have all the cases that cite a federal statute, you may want to search on WESTLAW for code references in case law. When you know the citation of a statute or code section, search for references to that citation. For example, to retrieve federal circuit court cases that cite 12 U.S.C. 1702, access the U.S. court of appeals (**CTA**) case law database and type **he(12 +5 1702).**

How to Use the *U.S.C.A.*

If you need a specific statute but know only the subject of the law, you will need to use the multivolume general index for the *U.S.C.A.* It is very important to consider as many terms as possible when using the index. You will find the index includes many cross-references that lead you to the correct section. For example, your client has lost his credit card. Unfortunately, he did not report the loss to the bank that issued the card. The bank claims that your client is responsible for the unauthorized purchases. Check the index to the *U.S.C.A.* under "credit cards" to find the appropriate statutes. The heading "Credit Cards and Plates" refers you to "Consumer Credit Protection." Going to this heading, you will find the laws that you need under the term "Loss or theft" (Figure 4.8).

If you know the popular name of the act, that is, the name that it is commonly known by, such as Title VII or the FOIA Act, you can check the Popular Name Table located at the end of the General Index. We use "popular" in a special sense here—it is not as if these laws have been on MTV. The popular name of an act is sometimes just the author of the act—for example, the Gramm-Rudman-Hollings Act named after the authors of the act in the U.S. Senate.

If you approach the *U.S.C.A.* with either the public law number or the *Statutes at Large* citation, you can check the volumes labeled "Tables" at the end of the set. These tables translate the public law number and the *Statutes at Large* citation, broken down into its component section numbers, into its corresponding *U.S.C.A.* citation (Figure 4.9).

Updating the *U.S.C.A.*

The constant possibility of change in legislation makes it *mandatory* for you to check for the very latest amendments to a law. Always check the publication

Figure 4.8 Using the *U.S.C.A.* Index

CREATIVE 972

CREATIVE WRITING
"Arts" as including, National Foundation on the Arts and the Humanities Act of 1965, **20 § 952**

CREDIT (PAYMENT OF INDEBTEDNESS) —Cont'd
Regional Agricultural Credit Corporations, generally, this index

Equal credit opportunity. Consumer Credit Protection, generally, this index
Extortionate Credit Transactions, generally, this index
Fair credit billing. Consumer Credit Protection, generally, this index
Farm credit,
Agricultural Credit, generally, this index
Farm Credit Administration, generally, this index
Farm Credit Bank, generally, this index
Farm Credit Banks, generally, this index
Farm Credit System, generally, this index
Farm Credit Administration, generally, this

CREDIT CARD FRAUD ACT OF 1984
Text of Act, **18 §§ 1029, 1029 nt**
Credit cards or plates. Consumer Credit Protection, generally, this index
Short title, **18 § 1001 nt**

CREDIT CARDS AND PLATES
Consumer Credit Protection, this index
Credit billing. Consumer Credit Protection, this index
Fair credit billing. Consumer Credit Protection, generally, this index
System, person operating, financial records, maintenance of, **12 § 1953**

Cross-Reference

Figure 4.8 Using the *U.S.C.A.* Index (continued)

583 **CONSUMER**

CONSUMER CREDIT PROTECTION
—Cont'd
Credit billing—Cont'd
Statement,
Effect of failure of timely mailing or delivery of, **15 § 1666b**
Required with each billing cycle, **15 § 1637**
Surcharge,
Defined, prohibition, surcharge on cardholders, **15 § 1602**
"Discount" as excluding, inducements to cardholders by sellers of cash discounts for payments by cash, etc., **15 § 1602**
On cardholder electing to use card prohibited, **15 § 1666f**
Time, notice, correction of billing errors, **15 § 1666**
Transmit statement to last address of obligor, **15 § 1666**
Treatment of credit balances, **15 § 1666d**
Use of,
Annual percentage rate in oral disclosures, exceptions, **15 § 1665a**
Cash discounts, **15 § 1666f**
Usury laws of State, etc., cash discounts not considered as finance charge or other charge for credit for sales transactions, **15 § 1666j**
Credit cards and plates,
Accepted credit card, defined, **15 § 1602**
Access device,

CONSUMER CREDIT PROTECTION
—Cont'd
Credit cards and plates—Cont'd
"Credit device" existing for purpose of obtaining money, property, etc., as meaning, **15 § 1602**
Defined, **15 § 1602**
Device-making equipment, defined, **18 § 1029**
Direct mail applications and solicitation, disclosure requirements, **15 § 1637**
Exclusiveness of liability of cardholder, **15 § 1643**
Fraud,
Access devices, **18 § 1029**
Interception of wire, etc., communications, authorization, **18 § 2516**
Secret Service arrests, **18 § 3056**
Fraudulent use, **15 § 1644**
General information without specific term, applications and solicitations, disclosure requirements, **15 § 1637**
Issuance, **15 § 1642**
Issuers, access to open end consumer credit plans, disclosure requirements, **15 § 1637**
Liability of cardholder, **15 § 1643**
Liability of issuer, violation of disclosure requirements, **15 § 1640**
Limits on liability of cardholder, **15 § 1643**
Loss or theft, liability of cardholder for unauthorized use in event of, **15 § 1643**
Other laws or agreement with issuer, liabili-

Reference to the Statute

date (copyright date on the back of the title page) of the hard-copy volume to determine if your law needs updating. To check for amendments, deletions, and new annotations that have appeared since the bound volume was published, check the supplementary pamphlets inserted in the back of each volume; these are called "pocket parts" because they fit into pockets in the cover of each volume. *Always, always, check the pocket part.* Do you catch our drift? Check it. The pocket parts are arranged by the same section numbers as the bound volume.

Because pocket parts to the *U.S.C.A.* only appear once a year, there are many times when a new law or amendment is not yet included. To fill this gap, the *U.S.C.A.* issues bimonthly noncumulative pamphlets of the newest laws and amendments arranged in *U.S.C.A.* classification. All of the new annotations also appear in these pamphlets. Usually, two additional pamphlets, as needed, will also be issued. These are the *U.S.C.A. Statutory Supplements* containing all amendments to the code through the last law of the session signed by the president. These two pamphlets are not arranged in *U.S.C.A.*

Figure 4.9 Finding the *U.S.C.A.* Citation from the Tables

1968 **STATUTES AT LARGE**

1968—90th Cong.—82 Stat.				USCA		
Apr.	P.L.	Sec.	Page	Tit.	Sec.	Status
29	90–296	1	109	28	1407	
		2	110	28	prec. 1391	
	90–297	1	110	42	1958	Rep.
		2, 3	111	42	1958 nts	Elim.
	90–298	—	111	46	817	
May						
3	90–299	1	112	47	223	
		2	112	47	153	
4	90–300	—	113	12	355	
7	90–301	1(a)	113	38	1810	
		1(b)	113	38	1811	
		2(a)	113	38	1810	
		2(b)	113	38	1822	Rep.
		3(a)	113	12	1709—1	Rep.
		3(b)	114	12	1713	
		3(c)	114	12	1715e	
		3(d)	114	12	1715v	
		3(e)	114	12	1715y	
		4	114	12	1709—1 nt	
		5(a)	116	38	1827	
		5(b)	116	38	prec. 1801	
8	90–302,	1	117	42	1752, 1752 nt	
		2(a)	117	42	1755	
		2(b)	117	42	1758	
		3	117	42	1761	
		4	119	42	1776	
		5	119	42	1773	
17	90–308	—	123	25	331 nt	
	90–309	2	123	25	396f nt	
18	90–311	1 to 3	124	43	615 to 615e nt	Elim.
	90–312	—	125	33	59f	
22	90–313	1–7	126–129	49	1653 nt	
23	90–314	—	129	22	2589	
24	90–318	—	131	16	1132 nt	
29	90–321	1, 101	146	15	1601 nt	
		102	146	15	1601	
		103	147	15	1602	
		104	147	15	1603	
		105	148	15	1604	
		106	148	15	1605	
		107	149	15	1606	
		108	150	15	1607	
		109	150	15	1608	
		110	151	15	1609	Rep.
		111	151	15	1610	
		112	151	15	1611	
		113	151	15	1612	
		114	151	15	1613	
		115	—	15	1614	Rep.
		121	152	15	1631	
		122	152	15	1632	
		123	152	15	1633	
		124	152	15	1634	
		125	152	15	1635	
		126	153	15	1636	Rep.
		127	153	15	1637	
		128	155	15	1638	
		129	156	15	1639	Rep.
		130	157	15	1640	
		131	157	15	1641	
		132	—	15	1642	
		133	—	15	1643	
		134	—	15	1644	
		135	—	15	1645	
		136	—	15	1646	
		141	158	15	1661	
		142	158	15	1662	
		143	158	15	1663	
		144	158	15	1664	
		145	159	15	1665	
		146	—	15	1665a	
		161	—	15	1666	
		162	—	15	1666a	
		163	—	15	1666b	

310

Public Law Number & Section No., and *U.S.C.A.* Citation

classification, but are in public law form. Late in any given year, you will have to check the main volume, the pocket part, and each of the year's pamphlets. An amazing number of people forget to check the pamphlets. Don't be one of them.

When we discussed the West publication *U.S.C.C.A.N.*, we noted that the bound volumes were supplemented on a monthly basis. You can also use the softbound monthly supplements to *U.S.C.C.A.N.* to update the code. The laws in *U.S.C.C.A.N.* are arranged in chronological order as they were passed by Congress. Remember that you can also update the code by checking the U.S. Public Laws database (**US-PL**) on WESTLAW. Public laws are on WESTLAW within a few working days of approval by the president. The update command on WESTLAW is a particularly easy method for updating the U.S. Code.

United States Code Service

The *United States Code Service (U.S.C.S.)* is published by Lawyers Co-op. Like the *U.S.C.A.*, the *U.S.C.S.* provides the researcher with references to authority, historical notes, cross-references, and case annotations. The *U.S.C.S.* also has a multivolume general index. The set is updated with annual pocket parts and quarterly cumulative supplements. The *U.S.C.S.* differs from the *U.S.C.A.* in that it is Lawyers Co-op's philosophy to be selective in its notes of case decisions. Therefore, the *U.S.C.S.* excludes case annotations that the editors at Lawyers Co-op deem to be obsolete, repetitive, or insignificant. On the other hand, the *U.S.C.S.* includes more notes of administrative decisions than the *U.S.C.A.* does. Therefore, if you are working on a subject area that is highly regulated, like occupational health and safety, you may want to check the *U.S.C.S.* (Figure 4.10), as well as other administrative decision sources on WESTLAW.

State Codes

At times when you are using the federal codes, you will also need to refer to the state codes. For example, although most aspects of labor law are subject to extensive federal law, some matters are not covered by federal law but are regulated by comprehensive state statutes concerning labor relations. For example, federal law specifically covers picketing by employees during labor controversies. Additionally, many states have comprehensive state statutes regulating violent conduct during picketing. It is this link between federal law and state law that may lead you to compare federal laws with state laws. If you search on WESTLAW, use the U.S. Code database (**USC**) and run the following query:

```
picket! & violen! danger! crim! weapon
firearm
```

This query retrieves four documents in the **USC** database—18 U.S.C. 1231 (Figure 4.11). Modify the query and run it in the multistate unannotated statutes database: type **qdb stat-all.** Change the "&" to a **/p**, so the query reads as follows:

```
picket! /p violen! danger! crim! weapon
firearm
```

Figure 4.10 Citations to Decisions in the *U.S.C.S.*

OCCUPATIONAL SAFETY AND HEALTH **29 USCS § 661**

Employer discharged employees as retaliation for filing safety charges, despite contention they were fired for taking extended lunch breaks, where there was no prior enforcement of tardiness rules and employees were not issued warnings. Donovan v Peter Zimmer America, Inc. (1982, DC SC) 557 F Supp 642.

plained to OSHA about health conditions in her workplace did not establish violation of nondiscrimination provisions (29 USCS § 660(c)), where no direct evidence of retaliation or employer animus was introduced and employer produced evidence that (1) it had taken actions to accommodate employee in resolving her com-

§ 661. Occupational Safety and Health Review Commission

(a) Establishment; membership; appointment; Chairman. The Occupational Safety and Health Review Commission is hereby established. The Commission shall be composed of three members who shall be appointed by the President, by and with the advice and consent of the Senate, from among persons who by reason of training, education, or experience are qualified to carry out the functions of the Commission under this Act. The President shall designate one of the members of the Commission to serve as Chairman.

(b) Terms of office; removal by President. The terms of members of the Commission shall be six years except that (1) the members of the Commission first taking office shall serve, as designated by the President at the time of appointment, one for a term of two years, one for a term of four years, and one for a term of six years, and (2) a vacancy caused by the death, resignation, or removal of a member prior to the expiration of the term for which he was appointed shall be filled only for the remainder of such unexpired term. A member of the Commission may be removed by the President for inefficiency, neglect of duty, or malfeasance in office.

[(c)](d) Principal office; hearings or other proceedings at other places. The principal office of the Commission shall be in the District of Columbia.

243

Source: Copyright© by The Lawyers Co-operative Publishing Company, Rochester, New York. Reprinted with permission of The Lawyers Co-operative Publishing Company.

This query retrieves approximately 37 documents from 20 states (Figure 4.12).

At other times, you will need just state law; for example, your client feels it is unfair that she cannot pay for her legal education by scalping tickets at concerts. If you search this problem on WESTLAW in the New York Statutes—unannotated database **ny-st** by typing

```
theat! concert event /s ticket! /p sell! sale
```

you will retrieve statutes on this issue (Figure 4.13).

You can also find the law in the hard-copy materials. Using the index to *McKinney's Consolidated Laws of New York Annotated,* look under "Tick-

Figure 4.10 Citations to Decisions in the *U.S.C.S.* (continued)

Law Review Articles:

Bangser, An Inherent Role for Cost-Benefit Analysis in Judicial Review of Agency Decisions: A New Perspective on OSHA Rulemaking. 10 Boston College Environmental Affairs L Rev 365, 1982.

Pleading and Practice Before the Occupational and Safety and Health Review Commission. 24 Labor LJ 779 (1973).

INTERPRETIVE NOTES AND DECISIONS

I. OSHRC

1. Judicial authority

Commission's function is to act as a neutral arbiter and determine whether the Secretary's citations should be enforced over employee or union objections, and its authority does not extend to overturning the Secretary's decision not to issue or to withdraw a citation. Cuyahoga V.R. Co. v United Transp. Union (1985) 474 US 3, 88 L Ed 2d 2, 106 S Ct 286, on remand (CA6) 783 F2d 58.

Congress intended that occupational safety and health review commission would have normal complement of adjudicatory powers possessed by traditional administrative agencies such as Federal Trade Commission. Brennan v Gilles & Cotting, Inc. (1974, CA4) 504 F2d 1255, 27 ALR Fed 925 (disagreed with by Marshall v Sun Petroleum Products Co. (CA3) 622 F2d 1176) and (disagreed with by Marshall v Occupational Safety & Health Review Com. (CA6) 635 F2d 544) and (disagreed with by Oil, Chemical & Atomic Workers International Union v Occupational Safety & Health Review Com., 217 App DC 137, 671 F2d 643, 33 FR Serv 2d 1223, 65 ALR Fed 580) and (disagreed with by Donovan v A. Amorello & Sons, Inc. (CA1) 761 F2d 61) and (disagreed with by United Steelworkers of America, etc. v Schuylkill Metals Corp. (CA5) 828 F2d 314, 13 BNA OSHC 1393, 1987 CCH OSHD ¶ 28059) and (disagreed with by Re Perry (CA1) 882 F2d 534, 14 BNA OSHC 1113, 1989 CCH OSHD ¶ 28625).

Decision on general contractor's joint responsibility for subcontractors' workmen is vested in occupational safety and health review commission, guided by "economic realities" in interpreting terms "employer" and "employee" in manner to achieve statutory objectives. Brennan v Gilles & Cotting, Inc. (1974, CA4) 504 F2d 1255, 27 ALR Fed 925 (disagreed with on other grounds Marshall v Sun Petroleum Products Co. (CA3) 622 F2d 1176, cert den 449 US 1061, 66 L Ed 2d 604, 101 S Ct 784) and (disagreed with by Donovan v Oil, Chemical, etc. Local 4-23 (CA5) 718 F2d 1341) and (disagreed with by Donovan v United Transp. Union (CA6) 748 F2d 340) and (disagreed with by Marshall v Occupational Safety & Health Review Com. (CA6) 635 F2d 544) and (disagreed with by Oil, Chemical & Atomic Workers International Union v Occupational Safety & Health Review Com., 217 App DC 137, 671 F2d 643, 33 FR Serv 2d 1223, 65 ALR Fed 580) and (disagreed with by Donovan v A. Amorello & Sons, Inc. (CA1) 761 F2d 61) and (disagreed with by United Steelworkers of America, etc. v Schuylkill Metals Corp. (CA5) 828 F2d 314, 13 BNA OSHC 1393, 1987 CCH OSHD ¶ 28059) and (disagreed with by Re Perry (CA1) 882 F2d 534,

Figure 4.11 A Document Retrieved by Using the USC Database

```
Citation                     Rank(R)        Page(P)      Database   Mode
18 USCA s 1231               R 1 OF 4       P 1 OF 2     USC        T
 18 U.S.C.A. s 1231

                      UNITED STATES CODE ANNOTATED
           COPR. (c) WEST 1990  No Claim to Orig. Govt. Works
                TITLE 18.  CRIMES AND CRIMINAL PROCEDURE
                            PART I--CRIMES--
                            CHAPTER 57--LABOR

 s 1231. Transportation of strikebreakers

  Whoever willfully transports in interstate or foreign commerce any person who
 is employed or is to be employed for the purpose of obstructing or interfering
 by force or threats with (1) peaceful PICKETING by employees during any labor
 controversy affecting wages, hours, or conditions of labor, or (2) the exercise
 by employees of any of the rights of self-organization or collective
 bargaining;  or
  Whoever is knowingly transported or travels in interstate or foreign commerce
 for any of the purposes enumerated in this section--
  Shall be fined not more than $5,000 or imprisoned not more than two years, or
 both.
  This section shall not apply to common carriers.
```

Figure 4.12 Thirty-Seven Documents Retrieved by Using the USC Database

```
CITATIONS LIST (Page 1)                            Total Documents:  37
Database: STAT-ALL

    1.   A.R.S. s 23-619.01   ARIZONA REVISED STATUTES ANNOTATED
 TITLE 23.  LABOR    CHAPTER 4.--EMPLOYMENT SECURITY   ARTICLE 1. DEFINITIONS
 s 23-619.01. Misconduct connected with the employment;  wilful misconduct;
 evaluation

    2.   A.R.S. s 23-1321   ARIZONA REVISED STATUTES ANNOTATED
 TITLE 23.  LABOR    CHAPTER 8.--LABOR RELATIONS
 ARTICLE 2. PICKETING AND SECONDARY BOYCOTTS    s 23-1321. Definitions

    3.   West's Ann.Cal.Penal Code s 70   WEST'S ANNOTATED CALIFORNIA CODES
 PENAL CODE    PART 1. OF CRIMES AND PUNISHMENTS
 TITLE 5.  OF CRIMES BY AND AGAINST THE EXECUTIVE POWER OF THE STATE
 s 70. Unauthorized emoluments, gratuities, or rewards;  prohibition against
 request or receipt by executive or ministerial officers or employees;
 exceptions;  peace officers
```

Figure 4.13 Retrieving a State Statute on WESTLAW

```
CITATIONS LIST (Page 3)                            Total Documents:  25
Database: NY-ST

    7.   McKinney's Arts and Cultural Affairs Law s 25.03
 MCKINNEY'S CONSOLIDATED LAWS OF NEW YORK ANNOTATED
 ARTS AND CULTURAL AFFAIRS LAW   CHAPTER 11-C OF THE CONSOLIDATED LAWS
 TITLE G--REGULATION OF SALE OF THEATRE TICKETS   ARTICLE 25--THEATRE TICKETS
 s 25.03. Reselling of tickets of admission;  licenses;  fees

    8.   McKinney's Arts and Cultural Affairs Law s 25.05
 MCKINNEY'S CONSOLIDATED LAWS OF NEW YORK ANNOTATED
 ARTS AND CULTURAL AFFAIRS LAW   CHAPTER 11-C OF THE CONSOLIDATED LAWS
 TITLE G--REGULATION OF SALE OF THEATRE TICKETS   ARTICLE 25--THEATRE TICKETS
 s 25.05. Ticket speculators

    9.   McKinney's Arts and Cultural Affairs Law s 25.07
 MCKINNEY'S CONSOLIDATED LAWS OF NEW YORK ANNOTATED
 ARTS AND CULTURAL AFFAIRS LAW   CHAPTER 11-C OF THE CONSOLIDATED LAWS
 TITLE G--REGULATION OF SALE OF THEATRE TICKETS   ARTICLE 25--THEATRE TICKETS
 s 25.07. Bond
```

ets—Sales," which leads you to "Ticket Speculators—Selling or soliciting tickets" and to the statute Arts & Cult Aff § 25.05 (Figure 4.14).

Remember that you will use the same connectors in searching statutes on WESTLAW as in searching case law. It is most efficient to use a field restriction. The fields are the same for both the *U.S.C.A.* and for state codes. When searching by topic, restrict your search to the prelim and caption fields. For example, access the New York statutes–annotated database **ny-st-ann** and type

```
pr,ca(theat! concert event & ticket!
        & sell! sale)
```

This search uses the preliminary field (which includes the title, subtitle, chapter, and subchapter headings of each section) and the caption field (which includes the section number, followed by terms that generally describe its contents). Figure 4.15 shows the results of your search.

What we said earlier about the publications of federal legislation is true for state legislation. Most states publish their statutes initially in a slip law format. Many states publish slip laws in the form of an advance sheet service, which are softbound supplements to a code. All states publish bound session laws. Most states publish a bound official code, and at least one annotated code is published for every state. Court rules and constitutions, along with the laws, are usually included in state codes. State codifications may be called codes, revisions, compilations, or consolidations, and their format and numbering systems will vary from state to state.

When you practice law, you will find that on-line access to the full text of state laws is an enormous advantage since your law firm is unlikely to have the codes from all of the states. Statutes databases are being added or expanded all the time, so use the SCOPE command to see current coverage information. Most state statutes on WESTLAW can be searched in either an annotated or an unannotated database. If you want to see the summaries of the cases that have interpreted the statute, you should search in the annotated databases. You can also search in the unannotated databases and use the ANNOS service to retrieve the annotations and references as well as the statute text. The unannotated database focuses on specific legislative terminology and narrows your search considerably.

You can search for laws from individual states or from many states simultaneously. Use either ST-ANN-ALL for the annotated statutes from all available states or STAT-ALL for the unannotated statutes from all available states. For example, assume you are searching for legislation on the placement of smoke or heat detectors in hotels. To avoid retrieving a large number of irrelevant documents, search in the multistate unannotated statutes database, STAT-ALL and type

```
fire heat smok! /5 detect! & hotel motel inn
  lodg! resort ''public accommodation''
```

With this search, you will retrieve over 90 documents (Figure 4.16). Once you have retrieved the statute you want, read the statute and type **d** to view the

Figure 4.14 Finding a State Statute in the hard-Copy Materials

97 **TICKETS**

TIANA BAY
Fish and wildlife, marine fisheries, nets, restrictions on use, **ECL 13–0343**
Nets, restrictions on use, **ECL 13–0343**

TIBBETTS BROOK
Grant of former bed, **PUB L 75**

TICK-BORNE DISEASE INSTITUTE
Advisory committee, establishment, functions, membership, etc., **PUB HE 2799–a**
Chairman,
  Advisory committee, designation by governor, **PUB HE 2799–a**
  Research council, special meetings, power to call, **PUB HE 2799**
Committee, defined, **PUB HE 2796**
Compensation,
  Advisory committee, actual and necessary expenses, **PUB HE 2799–a**
  Research council, actual and necessary expenses, **PUB HE 2799**
Council, defined, **PUB HE 2796**
Definitions, **PUB HE 2796**
Director, appointment by health commissioner, **PUB HE 2797**
Establishment, **PUB HE 2797**
Governor, advisory committee, chairman of, designation by, **PUB HE 2799–a**
Health commissioner, powers, function, duties, etc., **PUB HE 2797 et seq.**
Health department, establishment of within, **PUB HE 2797**
Institute, defined, **PUB HE 2796**
Meetings,
  Advisory committee, number of, **PUB HE 2799–a**
  Research council, number of, **PUB HE 2799**
Members,
  Advisory committee, appointment by temporary president of senate, etc., **PUB HE 2799–a**
  Research council, appointment by health commissioner, **PUB HE 2799**
Power and duties, **PUB HE 2798**
Research council, establishment, membership, functions, etc., **PUB HE 2799**
Special meetings,
  Advisory committee, chairman to call, **PUB HE 2799–a**
  Research council, chairman to call, **PUB HE 2799**

TICKET AGENTS
Advertising, this index
Sporting Events, generally, this index
Theatre Tickets, generally, this index

TICKET SPECULATORS
Boxing and wrestling matches, **UNCON 8919**
Cities and Nassau county, selling or soliciting tickets in, misdemeanor, **ARTS&CA 25.05**
Index Reference — Selling or soliciting tickets, misdemeanor, **ARTS&CA 25.05**
Sporting Events, generally, this index
Theatre Tickets, generally, this index

TICKETS
Admission, excise tax in cities and villages for subsidies, **PUB HO 110**
Advertising sale of partially used non-transferable ticket, **GEN B 126**
Air transportation service, use of stolen or forged credit or debit card to obtain, presumption, stolen property, **PEN 165.55**
Airline Tickets. Money Laundering, generally, this index
Boxing and Wrestling, this index
Collateral loan brokers, lost ticket charge, etc., payments, **GEN B 44**
Common carriers. Passage Tickets, generally, this index
False description, misdemeanor, **GEN B 392–b**
Forgery, generally, this index
Gift of street railroad or omnibus transfer tickets, **GEN B 120**
Indecent material, dissemination to minors, **PEN 235.21**
Lotteries, generally, this index
Motor vehicles, traffic infractions or offenses, arraignment, **V&T 1807**
Omnibus transfer tickets, giving away or selling, **GEN B 120**
Passage Tickets, generally, this index
Passengers, collection by one without badge prohibited, **RR 65**
"Property" as including ticket or equivalent instrument, larceny provisions, **PEN 155.00**
Public service commission, ordering delivery to consumers for excessive charges, **PUB S 113**
Railroads,
  Passage Tickets, generally, this index
  Purchase or selling partially used non-transferable tickets, **GEN B 126**
  Redemption, unused tickets, **GEN B 116**
  Sale or purchase of partially used non-transferable ticket, **GEN B 126**
Sales,
  Partially used non-transferable railroad tickets as offense, **GEN B 126**
  Speculators. Ticket Speculators, generally, this index
  Street railroad or omnibus transfer tickets, **GEN B 120**
  Tax, state and local, entertainment and amusement facilities, charges for use of, **TAX 1105 nt**
Season, exemption, sales tax, **TAX 1105**
Soliciting, unauthorized, in behalf of civil service employees, purchase, etc., misdemeanor, **CIV S 156**
Sporting Events, generally, this index
Theatre Tickets, generally, this index
Theatrical Syndication Financing, generally, this index
Trade-Marks, Trade-Names and Service-Marks, generally, this index
Uniform Appearance Ticket and Simplified Information, generally, this index
Value of ticket or equivalent instrument, larceny provisions, **PEN 155.20**

Figure 4.15 The Results of a Search Using the Preliminary and Caption Fields

```
CITATIONS LIST (Page 1)                              Total Documents:  15
Database: NY-ST-ANN

    1.   McKinney's Arts and Cultural Affairs Law s 23.08
MCKINNEY'S CONSOLIDATED LAWS OF NEW YORK ANNOTATED
ARTS AND CULTURAL AFFAIRS LAW   CHAPTER 11-C OF THE CONSOLIDATED LAWS
TITLE F--THEATRICAL SYNDICATION FINANCING
ARTICLE 23--REGULATION OF THEATRICAL SYNDICATION FINANCING
s 23.08. Proceeds from advance ticket sales;  refunds

    2.   McKinney's Arts and Cultural Affairs Law s 25.01
MCKINNEY'S CONSOLIDATED LAWS OF NEW YORK ANNOTATED
ARTS AND CULTURAL AFFAIRS LAW   CHAPTER 11-C OF THE CONSOLIDATED LAWS
TITLE G--REGULATION OF SALE OF THEATRE TICKETS   ARTICLE 25--THEATRE TICKETS
s 25.01. Matters of public interest

    3.   McKinney's Arts and Cultural Affairs Law s 25.03
MCKINNEY'S CONSOLIDATED LAWS OF NEW YORK ANNOTATED
ARTS AND CULTURAL AFFAIRS LAW   CHAPTER 11-C OF THE CONSOLIDATED LAWS
TITLE G--REGULATION OF SALE OF THEATRE TICKETS   ARTICLE 25--THEATRE TICKETS
s 25.03. Reselling of tickets of admission;  licenses;  fees
```

documents preceding and following the displayed document by using the documents in sequence command.

The most important step in searching state statutes on-line is to use the UPDATE service. This service allows you to quickly determine whether a statute or rule on WESTLAW has been amended or repealed. Use this service to retrieve legislation that has been enacted after the last compilation of statutes in the statutes database. You can type **UPDATE** when you are viewing a statute to view session laws that amend or repeal the original section. For example, if you are interested in the Maryland statute on smoke detectors, you will find that the law has been amended (Figure 4.17). Eventually material in the UPDATE service will be incorporated into the statutory databases.

The Related Materials (RM) service lists materials related to the specific state statutory document that you are viewing. To see the Related Materials directory for a particular document, type **RM** from any screen.

The legislative service databases contain laws passed in the current or recent sessions. These materials are eventually incorporated into the statutory databases. This service is useful if you recently learned about a new law and want to view it on-line. We also recommend that you run previous searches in a legislative service database to assure that you have the most current information. After returning to the previous search regarding smoke detectors in STATE-ALL, type

```
sdb legis-all
```

This search retrieves several documents in addition to the Maryland statute retrieved by the previous UPDATE request.

When you know a statute's citation, FIND is the easiest method for retrieving the statute. For example, to retrieve section 34-15-4 from the *Code of Alabama*

```
fi al st s 34-15-4
```

Figure 4.18 shows the result of your search.

Figure 4.16 Documents Retrieved by Searching All States Simultaneously

```
CITATIONS LIST (Page 1)                         Total Documents:  99
Database: STAT-ALL

   1.   Code 1975 s 34-15-4    CODE OF ALABAMA 1975
TITLE 34. PROFESSIONS AND BUSINESSES.
CHAPTER 15. HOTELS, INNS AND OTHER TRANSIENT LODGING PLACES.
s 34-15-4. Duty of hotel owners, operators, etc., to maintain conditions, smoke
detectors, etc.

   2.   A.R.S. T. 36, Ch. 13, Art. 3.1, Refs & Annos
ARIZONA REVISED STATUTES ANNOTATED    TITLE 36.   PUBLIC HEALTH AND SAFETY
CHAPTER 13.--SAFETY    ARTICLE 3.1. HOTELS AND MOTELS;  SMOKE DETECTORS

   3.   A.R.S. s 36-1645    ARIZONA REVISED STATUTES ANNOTATED
TITLE 36.   PUBLIC HEALTH AND SAFETY    CHAPTER 13.--SAFETY
ARTICLE 3.1. HOTELS AND MOTELS;  SMOKE DETECTORS    s 36-1645.  Definitions

   4.   A.R.S. s 36-1646    ARIZONA REVISED STATUTES ANNOTATED
TITLE 36.   PUBLIC HEALTH AND SAFETY    CHAPTER 13.--SAFETY
ARTICLE 3.1. HOTELS AND MOTELS;  SMOKE DETECTORS
s 36-1646. Smoke detectors;  hotels and motels
```

Figure 4.17 An Example of an Updated Statute

(a) Maryland Statute Retrieved by the Original Search

```
Citation                    Rank(R)          Page(P)        Database    Mode
MD CODE 1957, Art. 38A      R 30 OF 99       P 1 OF 7       STAT-ALL    T
 Code 1957, Art. 38A, s 12A

                    ANNOTATED CODE OF MARYLAND, 1988
      Copyright (c) 1957-1990 by The Michie Company.  All rights reserved.
                   ARTICLE 38A. FIRES AND INVESTIGATIONS.
               FIRE PREVENTION COMMISSION AND FIRE MARSHAL
                         SMOKE DETECTION Systems

 s 12A. SMOKE DETECTION systems.

   (a) SMOKE DETECTOR required in sleeping area; light signal for deaf or
 hearing impaired occupants; compliance by HOTELS and multi-family
 buildings. -- (1) Each sleeping area within all occupancies classified
 residential, as defined in the National Fire Protection Association Life Safety
 Code, 1981 Edition, shall be provided with a minimum of one approved SMOKE
 DETECTOR sensing visible or invisible particles of combustion installed in a
 manner and location approved by the Fire Prevention Commission. When activated,
 the detector shall provide an alarm suitable to warn the occupants.
   (2) (i) Dwelling units within existing HOTELS and multifamily buildings that
 were exempt from the provisions of this section because there were 10 units or
 more constructed before 1975 which conformed with the exiting requirements of
```

(b) Update of Maryland Statute

```
Citation                    Rank(R)          Page(P)        Database    Mode
MD LEGIS 423 (1990)         R 1 OF 1         P 1 OF 8       MD-LEGIS    T
 1990 Maryland Laws Ch. 423

                 MARYLAND 1990 SESSION LAWS AND RESOLUTIONS
                         Maryland General Assembly
              Copr. (C) West 1990 No Claim to Orig. Govt. Works


          Additions are indicated by  <<+  Text  +>> ; deletions by
      <<-  Text  ->> .  Changes in tables are made but not highlighted.

                                 Ch. 423
                                S.B. No. 6
                 SMOKE DETECTORS--NEW RESIDENTIAL CONSTRUCTION


   AN ACT concerning

                         Fire Safety--Smoke Detectors

   FOR the purpose of expanding certain provisions of law relating to smoke
 detectors by requiring the installation of smoke detectors that operate by
```

Figure 4.18 Retrieving a Statute When You have a Citation

```
Citation                    Rank(R)        Page(P)        Database    Mode
AL ST s 34-15-4             R 1 OF 1       P 1 OF 3       AL-ST-ANN   T
 Code 1975 s 34-15-4

                           CODE OF ALABAMA 1975
       Copyright (c) 1977-1990 by State of Alabama.  All rights reserved.
                  TITLE 34. PROFESSIONS AND BUSINESSES.
         CHAPTER 15. HOTELS, INNS AND OTHER TRANSIENT LODGING PLACES.

s 34-15-4. Duty of HOTEL owners, operators, etc., to maintain conditions, SMOKE
  DETECTORS, etc.

   (a) Every owner, manager or operator of a hotel shall maintain the physical
and sanitary condition of the structure, its equipment, water supply and human
waste disposal and shall conduct the operations thereof in such manner as to
render services and accommodations to travelers in compliance with rules and
regulations governing hotels and hotel operation adopted by the state board of
health.
   (b) Every owner, manager, or operator of a HOTEL shall install and maintain
in operating condition a battery or electrically operated SMOKE DETECTOR device
in each HOTEL guest sleeping room. The detectors shall have received an
approval from a nationally recognized testing organization.
   (c) HOTEL owners or operators shall be required to test each SMOKE DETECTOR
```

Constitutions

The U.S. Constitution is the foundation of our judicial system. As you will learn in your course on Constitutional Law, the wording of the U.S. Constitution is very general. Consequently, most of the law in this area has been made by the courts, especially by decisions of the U.S. Supreme Court. Finding the Constitution is easy and keeping up with the amendments is not a problem, but locating these cases can be a trial. You can locate the Constitution in the *U.S. Code* and as separate volumes of the two annotated versions, *U.S.C.A.* and *U.S.C.S.* The two annotated codes are perhaps the easiest way to find citations to cases that have interpreted the Constitution. Most parts have been interpreted so frequently, however, that you will need more help than the cases alone can provide. Fortunately, there are many other materials that you can use, including treatises, encyclopedias, and periodicals.

The *U.S.C.A.* provides extensive coverage by including annotations to both the federal and state decisions regarding each article or amendment to the U.S. Constitution. Over four thousand annotations to the fourth Amendment alone are listed in the *U.S.C.A.* The digests, either the one devoted to the U.S. Supreme Court or the federal digests, will also prove useful in locating cases that interpret the Constitution.

Additionally, WESTLAW can be useful in retrieving case law that interprets the Constitution. You can search by a particular section or by an amendment or perhaps combine the citation with relevant terms. WESTLAW also has specific First Amendment databases. For example, to obtain Supreme Court cases concerning a city's right to display religious scenes on public grounds, a topic that is constantly in the news, you would access the First Amendment–Supreme Court cases database (**FCFA-SCT**) and type

```
religio** nativity christmas hanukkah holiday /s
              display scene show
```

This query will retrieve cases such as *County of Allegheny v. ACLU,* 109 S.Ct. 3086 (1989) that discuss the issue.

State constitutions also have provisions that parallel the basic rights guaranteed by the U.S. Constitution. There is an interrelationship between the state and federal constitutions that protects all of us regardless of our residence. State constitutions can usually be found in the state codes. The constitutions for most states are available on WESTLAW in the state statutes database.

Court Rules

Court rules guide the operation of courts in solving legal controversies. Court rules typically cover such matters as selecting a proper court, commencing the action, pleadings, discovery, jury selection, the trial, and the judgment. The various federal court rules may be found in a variety of practitioners' manuals, rules services, and formbooks. The two most accessible sources are the two annotated codes, *U.S.C.A.* and *U.S.C.S.* Both of these annotated codes have special volumes containing the federal court rules, including the Federal Rules of Civil Procedure, Criminal Procedure, Appellate Procedure, and Evidence. In the *U.S.C.A.*, you will find these rules in special volumes accompanying Title 28 "Judiciary and Judicial Procedure" and Title 18 "Crimes and Procedure." These forms of statutory publication are crucial parts of the research process. You should come to understand how they are created and organized—they are the real world.

On WESTLAW, the **US-RULES** database contains documents from the *United States Code.* State court rules are in the state statutory databases. For individual states, type the state identifier, followed by **RULES.** You would search the rules databases for the states using the same techniques as in statute databases. To retrieve motions to quash, for example, access the California Rules database (**CA-RULES**) and type

```
quash! /p sub-poena!
```

The Documents in Sequence command (**d**) is useful when you are viewing a document that contains a reference to a nearby statute that you want to see. In the preceding group of documents from California, Rule 307 contains a reference to Rule 305. To view this rule, type **d-2.**

Conclusion

This chapter has explained how to find federal laws as they are passed by Congress and then as they appear in a codified form. We discussed several titles and formats, including on-line databases, each of which is suited to a different purpose. We also discussed state legislative materials, with a special emphasis on state law on WESTLAW. Once you have taken a few legislative courses, you will want to review this chapter since you may not have the opportunity to use federal or state legislative materials during your first year.

5 Administrative Law

Legislatures, including the U.S. Congress, pass broadly written laws that need to be enforced. To make such broad and often highly technical laws work, the legislature has to delegate some of its power to administrative agencies. These agencies, which are part of the executive/administrative branch of government, are responsible for writing specific rules and regulations (these terms have the same meaning) that enforce the statutes that are written by the legislatures. Think of the Federal Aviation Administration (FAA). Congress knows that it wants to enforce rules to govern air travel, but it also knows that it needs people with technical expertise to do it. Hence, Congress turns to the FAA.

Federal agencies regulate key areas of the economy: transportation (Interstate Commerce Commission), communications (Federal Communications Commission), the securities markets (Securities and Exchange Commission), labor relations (National Labor Relations Board), and competitive trade practices (Federal Trade Commission). The regulations issued by these agencies are just as binding as statutes and, from a practical viewpoint, affect the lives of everyone. A violation of a regulation may be as serious as a violation of a statute.

In addition to writing rules and regulations, agencies issue orders, licenses, and advisory opinions and conduct hearings. These functions are called quasi-judicial because the administrative agencies act like courts. If you take a course in Administrative Law, you will learn the procedures through which the government officials exercise their power, and the checks the other branches of government have on the administrative branch.

We are concerned here not so much with procedure as with what the agencies do, an aspect of the law that is often ignored in law school. In this chapter, we will try to give you a brief look at administrative materials. We will examine the materials of federal agencies, their rules that implement legislation, and their power to adjudicate disputes concerning parties they regulate. The president's lawmaking actions will also be noted. State materials will be discussed briefly at the end of the chapter.

The *Federal Register* in Print Format

The U.S. Government Printing Office issues two publications that provide you with federal administrative regulations: the daily *Federal Register* and the annual *Code of Federal Regulations*. You need to understand both publications

Figure 5.1 The *Federal Register*

as well as the relationship between the two. In our examination of these publications, we will discuss both the print versions and the on-line version, WESTLAW.

Federal regulations are published *chronologically* in the *Federal Register (Fed. Reg.)* on a daily basis (Figure 5.1). In addition to publishing rules and regulations, the *Federal Register* publishes presidential documents; that is, presidential proclamations and executive orders. The *Federal Register* also publishes proposed rules. People are given the opportunity to comment on these proposed regulations before they are either adopted or rejected by federal agencies. The largest section of the *Federal Register* is the notice section, which contains information about agencies including orders, opinions, agency changes, and notices of meetings. The *Federal Register* may fill as many as 50,000 pages a year. It will look boring and confusing at first, but if you practice law in a heavily regulated area, you will come to realize its utility.

Since the *Federal Register* (published since 1936) consumes an enormous amount of shelf space, you will be able to find it with ease in your library. Its size and fineness of print are reminiscent of a bit city telephone directory. Because of its size and its newsprint paper, many libraries have the historical volumes of the *Federal Register* on microfiche.

The *Code of Federal Regulations* in Print Format

The same regulations that appear in the *Federal Register* are arranged by *subject* in the *Code of Federal Regulations* or *C.F.R.* (Figure 5.2). The *C.F.R.* includes only regulations that are currently in force. The entire *C.F.R.* is recompiled annually with any new amendments added. Regulations that have been withdrawn are deleted. If a proposed regulation is never adopted, it will not appear in the *C.F.R.*—it will only appear as a proposed regulation in the *Federal Register*.

Figure 5.2 The *Code of Federal Regulations*

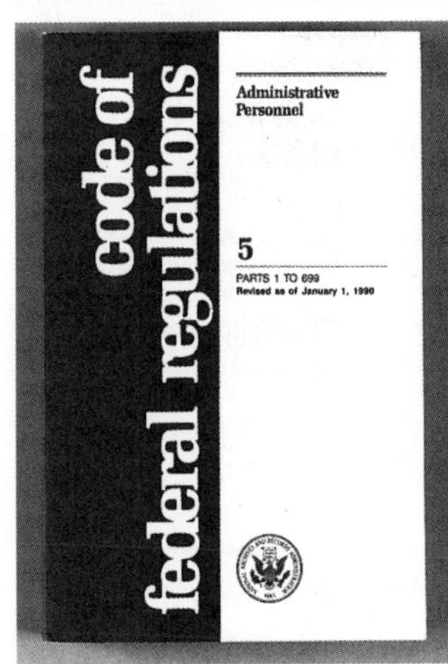

The *C.F.R.* is organized by titles, each of which represents a broad topic. Therefore, when you need to find all the federal regulations on electronic banking, you will look in the *C.F.R.* because it is arranged by subject. You will find that electronic banking is included in Title 12, which is dedicated to banking regulations. Using the *Federal Register* to find all of the regulations on a particular subject would be extremely difficult and time-consuming because the *Federal Register* is arranged chronologically. Therefore, you would have to search through approximately fifty-five years of the publication, page by page.

Within each title of the *C.F.R.*, regulations are divided into chapters, each of which is devoted to the regulations of a particular agency. The chapters are further divided into parts, consisting of a body of regulations on a particular topic or agency function. Parts are divided into sections, the basic unit of the *C.F.R.*, and if further breakdown is necessary, paragraphs are used (Figure 5.3).

Prefacing each part of the *C.F.R.* are notes provided by the agency that outline the statutory (legislative) authority under which the regulations are issued. Remember that regulations are adopted to implement specific pieces of legislation. The *authority note* is useful when you want to trace the regu-

Figure 5.3 The Organization of the C.F.R.

(g) *Reciprocal arrangements.* Finally, while a depository institution may enter into an arrangement with an unaffiliated third party wherein the third party agrees to stand ready to purchase time deposits held by the depository institution's customers, the Board will regard a reciprocal arrangement with another depository institution for purchase of each other's time deposits as a circumvention of the early withdrawal penalty rule and the purposes it is designed to serve.

[52 FR 47697, Dec. 16, 1987]

§ 204.132 Treatment of Loan Strip Participations.

(a) Effective March 31, 1988, the glossary section of the instructions for the Report of Condition and Income (FFIEC 031-034; OMB No. 7100-0036; available from a depository institution's primary federal regulator) ("Call Report") was amended to clarify that certain short-term loan participation arrangements (sometimes known or styled as "loan strips" or "strip participations") are regarded as borrowings rather than sales for Call Report purposes in certain circumstances. Through this interpretation, the Board is clarifying that such transactions should be treated as deposits for purposes of Regulation D.

(b) These transactions involve the sale (or placement) of a short-term loan by a depository institution that has been made under a long-term commitment of the depository institution to advance funds. For example, a 90-day loan made under a five-year revolving line of credit may be sold to or placed with a third party by the depository institution originating the loan. The depository institution originating the loan is obligated to renew the 90-day note itself (by advancing funds to its customer at the end of the 90-day period) in the event the original participant does not wish to renew the credit. Since, under these arrangements, the depository institution is obligated to make another loan at the end of 90 days (absent any event of default on the part of the borrower), the depository institution selling the loan or participation in effect must buy back the loan or participation at the maturity of the 90-day loan sold to or funded by the purchaser at the option of the purchaser. Accordingly, these transactions bear the essential characteristics of a repurchase agreement and, therefore, are reportable and reservable under Regulation D.

(c) Because many of these transactions give rise to deposit liabilities in the form of promissory notes, acknowledgments of advance or similar obligations (written or oral) as described in § 204.2(a)(1)(vii) of Regulation D, the exemptions from the definition of "deposit" incorporated in that section may apply to the liability incurred by a depository institution when it offers or originates a loan strip facility. Thus, for example, loan strips sold to domestic offices of other depository institutions are exempt from Regulation D under § 204.2(a)(1)(vii)(A)(*1*) because they are obligations issued or undertaken and held for the account of a U.S. office of another depository institution. Similarly, some of these transactions result in Eurocurrency liabilities and are reportable and reservable as such.

[53 FR 24931, July 1, 1988]

PART 205—ELECTRONIC FUND TRANSFERS

AUTHORITY: Pub. L. 95-630, 92 Stat. 3730 (15 U.S.C. 1693b).

107

lation back to its statutory authority. A *source note,* which lists the volume, page, and date of the *Federal Register* in which the regulation was published, follows the authority note (Figure 5.4). These two notes comprise the "administrative history" of the regulation.

The *C.F.R.* is published once a year on a staggered basis; that is, all of the volumes are not issued at one time. Instead, the titles are issued at four different times of the year:

- Title 1 through Title 16—as of January 1
- Title 17 through Title 27—as of April 1
- Title 28 through Title 41—as of July 1
- Title 42 through Title 50—as of October1

Because of these staggered dates, you must be careful to check the softbound cover of each title to determine the date of revision.

Fortunately, the U.S. Government Printing Office uses distinct colors for the covers of the *C.F.R.*—for example, 1988 was purple, 1989 gray, and 1990 blue. These boldly colored covers make it easy for you to see whether you have the correct year.

Finding Regulations in the Print Format of the *Federal Register* and the C.F.R.

Obviously, the easiest way to find a regulation is to get the citation to the *Federal Register* or the *C.F.R.* from a secondary source, such as a law review article. If you do not already have the *Federal Register* or the *C.F.R.* citation, you can either use the print indexes or access WESTLAW. The *Federal Register* has its own index. Each daily index contains a table of contents arranged by agency. There are also monthly and quarterly indexes and an annual index. These indexes are set up primarily by agency rather than by subject (Figure 5.5).

The *C.F.R.* publishes a single volume called *Index and Finding Aids,* which is revised once a year. However, this index suffers from several shortcomings—the main one being that it is not really a subject index at all! It is basically an agency index with a few subject terms interspersed (Figure 5.6).

To see how the index works, consider the following situation: Assume that your client, Jim, bought a new car from a dealer. The first time Jim washed his car, some of the paint rubbed off. Upon closer inspection, Jim discovered that the car had been in a wreck and had been painted to conceal the damage. Armed with a signed statement that the car was free from defect, Jim stormed into the dealer's office. The dealer claimed that she did not know that the car had been damaged. Furthermore, the dealer told Jim that since he did not receive a written warranty, he was out of luck.

Will a federal agency be able to help with this problem? To find out, you would look in the *Index and Finding Aids* under "Warranties." If you were

Figure 5.4 Authority and Source Note in the C.F.R.

§ 205.1 12 CFR Ch. II (1-1-90 Edition)

§ 205.1 Authority, purpose, and scope.

(a) *Authority.* This regulation, issued by the Board of Governors of the Federal Reserve System, implements title IX (Electronic Fund Transfer Act) of the Consumer Credit Protection Act, as amended (15 U.S.C. 1601 *et seq.*).

(b) *Purpose and scope.* In November 1978, the Congress enacted the Electronic Fund Transfer Act. The Congress found that the use of electronic systems to transfer funds provides the potential for substantial benefits to consumers, but that the unique characteristics of these systems make the application of existing consumer protection laws unclear, leaving the rights and liabilities of users of electronic fund transfer systems undefined. The Act establishes the basic rights, liabilities, and responsibilities of consumers who use electronic money transfer services and of financial institutions that offer these services. This regulation is intended to carry out the purposes of the Act, including, primarily, the protection of individual consumers engaging in electronic transfers. Except as otherwise provided, this regulation applies to all persons who are financial institutions as defined in § 205.2(i).

(Information collection requirements contained in this regulation have been approved by the Office of Management and Budget under the provisions of 44 U.S.C. 3501 *et seq.* and have been assigned OMB number 7100-0200)

[44 FR 18480, Mar. 28, 1979, as amended at 49 FR 40797, Oct. 18, 1984]

§ 205.2 Definitions and rules of construction.

For the purposes of this regulation, the following definitions apply, unless the context indicates otherwise:

(a)(1) "Access device" means a card, code, or other means of access to a consumer's account, or any combination thereof, that may be used by the consumer for the purpose of initiating electronic fund transfers.

(2) An access device becomes an "accepted access device" when the consumer to whom the access device was issued:

(i) Requests and receives, or signs, or uses, or authorizes another to use, the access device for the purpose of transferring money between accounts or obtaining money, property, labor or services;

(ii) Requests validation of an access device issued on an unsolicited basis; or

(iii) Receives an access device issued in renewal of, or in substitution for, an accepted access device, whether such access device is issued by the initial financial institution or a successor.

(b) "Account" means a demand deposit (checking), savings, or other consumer asset account (other than an occasional or incidental credit balance in a credit plan) held either directly or indirectly by a financial institution and established primarily for personal, family, or household purposes.

(c) "Act" means the Electronic Fund Transfer Act (Title IX of the Consumer Credit Protection Act, 15 U.S.C. 1601 et seq.).

(d) "Business day" means any day on which the offices of the consumer's financial institution are open to the public for carrying on substantially all business functions.

(e) "Consumer" means a natural person.

(f) "Credit" means the right granted by a financial institution to a consumer to defer payment of debt, incur debt and defer its payment, or purchase property or services and defer payment therefor.

(g) "Electronic fund transfer" means any transfer of funds, other than a transaction originated by check, draft, or similar paper instrument, that is initiated through an electronic terminal, telephone, or computer or magnetic tape for the purpose of ordering, instructing, or authorizing a financial institution to debit or credit an account. The term includes, but is not limited to, point-of-sale transfers, automated teller machine transfers, direct deposits or withdrawals of funds, and transfers initiated by telephone. It includes all transfers resulting from debit card transactions, including those that do not involve an electronic terminal at the time of the transaction. The term does not include payments made by check, draft, or similar paper instrument at an electronic terminal.

108

Figure 5.5 The *Federal Register* Index

Agency

NIH

NOTICES
Auto theft and comprehensive insurance premiums, Federal regulation; public review and comment on report, 30786
Fuel economy program, automotive; annual report to Congress, 11484
Fuel economy standards; exemption petitions, etc.:
 Officine Alfieri Maserati, S.p.A., 22879, 25767
Grants and cooperative agreements; availability, etc.:
 National occupant protection and impaired driving prevention programs, 7622
 School bus safety projects; assistance to States, 32554
 School bus safety; State matching of planning and administration costs, 40975
Highway safety analysis; police traffic accident reports; critical automated data reporting elements; list, 18220, 27327
Highway safety program; breath alcohol testing devices:
 Evidential devices; model specifications and conforming products list, 6865, 32343
Highway traffic safety improvement; priority plan 1990-1992; availability, 47824
Meetings:
 International Harmonization of Safety Standards, 13690
 Motor Vehicle Safety Research Advisory Committee, 1764, 34639, 43060
 National Driver Register Advisory Committee, 15096, 38186
 Rulemaking, research, and enforcement programs, 9818, 25920, 40977, 41782
Motor vehicle defect proceedings; petitions, etc.:
 Center for Auto Safety, 10570
 Ditlow, Clarence M., III, 21140
 Faircloth, Harvey G., et al., 6865
 Fujimori, Warren W.T., 47600
 Institute for Injury Reduction, Public Citizen, et al., 42144
 Jarvis, Brian, 17348
 Rand, M. Kristen, 42301
 Roupinian, Paul, 21140
 Skreba, Leonard T., 30072
 Stewart, Gloria Jean, 20674
 Sweeney, Harry M., 20382
 Toyota Motor Co., 17349
Motor vehicle safety standards:
 Nonconforming vehicles—
  Final determinations, 32988
  Importation eligibility; tentative determinations, 17518, 47418
 Rear seat lap/shoulder belt retrofit kits, 35241
Motor vehicle safety standards; exemption petitions, etc.:
 Automobiles Peugeot, 20382
 Bridgestone (U.S.A.) Inc., 3297, 12617
 Budd Co., 8632
 Cadillac Plastic & Chemical Co., 11497, 28340
 Cantab Motors, 11714, 21141
 Consulier Industries, Inc., 5712, 12982
 Cooper Tire & Rubber Co., 47823
 Ferrari S.p.A., 3785
 General Motors Corp., 21297, 34639, 40977
 Goodyear Tire & Rubber Co., 2915
 Hella, Inc., 37601
 Marmon Motor Co., 7404
 Mazda Motor Corp., 7404
 Mazda Motor Corp. of Japan, 28341
 Mazda Research & Development of North America, Inc., 26528, 49365
 Officine Alfieri Maserati S.p.A., 78, 7405
 Supreme Corp., Inc., 38186
 Takata-Gerico Corp., 28341
 Uniroyal Goodrich Tire Co., 40506
Motor vehicle theft prevention standard; exemption petitions, etc.:
 American Honda Motor Co., Inc., 4746, 22004, 46126
 General Motors Corp., 17854
New car assessment program:
 Crash test results and analysis; deformable moving barrier, 40595
Passenger motor vehicle theft data, 7406, 18794, 41149

National Institute for Occupational Safety and Health

See Centers for Disease Control

National Institute of Corrections

NOTICES
Grants and cooperative agreements; availability, etc.:
 Program plan/academy training schedule (1991 FY), 32980
Meetings:
 Advisory Board, 5086, 24672, 39747

National Institute of Justice

NOTICES
Body armor users workshop, 17681
Drug program evaluations; special initiative, 7387
Grants and cooperative agreements; availability, etc.:
 Boot camps for juvenile offenders; constructive intervention and early support, 28718, 32980
 Discretionary programs (1990 FY), 10146
 Technology assessment program information center, 31908

National Institute of Standards and Technology

RULES
Manufacturing technology transfer; regional centers establishment transfer, 38274
Organization, functions, and authority delegations:
 National Institute of Standards and Technology, 38314
PROPOSED RULES
Manufacturing technology transfer; centers establishment transfer, 18124
NOTICES
Grants and cooperative agreements; availability, etc.:
 Advanced structural ceramics, 20620
 Fire research program, 29877
 Manufacturing technology transfer; regional centers, 38280
 Precision measurement program, 48665
 Standard reference data program, 47789
Information processing standards, Federal:
 COBOL, 1243, 2733
 Computer output microform formats and reduction ratios, 7516, 9824
 Database language SQL, 3627
 Electronic data interchange (EDI), 28274, 29146
 Family of input/output interface standards, 10272
 Government Open Systems Interconnection Profile (GOSIP), 27666, 32451
 Graphical kernel system (GKS), 10273, 12444
 Interface between data terminal equipment (DTE) and data circuit-terminating equipment (DOE) for operation with packet-switched data networks, or between two DTEs by dedicated circuit, 10276
 POSIX; portable operating system interface for computer environments, 11424, 12778, 23959
 POSIX shell and utility application interface for computer operating system environments, 23959
 Programming language C, 19768
 Programming language MUMPS, 10278
Laboratory Accreditation Program, National Voluntary:
 Airborne asbestos analysis, 38734
 Directory of accredited laboratories; supplement, 32452
Meetings:
 Advanced Technology Visiting Committee, 5644, 7019, 23455, 27667, 33948, 47504
 Broadband Integrated Services Digital Network (B-ISDN) users and implementors workshop, 5046
 Computer courseware standards, architectural proposals; discussion, 20620
 Computer System Security and Privacy Advisory Board, 5045, 32452, 46093
 Eighth North American ISDN Users' Forum, 5046
 FORTRAN programming language standard test suit; workshop, 6676
 Intergrated Services Digital Network (ISDN) users and implementors workshop, 27668
 International Laboratory Accreditation Conference, 33741
 International standards activities, U.S. participation, 12252
 Malcolm Baldrige National Quality Award's Board of Overseers, 49558
 Malcolm Baldrige National Quality Award's Panel of Judges, 6035, 23456, 28080, 33948, 49325
 OSI Implementors workshop, 2256
 Weights and Measures National Conference, 1245, 27294
National Fire Codes:
 Fire safety standards, 3991, 32679
 Technical committee reports, 3991, 32678
Senior Executive Service:
 General and Limited Performance Review Boards; membership, 29878

National Institutes of Health

NOTICES
Committees; establishment, renewal, termination, etc.:
 AIDS and Related Research Study Sections et al., 2705
 American Stop Smoking Intervention Study (ASSIST) Committee, 40945
 Biological and Clinical Aging Review Committee et al., 15021
 Genome Research Review Committee, 26265
 Human Genome Research National Advisory Council, 17309

January—November 1990, FEDERAL REGISTER INDEX 95

aware that the Federal Trade Commission was involved with warranties, you could look under that commission. Looking under "Warranties" in the *Index and Finding Aids* leads you to the Magnuson-Moss Warranty Act, which then refers you to 16 C.F.R. 700 (Figure 5.7).

Fortunately, under 700.3(a) is a footnote that states that "a 'written warranty' is also created by a written affirmation of fact or a written promise that the product is defect free . . ." It appears that Jim is not out of luck.

Figure 5.6 The C.F.R. Index

227

Figure 5.7 Using the C.F.R. Index

Look under Warranties

Find the Magnuson-Moss Warranty Act

16 C.F.R. 700

Commercial indexes are also available that are vastly superior to those of the *Federal Register* and the *C.F.R.* Congressional Information Service has published an *Index to the Code of Federal Regulations* since 1981 and a *Federal Register Index* since 1984, and R. R. Bowker's *Code of Federal Regulations Index* has been published since 1988. With these publications, you can locate regulations by subject, agency, industry, geographic area, or authorizing legislation.

You may recall that in our discussion of the federal annotated codes in Chapter 4, we noted that both *U.S.C.A.*, a West publication, and *U.S.C.S.*, published by Lawyers Co-op, list citations to the *C.F.R.* in the annotations after each section. Actually, if you are already working with a federal law, the easiest way to locate the regulations that will implement the law is to use one of the annotated codes. For example, the federal laws on warranties can be located in 15 U.S.C.A. 2301. This section of the *U.S.C.A.* refers you to the governing regulations in 16 C.F.R. 700.1 (Figure 5.8).

If you are not using the *U.S.C.A.*, you can check the *C.F.R. Index and Finding Aids* for its useful Parallel Table of Authorities and Rules. This table allows you to locate the *C.F.R.* citation if you already have the *U.S.C.A.* citation (Figure 5.9).

Finding Regulations on WESTLAW

Fortunately, the full text of the *Federal Register* and the *C.F.R.* are on WESTLAW and other on-line services. On WESTLAW, the *Federal Register* is in the **FR** database, and the *C.F.R.* is in the **CFR** database.

The *Federal Register* (**FR**) database on WESTLAW dates from August, 1980. The full text of the *Federal Register* is on-line within five days of the day issued. You would use the **FR** database when you are looking for a current document, one issued during the current year that has not yet appeared in the *C.F.R.* In an area such as asbestos regulation under the Clean Air Act, which changes on a weekly basis, you would want to search the daily **FR** database since the **CFR** database would be a year out of date. Type

```
asbestos & "clean air act" & da(1991)
```

and you will retrieve many documents in the 1991 *Federal Register.*

You would also use the **FR** database to search for material that is not included in the *C.F.R.* including proposed regulations (those never adopted by an agency) and agency notices. For example, suppose you want to locate the Department of Transportation's proposed rule of June 13, 1986, dealing with "replacement lighting equipment." Because this proposed rule was never adopted, it will only appear in the *Federal Register.* Access the **FR** database and type

```
replac! /p light! & da(June 13, 1986)
```

Figure 5.10 shows the results of your search.

On WESTLAW, the current year of the *C.F.R.* has the database identifier **CFR.** To illustrate how you can search by either a *U.S.C.* citation or term, let

Figure 5.8 Finding Citations to the C.F.R. in the U.S.C.A.

15 § 2225a **COMMERCE AND TRADE**

the publication in the Federal Register of the master list referred to in section 2224(b) of this title.

(Pub.L. 101–391, § 6, Sept. 25, 1990, 104 Stat. 751.)

Historical and Statutory Notes

Codification. Section was enacted as part of the "Hotel and Motel Fire Safety Act of 1990", and not as part of the "Federal Fire Prevention and Control Act of 1974", which enacted this chapter.

Effective Date

Section effective on the first day of the first fiscal year that begins after the expiration of the 425-day period that begins on the date of the publication in the Federal Register of the master list referred to in section 2224(b) of this title, pursuant to subsec. (d) of this section.

Legislative History. For legislative history and purpose of Pub.L. 101–391, see 1990 U.S.Code Cong. and Adm.News, p. 1173.

§ 2226. Dissemination of fire prevention and control information

The Director, acting through the Administrator, is authorized to take steps to encourage the States to promote the use of automatic sprinkler systems and automatic smoke detection systems, and to disseminate to the maximum extent possible information on the life safety value and use of such systems. Such steps may include, but need not be limited to, providing copies of the guidelines described in section 2225 of this title and of the master list compiled under section 2224(b) of this title to Federal agencies, State and local governments, and fire services throughout the United States, and making copies of the master list compiled under section 2224(b) of this title available upon request to interested private organizations and individuals.

(Pub.L. 93–498, § 30, as added Pub.L. 101–391, § 3(a), Sept. 25, 1990, 104 Stat. 748.)

Historical and Statutory Notes

Legislative History. For legislative history and purpose of Pub.L. 101–391, see 1990 U.S.Code Cong. and Adm.News, p. 1173.

CHAPTER 50—CONSUMER PRODUCT WARRANTIES

Law Review Commentaries

Concept of warranty duration: A tangled web. Max E. Klinger, 89 Dick.L.Rev. 935 (1985).

Effect of warranty disclaimers on revocation of acceptance under the Uniform Commercial Code. Manning Gilbert Warren III and Michelle Rowe, 37 Ala.L.Rev. 307 (1986).

New Mexico's "Lemon Law": Consumer protection or consumer frustration? Joseph Goldberg, 16 New Mexico L.Rev. 251 (1986).

§ 2301. Definitions

Federal Practice and Procedure

Jurisdictional amount in controversy, see Wright, Miller & Cooper: Jurisdiction § 3701 et seq.

C.F.R. Citation

Code of Federal Regulations

Interpretations, see 16 CFR 700.1.

Law Review Commentaries

A comparative analysis of three lemon laws. Anne V. Swanson, 75 Ill.B.J. 436 (1987).

An informal resolution model of consumer product warranty law. Jean Braucher, Wis.L. Rev. 1405 (1985).

Consumer leases under Uniform Commercial Code Article 2A. Fred H. Miller, 39 Ala.L.Rev. 957 (1988).

Examining restraints on freedom to contract as an approach to purchaser dissatisfaction in the computer industry. 74 Cal.L.Rev. 2101 (1986).

Illinois lemon car buyer's options in a breach of warranty action. Lisa K. Jorgenson, 20 John Marshall L.Rev. 483 (1987).

Implied warranty and the Used Car Rule. 46 La.L.Rev. 1239 (1986).

Is revision due for Article 2? Fairfax Leary, Jr. and David Frisch, 31 Vill.L.Rev. 399 (1986).

Legislative responses to plight of new car purchasers. Richard L. Coffinberger and Linda B. Samuels, 18 UCC L.J. 168 (1985).

Product quality laws and the economics of federalism. David A. Rice (1985) 65 Boston U.L. Rev. 1.

84

us return to our warranty problem involving the car that was painted to conceal the damage. Type

```
15 +5 2301 & writ! /s warrant!
```

Figure 5.9 The *C.F.R.* Parallel Table of Authorities and Rules

CFR Index

15 U.S.C.—Continued	CFR
2032	49 Part 544
2051 et seq	16 Part 1032
2051—2081	16 Parts 1011, 1012, 1016, 1028, 1031
2051—2052	16 Parts 1201, 1202, 1204, 1205
2051	16 Parts 1009, 1015, 1207, 1401, 1402, 1404, 1406
2053	16 Part 1009
2054	16 Part 1204

15 U.S.C.—Continued	CFR
2611—2612	40 Part 707
2611	40 Parts 761, 762, 795, 799
2612	19 Part 12
2613	40 Part 720
2614	40 Part 761
2616	40 Part 761
2618	40 Part 23
2619	40 Part 702
2621	19 Part 12
2622	29 Part 24

U.S.C. Citation

CRF Citation

2111	16 Part 1009
2210	44 Part 151
2214	44 Part 150
2218	44 Part 151
2301	16 Part 700
2302	16 Parts 701, 702
2309	16 Parts 455, 701-703
2310	16 Part 703
2501 et seq	10 Part 476
2601 et seq	19 Part 12 40 Parts 22, 30-33
2603	40 Parts 766, 790-792, 795-799
2604	40 Parts 720, 721, 723, 747
2604f	40 Part 747
2605	40 Parts 704, 747, 750, 761-763
2607	40 Parts 2, 704, 710, 716, 717, 720, 721, 761-763, 766, 791
2610	40 Part 2

5	36 Parts 14
9a	36 Parts 1, 2, 4, 5, 7, 8, 12, 25
20 et seq	36 Part 51
36—36a	36 Part 10
40a	43 Part 17
47-1	36 Part 34
47a	43 Part 17
57a	16 Part 424
79	36 Part 14
90c et seq	43 Parts 3500, 3510, 3520, 3530, 3540, 3560, 3580, 3590
113—136	36 Part 293
141c	36 Part 10
241 et seq	36 Part 9
291—628	18 Part 6
363	36 Part 21
406d-3	43 Part 17
408k	36 Part 20
410 et seq	36 Part 9
431—433	43 Part 2300

790

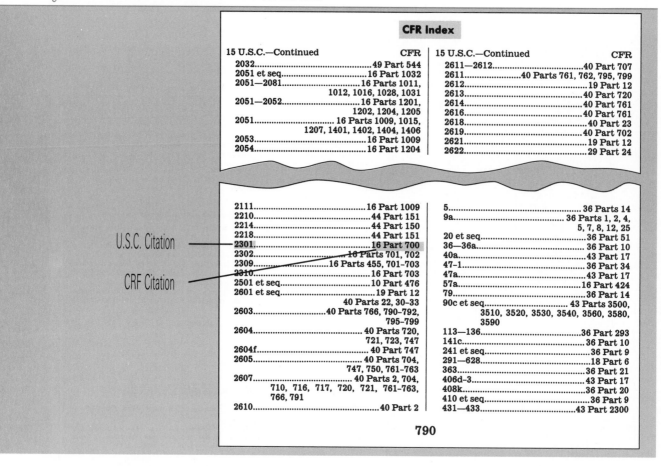

Figure 5.10 Finding a Proposed Regulation on WESTLAW

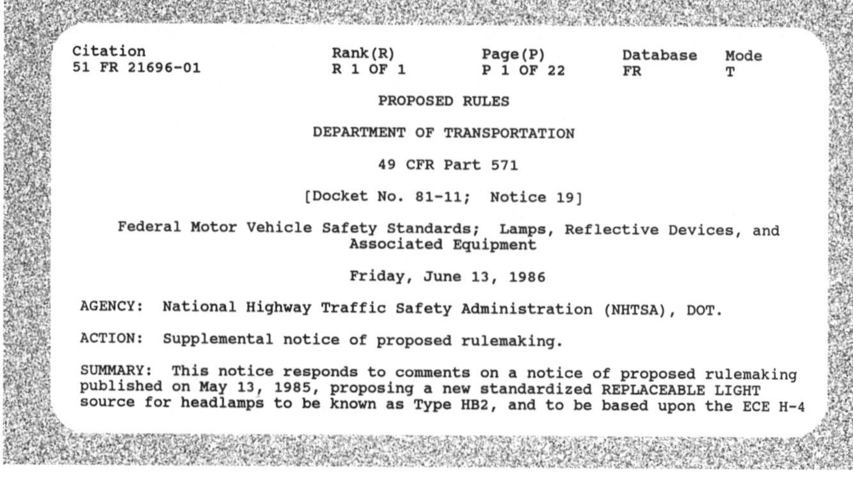

Citation	Rank(R)	Page(P)	Database	Mode
51 FR 21696-01	R 1 OF 1	P 1 OF 22	FR	T

PROPOSED RULES

DEPARTMENT OF TRANSPORTATION

49 CFR Part 571

[Docket No. 81-11; Notice 19]

Federal Motor Vehicle Safety Standards; Lamps, Reflective Devices, and Associated Equipment

Friday, June 13, 1986

AGENCY: National Highway Traffic Safety Administration (NHTSA), DOT.

ACTION: Supplemental notice of proposed rulemaking.

SUMMARY: This notice responds to comments on a notice of proposed rulemaking published on May 13, 1985, proposing a new standardized REPLACEABLE LIGHT source for headlamps to be known as Type HB2, and to be based upon the ECE H-4

This query retrieves thirteen documents (Figure 5.11). Type **L** to view a list of document citations. Scanning the list, you can read the applicable regulation "700.3 Written warranty" by typing **3.**

Occasionally, you may need regulations that were in effect during a certain year. The **CFR** databases are retrospective to 1984. If you want to find out how the regulation was stated in 1987, you would search the database **CFR87.** For example, the rule requiring labels in wool products to carry certain information on the reverse side was revised in 1988. To see how the rule read in 1987, you would access the **CFR87** database and type

```
reverse alternat! /s side /s label & wool
```

This search retrieves 16 C.F.R. 300.10 (Figure 5.12).

If you have a citation for the *Federal Register* or the *C.F.R.*, you can retrieve it in a snap with FIND. For example, to retrieve 54 FR 33737, type

```
fi 54 fr 33737
```

Figure 5.11 Searching by Using a *U.S.C.A.* Citation or Term

(a) List of Document Citations

```
CITATIONS LIST (Page 1)                          Total Documents:  13
Database: CFR

   1.   s 239.1 Purpose and scope of the guides.   16 CFR s 239.1

   2.   s 700.1 Products covered.   16 CFR s 700.1

   3.   s 700.3 Written warranty.   16 CFR s 700.3

   4.   s 700.4 Parties "actually making" a written warranty.   16 CFR s 700.4

   5.   s 700.6 Designation of warranties.   16 CFR s 700.6

   6.   s 700.8 Warrantor's decision as final.   16 CFR s 700.8

   7.   s 700.10 Section 102(c).   16 CFR s 700.10

   8.
 s 700.11 Written warranty, service contract, and insurance distinguished for
 purposes of compliance under the Act.   16 CFR s 700.11

   9.   s 700.12 Effective date of 16 CFR, Parts 701 and 702.   16 CFR s 700.12
```

(b) Text of Document Ranked Number 3

```
Citation                  Rank(R)        Page(P)        Database   Mode
16 CFR s 700.3            R 3 OF 13      P 1 OF 4       CFR        T

                       TITLE 16--COMMERCIAL PRACTICES
                          Federal Trade Commission
  Subchapter G--Rules, Regulations, Statements and Interpretations Under the
                         Magnuson-Moss Warranty Act
           Part 700--Interpretations of Magnuson-Moss Warranty Act

 s 700.3 WRITTEN WARRANTY.

  (a) The Act imposes specific duties and liabilities on suppliers who offer
 WRITTEN WARRANTIES on consumer products.  Certain representations, such as
 energy efficiency ratings for electrical appliances, care labeling of wearing
 apparel, and other product information disclosures may be express warranties
 under the Uniform Commercial Code. However, these disclosures alone are not
 WRITTEN WARRANTIES under this Act. Section 101(6) provides that a WRITTEN
 affirmation of fact or a WRITTEN promise of a specified level of performance
 must relate to a specified period of time in order to be considered a "WRITTEN
 WARRANTY." [FN1] A product information disclosure without a specified time
 period to which the disclosure relates is therefore not a WRITTEN WARRANTY.  In
 addition, section 111(d) exempts from the Act (except section 102(c)) any
 WRITTEN WARRANTY the making or content of which is required by federal law.
```

Figure 5.12 Searching for a Regulation in a Particular Year

```
Citation                    Rank(R)      Page(P)      Database  Mode
16 CFR s 300.10             R 1 OF 3     P 1 OF 3     CFR87     T

                    TITLE 16--COMMERCIAL PRACTICES
                       Federal Trade Commission
          Subchapter C--Regulations Under Specific Acts of Congress
             Part 300--Rules and Regulations Under the WOOL Act
                               Labeling

 s 300.10 Arrangement of label information.

  (a) All items or parts of the information required to be shown and displayed
 in the label of the product, shall be set forth consecutively and separately on
 the outer surface of the label, in immediate conjunction with each other, and
 in type or lettering plainly legible and conspicuous, and all parts of the
 required fiber content information shall appear in type or lettering of equal
 size and conspicuousness;  such as for example:
 Distributed by:
 John Q. Doe Co., Inc.,
 New York, N.Y.
 Made of
 60% WOOL
 40% RECYCLED WOOL
```

Because federal administrative law frequently deals with very specific things, on-line, full-text searching can work wonders. If you have a client who is interested in importing Bactrian camels, a word search in the **CFR** database could be the easiest way to find the applicable regulations—try it.

Updating the C.F.R. with the List of Sections Affected and the *Federal Register*

Since the volumes of the *C.F.R.* are issued annually, you must always update your regulation by checking for new revisions and deletions in the *Federal Register*. Remember that regulations are revised constantly. You cannot rely on a regulation as it is printed in the *C.F.R.* or in the *C.F.R.* on WESTLAW without updating it.

You can easily update your WESTLAW *C.F.R.* search by using the **UPDATE** command from a *C.F.R.* section. This will automatically bring you to any Federal Register entries affecting the *C.F.R.* section.

If you do not have access to WESTLAW to update your *C.F.R.* citation, you can still update your citation by using print sources. The following instructions may appear very cumbersome, but the process is quite mechanical and will work if you follow the instructions carefully (Figure 5.13):

1. Look up your section in the most recent *C.F.R.* paperback volume. Note the date of revision on the front cover.
2. Consult the most recent monthly *List of C.F.R. Sections Affected (LSA)* pamphlet to see if your *C.F.R.* section is listed. The *LSA* directs you to changes in the *C.F.R.* that were published in the *Federal Register*. Entries

Figure 5.13 Updating a C.F.R. Citation by Using Print Sources

Step 2: Changes in 12 *C.F.R.* 563 listed is *LSA*

20 **LSA—LIST OF CFR SECTIONS AFFECTED**

CHANGES JANUARY 2 THROUGH MARCH 30, 1990

TITLE 12 Chapter II—Con. Page

220.18 (a) and (b) amended......... 11160
221 OTC margin stock list............ 2631
224 OTC margin stock list............ 2631
225 Authority citation revised.. 6790
225.71—225.73 (Subpart H) Added; interim........................... 6790
229 Appendix F amended............ 11358
264b.3 (a) revised........................... 3576
(a) amended................................. 11360

Chapter III—Federal Deposit Insurance Corporation

312 Technical correction............... 1912
312.1 (c) revised; (f) through added; interim........................... 10412
312.4 Revised; interim.................. 10413
312.5 Added; interim.................... 10413
312.6 Revised; interim.................. 10413
312.7 Revised; interim.................. 10413
312.8 Added; interim.................... 10414
312.9 Added; interim.................... 10414
312.10 Added; interim................. 10414
357 Added; interim....................... 11161

Chapter IV—Export-Import Bank of the United States

411 Added; interim.............. 6737, 6747

Chapter V—Office of Thrift Supervision, Department of the Treasury

510.5 Added...................................... 7695
528 Revised..................................... 1388
545.75 (b)(3) revised; interim...... 11307
563.75 (i) removed........................... 7300
563.80 (e)(2) revised........................ 7300
563.93 Revised; interim................. 11307
563.132 (c) and (d) removed; (e) redesignated as new (c)....... 4602
563d.2 Revised................................. 3041
567.13 Added.................................... 7478
571 Technical correction................. 696
571.19 (e) amended........................... 126

Chapter VI—Farm Credit Administration

600.10 (Subpart B) Regulation at 54 FR 50735 eff. 3-6-90.........7884
611.1162 Regulation at 54 FR 1148 corrected........................... 10042
611.1167 Regulation at 54 FR 1148 corrected........................... 10042
611.1172 Regulation at 54 FR 1148 corrected........................... 10042
611.1174 Regulation at 54 FR 1148 corrected........................... 10042
612.2150 Regulation at 54 FR 50736 eff. 3-6-90......................... 7884
612.2160 Regulation at 54 FR 50736 eff. 3-6-90......................... 7884
614.4280 Regulation at 54 FR 50736 eff. 3-6-90......................... 7884
614.4320 Regulation at 54 FR 50736 eff. 3-6-90......................... 7884
614.4321 Regulation at 54 FR 50736 eff. 3-6-90......................... 7884
614.4340 Regulation at 54 FR 50736 eff. 3-6-90......................... 7884
614.4345 Regulation at 54 FR 50736 eff. 3-6-90......................... 7884
614.4460 Regulation at 54 FR 50736 eff. 3-6-90......................... 7884
614.4511 Regulation at 54 FR 50736 eff. 3-6-90......................... 7884
614.5040 Regulation at 54 FR 50736 eff. 3-6-90......................... 7884
615.5104 Regulation at 54 FR 50736 eff. 3-6-90......................... 7884
615.5135 Regulation at 54 FR 50736 eff. 3-6-90......................... 7884
615.5143 Regulation at 54 FR 50736 eff. 3-6-90......................... 7884
615.5190 Regulation at 54 FR 50736 eff. 3-6-90......................... 7884
618.8060 Regulation at 54 FR 50736 eff. 3-6-90......................... 7884

Chapter VII—National Credit Union Administration

700 Authority citation revised.. 1794
700.1 (h) and (i) removed; (j) through (m) redesignated as (h) through (k)........................... 1794
701 Authority citation revised.. 1794
701.6 (d) added................................ 1799
701.21 (c)(7) revised........................ 1797
701.32 Heading revised; (d) added.. 1794
705 Authority citation revised.. 1794
705.3 Revised.................................. 1794
741 Authority citation revised.. 1794
741.5 Revised.................................. 1794
741.9 (k) added................................ 1799

Figure 5.13 Updating a C.F.R. Citation by Using Print Sources (continued)

ii **Federal Register / Vol. 55, No. 83 / Monday, April 30, 1990 / Reader Aids**

1011 ... 12369
1012 ... 12369
1013 ... 12369
1030 ... 12369
1032 ... 12369
1033 ... 12369
1036 ... 12369
1040 ... 12369
1044 ... 12369
1046 ... 12369
1049 ... 12369
1050 ... 12369
1064 ... 12369
1065 ... 12369
1068 ... 12369
1075 ... 12369
1076 ... 12369
1079 ... 12369
1093 ... 12369
1094 ... 12369
1096 ... 12369
1097 ... 12369
1098 ... 12369
1099 ... 12369
1106 ... 12369
1108 ... 12369
1120 ... 12369
1124 ... 12369
1126 ... 12369
1131 ... 12369
1132 ... 12369
1134 ... 12369
1135 ... 12369
1137 ... 12369
1138 ... 12369
1139 ... 12369, 12848
1485 ... 17618
1494 ... 17443
1714 ... 12194, 12199

8 CFR

103 ... 12627, 12628, 12815
210 ... 12629
235 ... 14234
242 ... 12627
287 ... 12627
299 ... 12628
499 ... 12628
Proposed Rules:
103 ... 12666

9 CFR

1 ... 12630
71 ... 12631, 15320–15900
75 ... 13504
78 ... 12163, 15320–15900
82 ... 12631
91 ... 12632
92 ... 12632
Proposed Rules:
3 ... 12202, 12667
78 ... 12848
101 ... 15233
113 ... 15233
166 ... 15236
201 ... 13796
318 ... 12203
381 ... 12203

10 CFR

11 ... 14288
25 ... 14288
50 ... 12163
72 ... 13883
95 ... 14288
590 ... 14916
Proposed Rules:
2 ... 12370
30 ... 12374, 13542
40 ... 12374, 13542
50 ... 12374, 13542
55 ... 14288
60 ... 12374, 13542
61 ... 12374, 13542, 13797
70 ... 12374, 13542
72 ... 12374, 13542
110 ... 12374, 13542
150 ... 12374, 13542
708 ... 12668, 17453
725 ... 15237

11 CFR

110 ... 13507
Proposed Rules:
106 ... 12499
9003 ... 12499
9007 ... 12499
9033 ... 12499
9035 ... 12499
9038 ... 12499

12 CFR

19 ... 13010
202 ... 12471, 14830
205 ... 12635
226 ... 13103, 17749
500 ... 13507
543 ... 13507
544 ... 13507
545 ... 13507
546 ... 13507
550 ... 13507
552 ... 13507
563 ... 13507
563b ... 13507
563f ... 13507
567 ... 13507
574 ... 13507
584 ... 13507
614 ... 12472
615 ... 12473
620 ... 12472
621 ... 12472
1609 ... 14081
Proposed Rules:
21 ... 14424
216 ... 12850
226 ... 13282
701 ... 12852
741 ... 12852
747 ... 12855
1611 ... 13543, 17715

13 CFR

121 ... 17419
122 ... 17267
Proposed Rules:
120 ... 17280

14 CFR

13 ... 15110
14 ... 15110
21 ... 12328, 15214, 17589
23 ... 12328, 15214, 17589
25 ... 13474
39 ... 12332, 12473–12477, 12815–12817, 13259–13261, 13755–13760, 14411, 14412, 15217–15222, 17420, 17594, 17927–17930
71 ... 12336, 12482, 13263, 13264, 13761, 14234–14237, 15223, 15320–15900, 17421, 17422, 17595, 17931
73 ... 13761, 17931
75 ... 17423
91 ... 13444, 15320–15900, 17736
95 ... 13762
97 ... 15244, 17424
121 ... 13326–13332
125 ... 13332
129 ... 13332
135 ... 13444, 15320–15900
382 ... 12336
Proposed Rules:
Ch. I ... 12383, 13798, 15240, 17987
13 ... 15134
21 ... 12857
23 ... 12857
25 ... 12316, 13886
29 ... 12316
39 ... 12503, 12859–12863, 13284, 13799, 13801, 14290, 14292, 14426, 14428, 15243, 17453, 17631, 17860, 17987–17998
71 ... 12384, 13032, 13285–13287, 13802, 13803, 14293–14295, 17632
73 ... 13804
75 ... 13287
91 ... 12316
93 ... 17584
119 ... 14404
121 ... 12316, 13886, 14404
125 ... 12316, 14404
127 ... 14404
135 ... 12316, 13886, 14404, 17358
241 ... 14296
1266 ... 13912

15 CFR

776 ... 13121
779 ... 13121
799 ... 12635, 13121, 14089, 17530
Proposed Rules:
295 ... 12504

16 CFR

305 ... 13264
1700 ... 13123–13127
Proposed Rules:
1027 ... 13805
1700 ... 13157

17 CFR

1 ... 17932
30 ... 14238
200 ... 17933
230 ... 17933
241 ... 17949
Proposed Rules:
155 ... 13288
156 ... 13545

18 CFR

37 ... 14961
270 ... 17425
272 ... 17425
284 ... 12167
381 ... 12169, 13899

19 CFR

141 ... 17596
142 ... 12342
146 ... 14966
162 ... 17596
171 ... 17596
178 ... 12342, 17596
191 ... 17597
Proposed Rules:
101 ... 17633
141 ... 12385

20 CFR

404 ... 17530
416 ... 14916
626 ... 12992
636 ... 12992
638 ... 12992
675 ... 12992
676 ... 12992
677 ... 12992
678 ... 12992
679 ... 12992
680 ... 12992
684 ... 12992
685 ... 12992
688 ... 12992
689 ... 12992
Proposed Rules:
416 ... 17999

21 CFR

5 ... 14916
74 ... 12171
101 ... 17431
173 ... 12171
176 ... 13518
178 ... 12171, 12344, 13521
179 ... 14413
300 ... 14968
430 ... 14239
442 ... 14239
444 ... 14968
452 ... 14090
455 ... 14378
510 ... 13901, 13902, 14830, 17951
514 ... 14831
522 ... 13768, 13902
544 ... 13902
558 ... 15099, 17598, 17951
610 ... 14037
640 ... 14037
801 ... 17599
Proposed Rules:
101 ... 14429
872 ... 17455

23 CFR

658 ... 17952
Proposed Rules:
655 ... 17634
1327 ... 12509

24 CFR

882 ... 14243
885 ... 14243

26 CFR

1 ... 13521, 13769
301 ... 13289, 13521, 14244
602 ... 14244
Proposed Rules:
1 ... 13808, 14429, 14437, 17455, 17635, 17758
31 ... 17758
301 ... 12386
602 ... 14429, 14437, 17758

Step 3:
Check the CFR Parts
Affected Table

for rules are arranged numerically by *C.F.R.* title, chapter, part, section, and paragraph. If there has been a change, the *LSA* will refer you to the page numbers in the *Federal Register* where the action appears. There will also be a descriptive word or phrase indicating whether the change was an

Figure 5.13 Updating a *C.F.R.* Citation by Using Print Sources (continued)

Step 4: Check the CFR Parts Affected Table in the Most Recent *Federal Register*

i

Reader Aids

Federal Register
Vol. 55, No. 93
Monday, May 14, 1990

INFORMATION AND ASSISTANCE

Federal Register

Index, finding aids & general information	523-5227
Public inspection desk	523-5215
Corrections to published documents	523-5237
Document drafting information	523-5237
Machine readable documents	523-3447

Code of Federal Regulations

Index, finding aids & general information	523-5227
Printing schedules	523-3419

Laws

Public Laws Update Service (numbers, dates, etc.)	523-6641
Additional information	523-5230

Presidential Documents

Executive orders and proclamations	523-5230
Public Papers of the Presidents	523-5230
Weekly Compilation of Presidential Documents	523-5230

The United States Government Manual

General information	523-5230

Other Services

Data base and machine readable specifications	523-3408
Guide to Record Retention Requirements	523-3187
Legal staff	523-4534
Library	523-5240
Privacy Act Compilation	523-3187
Public Laws Update Service (PLUS)	523-6641
TDD for the deaf	523-5229

FEDERAL REGISTER PAGES AND DATES, MAY

18073-18302 1
18303-18584 2
18585-18716 3
18717-18850 4
18851-19046 7
19047-19232 8
19233-19616 9
19617-19716 10
19717-19870 11
19871-20110 14

CFR PARTS AFFECTED DURING MAY

At the end of each month, the Office of the Federal Register publishes separately a List of CFR Sections Affected (LSA), which lists parts and sections affected by documents published since the revision date of each title.

3 CFR

Proclamations:
6030 (See Proc. 6123) 18075
6122 18073
6123 18075
6124 18585
6125 18715
6126 18717
6127 19041
6128 19043
6129 19045
6130 19233
6131 19715
6132 20107
6133 20109
Executive Orders:
12675 (Amended by EO 12712) 18095
12712 18095
12713 18719
12714 19047
12715 19051
Administrative Orders:
Memorandums:
Apr. 26, 1990 18299
Presidential Determinations:
No. 90-17 of Apr. 25, 1990 18587
No. 90-18 of Apr. 25, 1990 18589
Order:
May 4, 1990 19235

5 CFR

1630 18851

7 CFR

2 18097
3 18591
13 18591
52 19001
210 18857
245 19237
301 19241
400 18097
704 19243
910 .... 18858, 19717
920 19717
927 18097
979 .... 19719, 19720
985 18859
993 19617
1012 18098
1139 18303
1478 19053
1980 19244
Proposed Rules:
220 .... 18908, 20023
300 20023
301 18342
911 19740
929 19741
953 18909
1762 18606
1941 18607
1943 18607
1945 18607
948 19631
982 19632

8 CFR

286 18860

9 CFR

71 18099
78 19054
82 18099
85 19245
92 19245
Proposed Rules:
78 19268
94 18342
114 18345
308 19888
318 19888
320 19888
381 19888

10 CFR

590 18227
Proposed Rules:
Ch. I 19633
20 19890
30 19890
40 19890
50 18608
70 19890

12 CFR

207 18591
220 18591
221 18591
224 18591
Proposed Rules:
563g 18610
741 18613
1611 20023

13 CFR

302 18593
309 18594
Proposed Rules:
120 18614
124 18615
125 19633

14 CFR

13 18800
14 18800
15 18704
21 19050

addition, revision, or removal. Make certain the coverage of the *LSA* pamphlet begins the day after the date of revision on the paperback *C.F.R.* volume, and note the month printed prominently on the front of the *LSA*.

3. Consult the last issue of the month of the *Federal Register* for each complete month since the month on the cover of the *LSA* pamphlet. Check the CFR Parts Affected During [month] table near the back of the issue. This table cumulates through the month so you only need to check the last issue for each month.
4. Consult the most recent issue of the *Federal Register* available and check the CFR Parts Affected During [month] table near the back. Note the date of the issue.
5. Finally, remember to check to see if the regulation is still valid. Check *Shepard's Code of Federal Regulation Citations* for cases that have interpreted the federal regulations.

Administrative Decisions

In addition to writing rules, agencies issue orders and opinions. Agencies report their opinions just as a court does. These reports are published by the U.S. Government Printing Office in either print format or microfiche.

An increasing number of agency decisions are available on-line on WESTLAW. These decisions can be found in topical databases, such as the Energy databases, which include decisions of the Federal Energy Regulatory Commission, the Nuclear Regulatory Commission, materials from two specialized publications, *Gower Federal Service* and the *Public Utilities Reports,* and applicable regulations from the *Federal Register* and the *Code of Federal Regulations,* among other materials.

An example of an administrative decision can be found in the case of *In re Sears, Roebuck and Co.,* 95 F.T.C. 406 (1980). In an advertisement for its dishwashers, Sears stated that its appliance would clean dishes, pots, and pans completely without prior rinsing and scraping. Furthermore, without substantiation, the store claimed that items placed in the top rack of the dishwasher would get as clean as those on the bottom rack. The Federal Trade Commission (FTC) issued a cease and desist order prohibiting Sears from making claims regarding the performance of any home appliance unless it could support those claims with reliable tests.

In addition to the official reports and WESTLAW, administrative decisions can be located in various loose-leaf services. Loose-leaf services are so named because they are published in binders with removable pages. A loose-leaf service is constantly kept current with new pages. Loose-leaf services generally follow one of two formats. In the newsletter format, new pages are added at the end of each unit. *United States Law Week (U.S.L.W.),* which we discussed in Chapter 1, is an example of a newsletter format. The second type of loose-leaf services replaces pages that are out of date in addition to adding new information. The major publishers of loose-leaf services are The Bureau of National Affairs, Inc. (BNA), Commerce Clearing House, Inc. (CCH), and Prentice-Hall (P-H). Many loose-leaf reporters are now published on-line as well as in print format.

Presidential Documents

In discussing administrative materials, we cannot overlook the administrative actions of the president, who may direct agency action by issuing executive orders. The president may also issue proclamations that are either ceremonial in nature, such as the observance of National Library Week, or of a more substantive nature, often concerning trade matters. Both types of actions have the effect of law.

The daily *Federal Register* prints presidential documents including proclamations and executive orders as well as other documents that the president orders to be published, such as determinations, letters, memoranda, and reorganization plans. All executive orders and proclamations published in the *Federal Register* are compiled annually in Title 3 of the *Code of Federal Regulations* and in West's *U.S. Code Congressional and Administrative News.* Proclamations and executive orders are available on WESTLAW in the Presidential Documents (**PRES**) database.

State Administrative Law Materials

Administrative powers comparable to those of federal agencies are vested in state agencies, based upon the power of the states to regulate their internal commerce. Typical state agencies include state Public Service commissions and Labor Relations Boards.

Many states have administrative codes similar in format to the *Code of Federal Regulations*. Many states also have registers similar to the *Federal Register*.

All Attorney General Opinions from all available states and the federal government and the *Public Utilities Reports* from all states are on WESTLAW in the **AG** and **PUR** databases, respectively. Recently, WESTLAW has begun to add administrative codes. This will make life easier for everyone. Additional administrative law materials from states are included in various topical areas, such as corporations or workers' compensation.

On the state level, the agency itself may be the best source of regulations and agency decisions. Often regulations and decisions are available directly from the agency even though they are not published in an organized manner.

Conclusion

Administrative law has intimidated people for years. Since law school courses generally avoid it, many new associates are surprised by administrative regulations and decisions. Nevertheless, the *Federal Register* can be your pal—well, sort of—and the *C.F.R.*, with its annual volumes and links to the *Federal Register* through the *Lists of Sections Affected,* is quite a decent tool. This may be an area, though, where the WESTLAW service *is* the best answer. It is updated for you, and you can search by unique terms. Try it for administrative law.

6 Background Legal Sources

Rather than beginning your research with one of the primary sources of the law, you may find it more productive—and less painful—to begin with various background materials. Just as you used secondary sources, such as encyclopedias and periodicals, for your college research papers, you can use legal background materials to become acquainted with a particular legal topic. An added advantage is that secondary materials, generally speaking, have good indexes. Consequently, the information is not only easy to understand, it is easy to get at as well.

Background materials are called secondary authority. These sources include annotations, legal periodicals, legal encyclopedias, treatises, restatements, dictionaries, and formbooks. All of these background materials include numerous citations to primary sources and narrative discussions of the principles of law; thus, they are tools for finding the primary authorities as well as commentaries on them.

Though they give excellent introductions to specific topics and related issues, secondary sources are not the law. These materials are not binding on the courts. Therefore, you should never limit your research to secondary materials; you must always follow through by reading the primary sources.

American Law Reports

We could have discussed the *American Law Reports (A.L.R.)* in the chapter on "Finding Cases" rather than in this chapter because the *A.L.R.* is used both as a means of finding cases and as a secondary source, meaning that it contains commentary material. A fountain of information, the *A.L.R.* is often an ideal starting place for your research (Figure 6.1).

The *A.L.R.*, which is published by Lawyers Co-op, is known for its thoroughly researched annotations written by an editorial staff who leave no citation uncovered. An *A.L.R.* annotation is a legal essay on a very specific point of law. It traces the development of that point of law and presents the judicial treatment in all jurisdictions. As a law student, you will be surprised at how narrow the annotation topics tend to be. However, when you practice law, you will be grateful for the very narrow, well-defined topics since your research will revolve around very specific issues.

Figure 6.1 *American Law Reports*

The *A.L.R.* does not attempt to cover every legal topic, so it is possible that your topic will not appear. Generally, the topics covered in the *A.L.R.* are of interest to attorneys of all jurisdictions, not just to those in the one in which the case was decided.

The *A.L.R.* includes several series, as shown in Table 6.1. In general, if you are dealing with a federal problem, you will use *A.L.R.Fed.;* if your issue is one arising primarily under state statutes or in state cases, you will use the third or four series. Annotations following the same format as those in the *A.L.R.* also appear in the *U.S. Supreme Court of Reports, Lawyers' Edition.*

To illustrate the features of the *A.L.R.*, let's examine the following problem. Assume that your client is a hospital administrator who is concerned about his hospital's responsibility for administering blood transfusions.

To answer this question by using the *A.L.R.*, you can access the *A.L.R.* either by using the multivolume *Index to Annotations* or on-line through the LEXIS service. The *Index to Annotations* provides subject access to all of the *A.L.R.* series (except the first). On LEXIS, you can access the full text of *A.L.R.*, or you can find references to *A.L.R.* annotations by using the LEXIS citator service known as Auto-Cite.

The *Index to Annotations* lists the entry "Liability of hospital, physician, or other individual medical practitioner for injury or death resulting from blood transfusion," which appears to be on target. Turning to the annotation in Volume 20 of the *A.L.R.4th,* you find that the text of one important representative case *(Fisher v. Sibley Memorial Hospital)* precedes the annotation. This case acts as the theme for the annotation. Following the case are an outline of topics covered in the annotation, a word index of topics for the annotation, and a table of jurisdictions represented so you can turn to cases of a specific state. Also included are references to treatment of the issue in other Lawyers Co-op publications (Figure 6.2). The most useful part of the annotation, however, is the case and statute analysis, where the weight of authority is noted along with the direction of emerging trends. Here the holdings of hundreds of cases are abstracted (Figure 6.3).

Updating Your Research in the *A.L.R.*

Since the annotations in the first and second series of the *A.L.R.* were written before 1965, many of them have been rewritten and superseded by later ones. The most important step in using *A.L.R.*, then, is to consult the Annotation

Table 6.1 A.L.R. Series

Series	Years	Coverage
ALR1st	1919–1948	State and federal issues
ALR2d	1948–1965	State and federal issues
ALR3d	1965–1980	State issues and federal issues until 1969
ALR4th	1980–date	State issues only
ALRFed.	1969–date	Federal issues only

Figure 6.2 An *A.L.R.* Annotation

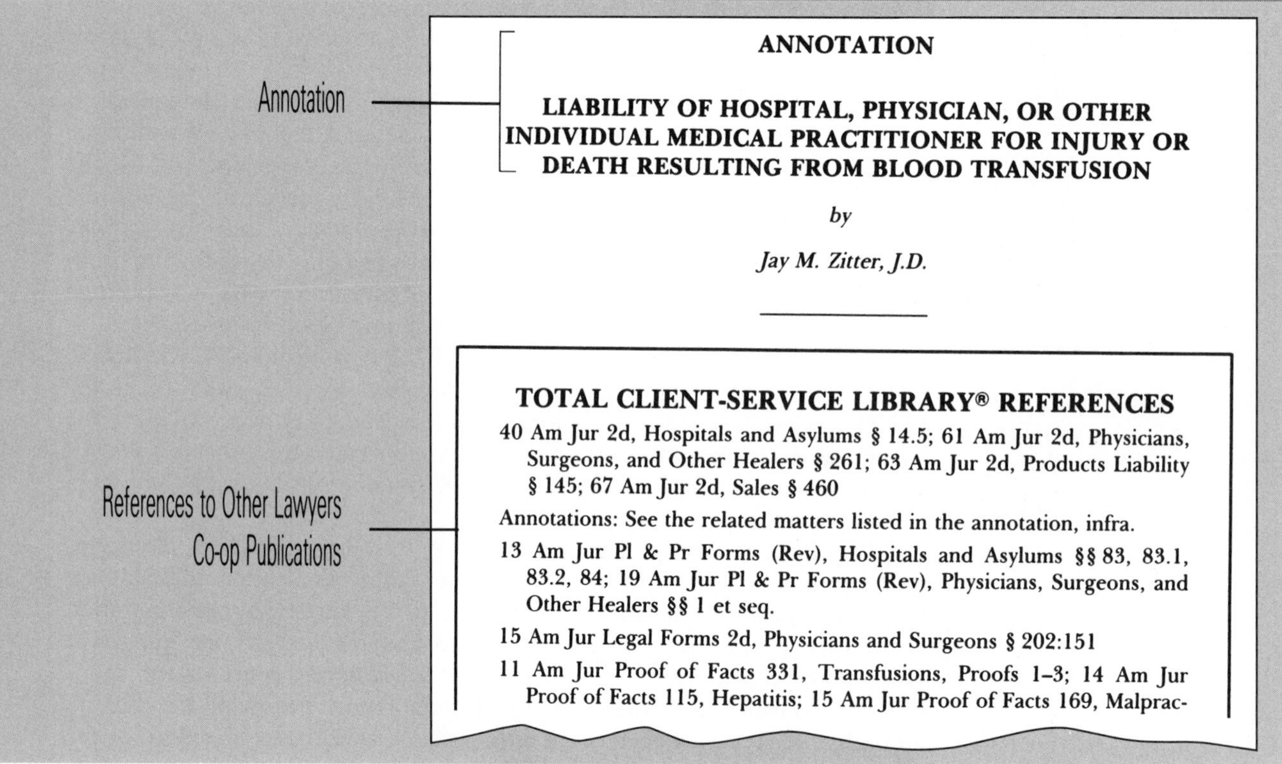

ANNOTATION

LIABILITY OF HOSPITAL, PHYSICIAN, OR OTHER INDIVIDUAL MEDICAL PRACTITIONER FOR INJURY OR DEATH RESULTING FROM BLOOD TRANSFUSION

by

Jay M. Zitter, J.D.

TOTAL CLIENT-SERVICE LIBRARY® REFERENCES

40 Am Jur 2d, Hospitals and Asylums § 14.5; 61 Am Jur 2d, Physicians, Surgeons, and Other Healers § 261; 63 Am Jur 2d, Products Liability § 145; 67 Am Jur 2d, Sales § 460

Annotations: See the related matters listed in the annotation, infra.

13 Am Jur Pl & Pr Forms (Rev), Hospitals and Asylums §§ 83, 83.1, 83.2, 84; 19 Am Jur Pl & Pr Forms (Rev), Physicians, Surgeons, and Other Healers §§ 1 et seq.

15 Am Jur Legal Forms 2d, Physicians and Surgeons § 202:151

11 Am Jur Proof of Facts 331, Transfusions, Proofs 1–3; 14 Am Jur Proof of Facts 115, Hepatitis; 15 Am Jur Proof of Facts 169, Malprac-

History Table, located in Volume 5 of the *Index to Annotations* (Figure 6.4). This table will tell you whether or not an annotation has been supplemented or superseded by a later annotation. It would be a terrible waste of your energy to read an outdated annotation. Always check the Annotation History Table before you read the annotation.

Obviously, the annotations in the *A.L.R.* would lose their appeal if the citations to cases became outdated. Fortunately, you can update the cases that are cited in the text of the annotations by various means, depending on the series. For the third, fourth, and federal series, use the cumulative pocket parts inserted in the back of each volume (Figure 6.5). To update the cases in the second series, use the *A.L.R.2d Later Case Service,* a separate supplemental set of books. For updates to the first series, check the set of books entitled *A.L.R.1st Blue Book of Supplemental Decisions.* For the latest cases, Use Insta-Cite—do not stop with the *A.L.R.* system for updating.

Legal Periodicals

Articles that appear in legal periodicals provide an in-depth treatment of a topic with numerous references to primary and secondary authorities. Other

Figure 6.3 Abstracts of Cases in an Annotation

20 ALR4th BLOOD TRANSFUSIONS § 3[a]
20 ALR4th 136

The fact that the consequences of improper transfusion techniques may not appear until a much later date raises obvious questions as to the time when the statute of limitations begins to run. Thus, counsel for the patient should be aware that in choosing among the various remedies available for recovery, he should consider whether questions of limitations would be avoided thereby.[16]

Counsel on either side may find the hospital's records a valuable source of evidence. In states adopting the Uniform Business Records as Evidence

II. Liability of hospitals or their employees

§ 3. Transfusing wrong or incompatible type of blood

[a] Application of view that transaction constitutes a service not giving rise to liability without fault

The courts have generally ruled that a supplier of a product may not be held liable without fault for injuries caused by the product, if the transaction involved the supplying of

15. The foregoing list of nonvalid reasons are utilized by some hospitals for the guidance of the staff. See 11 Am Jur Proof of Facts 331, Transfusions, Supplement.

16. See, for example, Smith v McComb Infirmary Asso. (1967, **Miss)** 196 So 2d 91, a statutory wrongful death action based upon negligence of a hospital in mistyping the blood of a mother, wherein the court held that the plaintiff's declaration was cast under the wrongful death statute and that the statute of limitations began to run from the date of the infant's death in December, 1964, and not from the time of the alleged negligent act in 1958, and that therefore the trial judge had erred in sustaining the plea of limitation, and the judgment was reversed and the cause remanded. The trial judge had based his opinion on the theory that the declaration of plaintiff was one charging malpractice and that the statute of limitations had run according to a rule that a cause of action for malpractice accrues and the statute begins to run on the date of the wrongful act or omission which constitutes the malpractice, and not from the time of the discovery thereof.

17. For example, the admissibility of hospital records tending to prove an incompatible blood transfusion was recognized in Joseph v W. H. Groves Latter Day Saints Hospital (1957) 7 **Utah** 2d 39, 318 P2d 330.

See, generally, 40 Am Jur 2d, Hospitals and Asylums § 43.

As to the admissibility of computerized hospital records, see § 8 of the annotation at 7 ALR4th 8.

143

articles, particularly those that appear in bar association periodicals, commercial journals, newsletters, and legal newspapers, include the most current topics not covered in other secondary sources. Usually, new developments in the law are discussed first in legal periodicals.

You may also find an article that proposes legal reforms. One famous article that falls into this category is a piece by Gerald Gunther entitled "The Supreme Court, 1971 Term—Foreword: In Search of Evolving Doctrine on a Changing Court: A Model for a Newer Equal Protection," which appeared in the *Harvard Law Review* in 1972 (Figure 6.6). The information in this article would be very useful in supporting a point of view not held by the courts.

Figure 6.4 The Annotation History Table

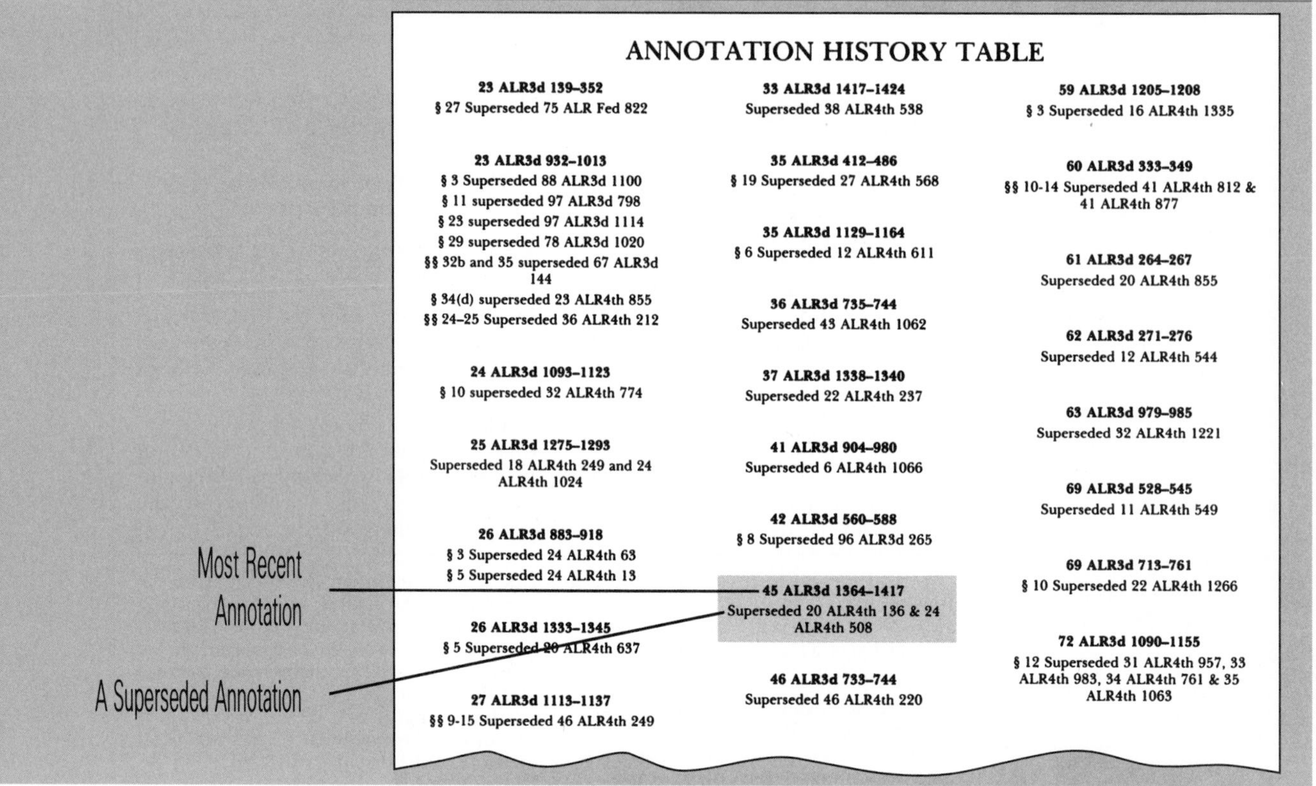

ANNOTATION HISTORY TABLE

23 ALR3d 139–352
§ 27 Superseded 75 ALR Fed 822

23 ALR3d 932–1013
§ 3 Superseded 88 ALR3d 1100
§ 11 superseded 97 ALR3d 798
§ 23 superseded 97 ALR3d 1114
§ 29 superseded 78 ALR3d 1020
§§ 32b and 35 superseded 67 ALR3d 144
§ 34(d) superseded 23 ALR4th 855
§§ 24–25 Superseded 36 ALR4th 212

24 ALR3d 1093–1123
§ 10 superseded 32 ALR4th 774

25 ALR3d 1275–1293
Superseded 18 ALR4th 249 and 24 ALR4th 1024

26 ALR3d 883–918
§ 3 Superseded 24 ALR4th 63
§ 5 Superseded 24 ALR4th 13

26 ALR3d 1333–1345
§ 5 Superseded 20 ALR4th 637

27 ALR3d 1113–1137
§§ 9-15 Superseded 46 ALR4th 249

33 ALR3d 1417–1424
Superseded 38 ALR4th 538

35 ALR3d 412–486
§ 19 Superseded 27 ALR4th 568

35 ALR3d 1129–1164
§ 6 Superseded 12 ALR4th 611

36 ALR3d 735–744
Superseded 43 ALR4th 1062

37 ALR3d 1338–1340
Superseded 22 ALR4th 237

41 ALR3d 904–980
Superseded 6 ALR4th 1066

42 ALR3d 560–588
§ 8 Superseded 96 ALR3d 265

45 ALR3d 1364–1417
Superseded 20 ALR4th 136 & 24 ALR4th 508

46 ALR3d 733–744
Superseded 46 ALR4th 220

59 ALR3d 1205–1208
§ 3 Superseded 16 ALR4th 1335

60 ALR3d 333–349
§§ 10-14 Superseded 41 ALR4th 812 & 41 ALR4th 877

61 ALR3d 264–267
Superseded 20 ALR4th 855

62 ALR3d 271–276
Superseded 12 ALR4th 544

63 ALR3d 979–985
Superseded 32 ALR4th 1221

69 ALR3d 528–545
Superseded 11 ALR4th 549

69 ALR3d 713–761
§ 10 Superseded 22 ALR4th 1266

72 ALR3d 1090–1155
§ 12 Superseded 31 ALR4th 957, 33 ALR4th 983, 34 ALR4th 761 & 35 ALR4th 1063

Using a legal periodical article is often the best way to begin your research, particularly in a developing area of the law.

Law school law reviews, a very special type of legal periodical, include lengthy essays written by scholars or practitioners. Every law school has at least one law review (Figure 6.7). The authors discuss, in meticulous detail, aspects of the law perhaps not covered in other sources. The extensive footnotes (literally hundreds to thousands) are a great aid in finding primary sources. In addition to the lengthy articles, law reviews generally include a "Notes and Comments" section, which contains short articles written by the law review staff.

You can locate periodical articles very easily either on-line through WESTLAW or other on-line services, on laser disc, or in print format. In print, you can use the *Index to Legal Periodicals,* published by the H. W. Wilson Company, which dates back to 1908, or the *Current Law Index,* published by Information Access Company, which dates back to 1980.

Law schools have access through WESTLAW to the *Current Index to Legal Periodicals* database (**CILP**), which is produced by the University of Washington Law Library and indexes the most recent information from three hundred legal periodicals; the *Index to Legal Periodicals* database (**ILP**); and

Figure 6.5 A Pocket Part for the *A.L.R.*

SUPPLEMENT **20 ALR4th 136–184**

For latest cases, call the toll free number appearing on the cover of this supplement.

whether, and the extent to which, a claimant qualifies for an award of reparations," was that police reports were to be considered as proof of truth of facts contained therein, and fact that such reports might contain conclusions, or that some statements might be first, second or third level hearsay, did not make any part of police report incompetent evidence; thus, award of panel of commissioners to claimant of full amount of work lost was contrary to manifest weight of evidence, and erroneously entered, where panel failed to consider police report. Re Grow (1983) 7 **Ohio** Misc 2d 26, 7 Ohio BR 175, 454 NE2d 618.

§ 19. [New] Appeal

See Re Application of Eader (1982) 70 **Ohio** Misc 17, 24 Ohio Ops 3d 83, 434 NE2d 757, § 15.

20 ALR4th 122–128

When statute of limitations commences to run on right of partnership accounting. 44 ALR4th 678.

Auto-Cite®: Cases and annotations referred to herein can be further researched through the Auto-Cite® computer-assisted research service. Use Auto-Cite to check citations for form, parallel references, prior and later history, and annotation references.

An Update to the Annotation in the Pocket Part

20 ALR4th 136–184

New sections and subsections added:

§ 11.5. Transfusing blood containing other injurious substances

---

§ 1. Introduction

[b] Related matters

Liability of blood supplier or donor for injury or death resulting from blood transfusion ... to herein can be further researched through the Auto-Cite® computer-assisted research service. Use Auto-Cite to check citations for form, parallel references, prior and later history, and annotation references.

§ 3. Transfusing wrong or incompatible type of blood

[b] Cases determined in circumstances presented—liability held established or supportable

In action against medical lab alleging negligence in typing plaintiff's blood incorrectly with result that RH incompatability occurred between plaintiff and her unborn child, summary judgment for defendant was precluded where fact question arose as to whether incorrect typing could have been result of defendant's failure to either possess or use degree of care ordinarily possessed by laboratories which perform blood typing; action would be joined to action against physicians based on same injury, and limitations in action commenced running, not when faulty test was performed, but from time injury resulted to plaintiff. Guthrie v Bio-Medical Laboratories, Inc. (1983, **Ala**) 442 So 2d 92.

See Walker v Humana Medical Corp. (1982, **Ala** App) 415 So 2d 1107, later app (Ala App) 423 So 2d 891, § 7[a].

§ 5. —Cases determined in circumstances presented

[a] Liability held established or supportable

Hospital which purchased from blood bank blood contaminated with non-A/non-B hepatitis, which plaintiff contracted after she was given five units of packed red blood cells, was strictly liable for defect in blood. Shortess v Touro Infirmary (1988, **La**) 520 So 2d 389, on remand (La App 4th Cir) 535 So2d 446.

In action by patient who developed chronic hepatitis following blood transfusions, hospi-

the *Legal Resource Index* database (**LRI**). The **LRI** database, includes all the material covered in the *Current Law Index*, plus legal newspapers and law-related articles from the popular press. These indexes are extremely convenient to use on-line.

Using the indexes on-line is preferable to searching through the printed volumes since all of the indexes cumulate in one place and you can print your results. You can search these periodical indexes on WESTLAW the same way

Figure 6.6 A Law Review Article Proposing Legal Reforms

VOLUME 86 NOVEMBER 1972 NUMBER 1

HARVARD LAW REVIEW

CONTENTS

Figure 6.7 Some Representative Law Reviews

you would search any other database. For example, to retrieve recent articles discussing insider trading, access either **LRI, CILP,** or **ILP** and type

```
inside* /s trad*** & da(aft 1988)
```

Figure 6.8 shows the results of your search.

Using the indexes on-line is the most efficient way to research a current issue. If, however, you are dealing with an issue that is more retrospective in scope, such as the topic "dower," you must use the print *Index to Legal Periodicals* since that index dates back to the early 1900s, with predecessors indexing to the early nineteenth century.

Figure 6.8 *Legal Resources Index* On-Line

```
                       COPR. (C) WEST 1991 NO CLAIM TO ORIG. U.S. GOVT. WORKS
CITATIONS LIST (Page 1)                               Total Documents:  185
Database: LRI

    1.   204 New York Law Journal 3
 TITLE: The Milken sentencing issues. (Michael R. Milken).
 AUTHOR: Morvillo, Robert G.   DATE: December 4, 1990.   Edition:  Tuesday.
 Column Number:  col 1.

    2.   204 New York Law Journal 3
 TITLE: Securities law statute of limitations.
 AUTHOR: Flumenbaum, Martin;  Karp, Brad S.   DATE: November 29, 1990.
 Edition:  Thursday.   Column Number:  col 1.

    3.   204 New York Law Journal 1
 TITLE: En banc review of key securities ruling.   AUTHOR: Squires, Deborah.
 DATE: November 13, 1990.   Edition:  Tuesday.   Column Number:  col 3.

    4.   204 New York Law Journal 3
 TITLE: From regulation to punishment: new SEC power.
 AUTHOR: Abramowitz, Elkan.   DATE: November 6, 1990.   Edition:  Tuesday.
 Column Number:  col 1.
```

You can also locate the *full text* of articles on WESTLAW. The Texts and Periodicals database **TP-ALL** on WESTLAW contains articles from law reviews, texts, and bar journals from about 1982. Articles are available in WESTLAW after a copyright release has been obtained from the author. You will be able to access every word in the text and footnotes.

Parts of articles that deal with subtopics of the main article can be searched on-line too. These subtopics would not normally be found in the standard indexes. For example, if you are interested in articles on test anxiety, access the **TP-ALL** database and type

```
test** exam /p anxi!
```

By searching in the **TP-ALL** database, you retrieve an article entitled "Law School Academic Support Programs" that appeared in 40 Hastings L.J. 771 (1989); you would not retrieve this article in the standard indexes under the subject "test anxiety."

If you are looking for a specific article and you already know its citation, access the appropriate database and search in the citation field. For example, if the cite is 74 ABA J. 55, access the ABA Journal database (**ABAJ**) and type

```
ci(74 +5 55)
```

Encyclopedias

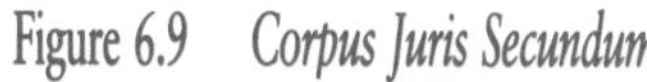
Figure 6.9 *Corpus Juris Secundum*

The two national encyclopedias, *Corpus Juris Secundum (C.J.S.)* and *American Jurisprudence 2d (Am. Jur.2d)*, provide an elementary, objective statement of the law and cite literally hundreds of thousands of state and federal cases. Encyclopedias tend to concentrate on case law and ignore statutory materials. *C.J.S.* and *Am. Jur.2d.* are similar to general encyclopedias in that both sets contain alphabetically arranged summaries of legal topics and a multivolume index that provides easy access to the material.

In its introductory "Explanation," *C.J.S.*, a West publication, defines its mission as ". . . a complete restatement of the entire American law as developed by all reported cases" (Figure 6.9). Due to this publishing philosophy, each page in *C.J.S.* contains about six lines of text and almost three-quarters of a page of citations to cases and materials. The citations to cases are arranged alphabetically by state. With such an arrangement, you can quickly find citations from your jurisdiction.

The editors of *C.J.S.* have undertaken a planned program of replacing volumes in subject areas that have seen substantial changes and developments, such the area of criminal law. The new volumes state West's philosophy as ". . . a contemporary statement of American law as derived from reported cases and legislation." As a result in the change in West's approach, the number of cases cited has been greatly reduced in the recompilation volumes, thus increasing the usefulness of *C.J.S.*

Because it supplies West topic and key numbers, *C.J.S.* is perhaps most useful as a springboard into the West research system. Finding the topic and key numbers in *C.J.S.* circumvents the need to search through the Descriptive Word Index when using the digests.

A five-volume *General Index* offers descriptive word entry into *C.J.S.* An alphabetical list of over 430 subjects, called "List of Titles," is located at the front of each volume. In using *C.J.S.*, look up the most appropriate terms for your topic in the index. For example, if you were interested in an explanation of "nolo contendere," after a check in the *C.J.S.* index you would turn to Criminal Law § 398 (Figure 6.10).

American Jurisprudence Second (Am. Jur.2d), published by Lawyers Co-op, is more selective and contains fewer footnote references, which cite only leading decisions. A *Desk Book* provides useful reference information, such as the United States Constitution, the organization of the federal court system, and various tables. *Am. Jur.2d* includes a ring-bound volume *New Topic Service*, which includes current topics, such as "Alternative Dispute Resolution."

The complaint most law students have with the legal encyclopedias is that some of the volumes are rather musty. The encyclopedias do not keep pace with the law as it grows and changes. Although both sets are kept up-to-date by pocket parts and replacement volumes, the sets are most useful for general information on traditional topics.

State Legal Encyclopedias

Many states have an encyclopedia that organizes and discusses the points of law applicable in that particular jurisdiction. State encyclopedias, are extremely

Figure 6.10 An Entry in *Corpus Juris Secundum*

22 C. J. S. CRIMINAL LAW § 398

ment or information is insufficient, from the standpoint of failing either to confer jurisdiction or to set forth facts sufficient to constitute a public offense, the plea of guilty confesses nothing,[62] and, accordingly, does not preclude accused from attacking the indictment or information on such grounds.[63] In fact, where the plea of guilty is to a void charge or one which fails to state facts sufficient to constitute a crime, the conviction is jurisdictionally defective and a nullity, and is not validated by the plea.[64]

A guilty plea does not waive a claim that the information or indictment, judged on its face, is constitutionally deficient in violation of the double jeopardy clause.[65]

Defects or irregularities in prior proceedings.

By pleading guilty to the charge contained in an indictment or information accused waives any technical defects or irregularities in prior proceedings[66] except such as go to jurisdiction.[67]

Involuntary plea.

Where a plea of guilty is so coerced that it is deprived of validity to support the conviction the coercion likewise deprives it of validity as a waiver of the right of accused to assail the conviction.[68]

Venue.

Since accused's plea of guilty is an admission of the material facts in the indictment or information, including the facts concerning the situs of the crime, the plea operates to waive any right to be tried in the county where the acts were actually committed, and the judgment cannot be collaterally attacked on that ground.[69]

Trial of accomplices.

Certainly, one who has pleaded guilty cannot question the procedure followed at the trial of his accomplices.[70]

2. Plea of Nolo Contendere

§ 398. In General

The so-called plea of "nolo contendere," also called "no contest," is not, strictly speaking, a plea, but a formal declaration by the accused that he will not contest the charge against him.

practical, timely, and a great way to find state cases, statutes, and formbooks. West publishes several state encyclopedias. They follow the pattern and style of *C.J.S.* in providing topic and key numbers, which makes it easy to access information in the state digests.

Legal Dictionaries

Undoubtedly, you have already had a need to consult a legal dictionary. Since the legal field has its own jargon, the need for a law dictionary is constant. Several legal dictionaries are available in your library. The two most prominent are *Black's Law Dictionary,* published by West, and *Ballentine's,* published by Lawyers Co-op.

Legal dictionaries may give case citations as well as defining terms. A citation may lead you to a good case as a starting point to understanding the meaning of the term. Additionally, these dictionaries include a very handy table of abbreviations for just about any citation you need to interpret. You will also find that legal dictionaries are an aid in using the on-line services, since they supply alternative words for you to add as synonyms in your queries.

Black's Law Dictionary, 6th ed. is also available on WESTLAW. If you are reading a case or statute, you can type **DI,** followed by your term, to learn its definition. To check the spelling of a term before using it as a search term in a query, type **DI** followed by a portion of the term followed by an exclamation point (**!**). For example, type **es!** if you want to check the spelling of escheat (Figure 6.11).

West also publishes *Words and Phrases,* an expanded multivolume dictionary. This set can be used to locate cases that have defined a particular term. Hundreds of thousands of definitions are alphabetically arranged, couched in the language of the court. For example, numerous courts have defined the term "enjoyment" (Figure 6.12).

Figure 6.11 Checking Spelling on WESTLAW in the *Black's Law Dictionary*

(a) List of Words Retrieved

```
BLACK'S LAW DICTIONARY  6TH EDITION

 1. Escalation clause.
 2. Escalator clause.
 3. Escambio
 4. Escambium
 5. Escape.
 6. Escape clause.
 7. Escape period.
 8. Escape warrant.
 9. Escapio quietus
10. Escapium
11. Eschaeta derivatur a verbo gallico eschoir, quod est accidere, quia accidit
    domino ex eventu et ex insperato
12. Eschaetae vulgo dicuntur quae decidentibus iis quae de rege tenent, cum non
    existit ratione sanguinis haeres, ad fiscum relabuntur
13. Escheat
14. Escheator

To see a definition, enter the number of the desired term.
To continue through the list of terms . . . . . . . Press ENTER .
To leave the Dictionary system. . . . . . . . . . . Enter GOBACK or GB
COPR. (C) WEST 1991 NO CLAIM TO ORIG. U.S. GOVT. WORKS
```

Figure 6.11 Checking Spelling on WESTLAW in the *Black's Law Dictionary* (continued)

(b) Definition of Escheat

```
BLACK'S LAW DICTIONARY  6TH EDITION                                P  1 OF  1

ESCHEAT

  A reversion of property to the state in consequence of a want of any
individual competent to inherit.
  Escheat at feudal law was the right of the lord of a fee to re-enter upon
the same when it became vacant by the extinction of the blood of the tenant.
This extinction might either be per defectum sanguinis or else per delictum
tenentis, where the course of descent was broken by the corruption of the
blood of the tenant.  As a fee might be holden either of the crown or from
some inferior lord, the escheat was not always to the crown.  The word
''escheat'', in this country, merely indicates the preferable right of the
state to an estate left vacant, and without there being any one in existence
able to make claim thereto.

To leave the Dictionary system. . . . . . . . . . . Enter GOBACK or GB
COPR. (C) WEST 1991 NO CLAIM TO ORIG. U.S. GOVT. WORKS
```

In a literal sense, both WESTLAW and LEXIS are gigantic dictionaries. The databases contain every word of every opinion. Most words appear far too often to make the full-text dictionary feasible, but if you have a unique term, you can give it a try.

Treatises and Hornbooks

Treatises, simply stated, are books that describe an area of law. A treatise may consist of a single volume or multiple volumes. In your law school library, you will find thousands of treatises. In your course work, you probably are acquainted with hornbooks, a type of treatise (Figure 6.13).

Hornbooks explain the rudiments of a legal topic. The term "hornbook law" is often used to refer to points of law that are well settled by the courts. Hornbooks can be an excellent introduction to a topic in the traditional areas of law and can provide you with citations to key cases. Several publishers produce hornbooks. The two largest are West and Foundation Press. The West hornbooks may provide keys to search strategies in WESTLAW.

West also publishes a series called *nutshells*. These are paperback volumes, each of which is devoted to a single legal subject. Nutshells present the topic in a simplified format; hence, they are an excellent introduction to a subject.

You can locate a treatise by checking your library's catalog. In most law libraries, the hornbooks and most popular treatises, or those titles recommended for a course, will be on reserve—ask for help.

Restatements

You have probably also been introduced to restatements in your class work. Restatements are written by scholars under the auspices of the American Law Institute. The purpose of the restatements is to state what the law "is" on a particular subject. Pertinent excerpts from restatements are usually included

Figure 6.12 Definitions in *Words and Phrases*

ENJOYED WITHOUT LIMITATIONS

In a deed conveying a lot of land and "a free right of way for an alleyway 12 feet wide, extending from the rear end of said lot across another lot owned by said K. to the alley running to L. street," the word "free" qualifies and relates to "right of way" and is descriptive of the right of way, the thing granted, and not of the use to be made of the right of way. According to Webst.Dict., the word "free," when used in relation to a thing to be enjoyed or possessed, means "thrown open, or made accessible to all; to be enjoyed without limitations; unrestricted; not obstructed, engrossed, or appropriated; open." Applying that definition, the word "free," as used in the deed, indicates the condition and character of the right of way, which is the thing granted, and the thing to be enjoyed and possessed and, as thus interpreted, it means an unobstructed right of way as far as any future act of the owner of the servient lot is concerned. Flaherty v. Fleming, 52 S.E. 857, 859, 58 W.Va. 669, 3 L.R.A., N.S., 461.

ENJOYMENT

Cross References

Accumulate; Accumulation
Adverse Enjoyment
Exclusive Enjoyment
Full Benefit and Enjoyment
Natural Use and Enjoyment
Necessary to the Enjoyment
Personal Enjoyment
Possession, Enjoyment or Right to Income from

A Court's Definition

The words "enjoyment" and "enjoy", as used in statutes relating to estate and gift taxes, are not terms of art, but connote substantial present economic benefit rather than technical vesting of title or estates. C. I. R. v. Holmes' Estate, Tex., 66 S.Ct. 257, 260, 326 U.S. 480, 90 L.Ed. 228.

Where trustees, including settlor had power to accomplish a complete diversion of trust income and an invasion of corpus,

ENJOYMENT—Cont'd

settlor had power to alter the "enjoyment" of trust property, within Revenue Act. Jennings v. Smith, D.C.Conn., 63 F.Supp. 834. 838.

"Enjoyment", within statute levying tax on succession to property by deed, sale, assignment or gift without consideration substantially equivalent to full value of property, if intended to take effect in possession or enjoyment at or after grantor's, vendor's, assignor or donor's death, is synonymous with comfort, consolation, contentment, ease, happiness, pleasure and satisfaction. In re Heine's Estate, Ohio Pb., 100 N.E.2d 545, 554.

The rule that income is not taxable until "realized" is founded on administrative convenience, and is only a rule of postponement of the tax to the final event of "enjoyment" of the income, usually the receipt of it by the taxpayer, and not a rule of exemption from taxation where enjoyment is consummated by some event other than taxpayer's personal receipt of money or property. Helvering v. Horst, 61 S.Ct. 144, 147, 148, 311 U. S. 112, 85 L.Ed. 75, 131 A.L.R. 655.

The power to dispose of income is the equivalent of "ownership" and the exercise of that power to procure the payment of income to another is the "enjoyment", and hence the "realization" of the income by him who exercises it, so as to render the income subject to tax. Helvering v. Horst, 61 S.Ct. 144, 147, 148, 311 U.S. 112, 85 L.Ed. 75, 131 A.L.R. 655.

Under Internal Revenue Acts defining "gross income" in broad language, the power to dispose of income is tantamount to "ownership" of it, and exercise of that power in procuring payment to an assignee or nominee is the equivalent of the "enjoyment" of the income on part of him who exercises the right. Duran v. Commissioner of Internal Revenue, C.C.A.10, 123 F.2d 324, 326.

A use of economic gain, the right to receive income, to procure a satisfaction which can be obtained only by the expenditure of money or property, would seem to be the "en-

Figure 6.13 Hornbooks and Nutshells

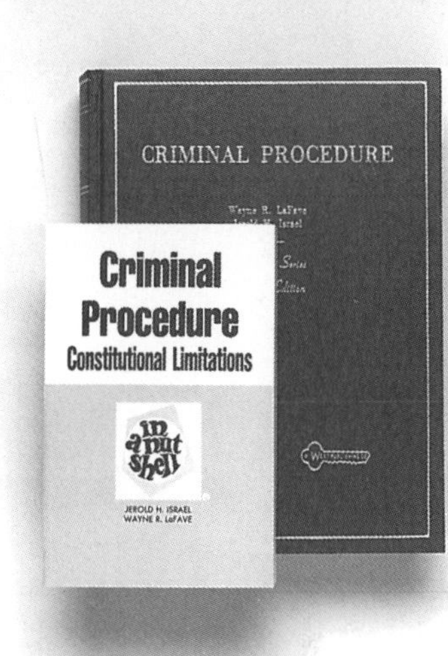

in casebooks or reprinted as supplements to your casebooks; for example, Section 402A from the *Restatement of Torts* will be included in your torts casebook.

Restatements cover only ten fields of law, which include several first-year courses, such as Contracts, Torts, and Property. Each section begins with a boldface statement of principles, followed by comments intended to explain the statement. Since the series has a great deal of prestige among judges and scholars, you may want to present an issue using the "restatement view."

Formbooks and Practice Manuals

At some point, you may need works that deal with legal procedure. Although some works are written for the practicing attorney, they can be very useful in your procedure and litigation courses. For federal law, you may look to Wright and Miller's *Federal Practice and Procedure* published by West or *West's Federal Forms*.

Conclusion

This chapter has introduced background legal sources, including annotations, legal periodicals, legal encyclopedias, dictionaries, treatises, and restatements, and formbooks. You may feel more comfortable with these sources than with primary sources at this point in your law school career because they are the same types of materials that you used in your undergraduate or graduate days. Even though they are considered "secondary," you will more than likely use them first.

7 The Research Process

This book has tried to present you with an introduction to the full array of information that is available in the law library. We have talked about books and about computer databases. This material will not become meaningful or really useful to you, however, until you actually work through it. The great Zen koan of legal research is that you can't understand the materials without using them, and you can't use them very well without understanding them. Fortunately in the coming months, you will probably be assigned a series of research problems and undoubtedly will be subjected to an agonizing moot court experience, both of which will force you to plunge into the lake of legal research. This may be one of the few times when throwing the nonswimmer into the water and watching what happens is an historical inevitability. This book has attempted to provide you with a series of ideas, explanations, and overviews that should make the shock of the water a little less traumatic.

To succeed, you must look at legal research materials functionally, understanding how they fit together and why they look the way they do. If you only understand one way of using the books, you will be lost when something goes awry. If you understand why the books work the way they do, however, you will be able to improvise when caught in a corner.

This final chapter presents a few ideas on research methodology, i.e., how to go about attacking a research problem. We can't offer you a simple solution, but we would like to present you with a working model. Feel free to modify it as you wish; you may have to do so if you are to be successful. The point is that *some* model or plan is necessary. You have to have some overall concept of what you are doing, or you will simply drown in the mass of cases, statutes, administrative rules and regulations, and secondary sources that are available. Therefore we propose the following four-step model.

Step 1: Deciding Where to Start

A large portion of your first year of law school will be devoted to wading through facts and law, developing skills in how to attack a situation and how to distinguish what is important from what is not. This is a necessary first step in any research process as well. We urge that you carry this procedure one step further. Once you have extracted the necessary issues, ask yourself what the "ideal" answer would be. In other words, *what* are you looking for?

You would be surprised how many people plunge into the research process without really knowing where they want to end up. This is dangerous because many bears are lurking in the forest of the library. You have to know up front what you expect to find when you get in there. Do you want a statute? A case? An administrative rule or regulation? A clear explanation of a new area? Some guidance on how to update certain citations? There are probably a thousand different types of answers that you can pursue.

Only if you understand what your ideal answer is can you set out in search of it. It may turn out that your initial guess was incorrect, that once you get deeper into the problem, your ideal answer turns out to be not so ideal after all. But unless you have a goal in mind when your research begins, you will never reach a successful end.

Step 2: Thinking about How to Proceed

One thing that we hope this book has made you realize is that a whole host of research systems are available out there. West Publishing Company has an intricate self-referencing system of materials. Based on the National Reporter System, it flows into the American Digest System and the WESTLAW databases and filters into the family of annotated codes and other West products. As we have pointed out, there is a coherent philosophy behind the West system. The same can be said of other publishers. Indeed, many law firms now have their own internal information systems, consisting of briefs and memoranda that have been written on various matters.

The successful researcher must understand how to exploit these various systems. Part of that means understanding where to enter them. As you begin your research, once you know what your ideal answer is, you must decide which research process and which research *system* make sense for you. Oftentimes understanding this second step can save you enormous amounts of time. If what you really need is background information, you are far better off using an encyclopedia like *Corpus Juris Secundum* or *American Jurisprudence 2d* than you are starting out reading cases. If you need background on a particular case, you should probably begin by reading the hornbook explanation of that case rather than plunging into the dense verbiage of the case itself.

The point is that you should follow one of our first rules of research—find someone who has done the work for you. Use the collective wisdom of legal publishers, legal scholars, and your own colleagues and professors as much as you possibly can. At the same time, you must never lose sight of the distinction between a primary source (i.e., the law itself) and a secondary source (i.e., an interpretation of the law). Nevertheless, if you understand where to enter the research systems, you can save yourself grief, time, and money.

Step 3: Legal Research and Economics

Economics and the law is a very hot topic in substantive law school courses these days. In fact, we think it has a great deal to do with legal research. Once you are in practice, you will find that questions come with price tags attached. A partner may assign you a question where you will be allowed to do only $500 worth of research. It is just as bad to do $5,000 worth of research on a $50 problem as it is to do $50 worth of research on a $5,000 problem.

Law students often have difficulty understanding this concept, partly because of their experiences in law school. Law professors assume that law students have an infinite amount of time. A professor can ask you to rewrite, reresearch, and totally redo without giving any thought to how much available time you actually have. Once you are in practice, the rules of the game will change. You will be up against a very hard edge of billable hours in a private firm, an overwhelming caseload in a public interest practice, or a stack of files from a government agency, and you will have to complete the assignment before the deadline. To do so, you will have to allocate and budget your research time correctly. Start doing this now. Be an economist when it comes to your research. Plan how much time you can allocate to each part of the research process. Set goals for yourself. This will make the whole process easier.

If you have defined your question as we recommended in step 1 and picked the quick entry places as we suggested in step 2, then you can devise a time budget in step 3. Doing so will allow you to be an efficient, effective researcher and will lead to far better research results. There is no sadder sight than a student surrounded by piles of case reporters and statutory volumes working away late into the night in the law library. The student may have no concept of what to do with the problem or how much time should be spent on it.

The truly creative act is not locating materials, but reading and synthesizing them. That is why legal writing is such an important part of your first year. Remember, though, that you can't start on the truly creative part until you have assembled your materials. Factoring in time as a realistic constraint is part of that process.

Step 4: Knowing When to Stop

One of the things law schools often fail to teach is how to judge when you should stop your research process. Once again, this is due to the idea that student time is infinitely elastic. In law school, you are asked to go back to the beginning and reinvent every wheel, to build each new research edifice from brick number one. In other words, you are expected to look at every case ever decided in the history of humankind when writing your brief. In the real world, including the world in which you must live during your first year, you will have to make judgments as to when you can successfully stop your research process. Devising stop rules is one of the current items in legal research training. We suggest the following stop rules for your consideration:

1. *Economic analysis or diminishing returns model.* This model suggests that when you are investing more in your research than you are getting in research returns, you should stop. The classic example of diminishing returns is the student in the library at 10:30 P.M. on Friday night, continuing

to read cases that seem to be less and less useful. Because of the built-in paranoia that goes with being a law student, students feel that if they stop the very next case they would have read will turn out to be the perfect case, the one that defines the problem in clear, sharp prose. The wily, experienced researcher has a feel for when less is coming back than is being put in. This is a very tough rule to follow, however. To adhere to it, you must have confidence in your research abilities and must understand the relationship between what the materials can tell you and the time you can expend. This is a hard-body rule, one that is difficult for first-year students. But if you want to be an efficient researcher, you should consider using it.

2. *The Loop Rule.* This is the simplest rule for a first-year student to apply. When you start to see the same materials over and over again—the same cases, the same statutes, the same administrative agency rulings or regulations, the same types of citations in *Shepards*—you should realize that you are probably done. This kind of loop can be dangerous, however, unless you are using the products of more than one publisher. Any publisher will have an internal cross-referencing system. We have already urged you to use the dynamics of the system in your research, but you should also use other research tools. However, once you recognize that you understand the cases, statutes, and rulings in your area, and you have updated everything, you will know that you are in control of the relevant literature. When you reach the point in your research where you know—or can guess—what you are going to see next, you have probably caught yourself in a loop. Remember there is almost never a "perfect" case, and once you have read enough to know what others think is out there, you have probably done enough.

3. *The Zen Rule.*This is an aspirational rule, one for you to look forward to in the future. When you are in practice and have been working in one area for a long time, you will simply "know" when you are done. After a while you will become so familiar with the statutory and administrative architecture of your area—the common law implications of what is going on and the rule of the law makers and law interpreters in your particular specialty—that you will be the expert resource. This is why we urge you to use a human being in your research. Law school is often a very competitive experience, but it does not have to be. Instead of concentrating on competition, learn to exploit the utility and helpfulness of other humans. Ask a professor or another student for help. In practice, ask a senior partner, a more experienced associate, a colleague, or someone who works in the same department or division. A human being can enable you to avoid many research bottlenecks by telling you which research materials are universally accepted in your area and helping you find the answer that you need. At this point, you will be in the Zen stopping stage. You will have found a person who is a research resource, and eventually you will become one yourself. You will be transformed from the caterpillar of the new researcher to the butterfly of the information expert. You will still have to struggle to keep up with the newest developments in your area, but you will be a major player in the research game.

No amount of methodology can substitute for simple common sense. And common sense is what legal research is really all about. It is easy to get lost in the first-year experience, easy to be baffled by all the books on the shelves. But think back to the research skills that you mastered in high school and college and to all the intelligence and hard work that got you here, and you will find that legal research is not so bad. Think about the wealth of information that is available, see how the parts of the systems fit together, and you will ride the wave rather than being crushed by it. Enjoy.

Appendix

Query Formulation

When you search for documents on WESTLAW, your request must be in a format WESTLAW understands. WESTLAW, like most computer systems, is very literal minded. The result of your search will only be as good as your search request. These requests are called queries. This appendix describes the basics of query formulation. It explains how WESTLAW searches terms, how to use connectors, how to restrict your search, and how to edit queries.

How WESTLAW Searches Terms

When you run a query on WESTLAW, you ask it to retrieve all documents containing your search terms in the relationships you have specified. When choosing your search terms, you must consider the various forms they might take. When you search for the term **car,** for example, you may also wish to search for **cars** and **car's.** If you do not search for all variations of a term, you may miss relevant documents.

WESTLAW assists you in this by retrieving many word forms automatically; you can also retrieve other word forms by using special symbols. The methods for retrieving variant word forms on WESTLAW are outlined in the following sections.

Plurals

If you enter the singular form of a term, WESTLAW automatically retrieves the plural form as well; this is true for both regular and irregular plurals:

Term	Retrieves
car	car cars
memorandum	memorandum memorandums memoranda memorandas

This automatic pluralizer works only when you enter the singular form of a term. If you enter the plural form of a term, only the plural is retrieved.

Possessives

If you enter the nonpossessive form of a search term, WESTLAW automatically retrieves the possessive form as well. If you enter the possessive form, only the possessive form is retrieved:

Term	Retrieves
customer	customer customer's
customer's	customer's

Interchangeable Terms: Automatic Equivalencies

Some terms have interchangeable forms, or equivalencies; for example, **5** and **five** are equivalent terms. On WESTLAW, when you enter a term that has an equivalent term, both terms are retrieved along with their plurals and possessives.

Acronyms

Like compound words, an acronym may appear in various ways; it may or may not have periods or spaces. To retrieve all variations of an acronym, enter it with periods and without spaces:

Term	Retrieves
e.p.a.	E.P.A. E. P. A. E P A EPA

(Note: Uppercase and lowercase letters are interchangeable; they are read the same by WESTLAW.)

Root Expander (!)

To retrieve words with variant endings, use the root expander (!). When you place the ! at the end of a root term, you retrieve all forms of that root:

Term	Retrieves
know!	know known knowing knowingly knowingful knowable knows knowledge knowledgeable

The root expander does not retrieve related terms that do not begin with the root word; **know!** does not retrieve *knew*. To search for these forms, use the universal character (*) discussed in the next section. You can combine the universal character and the root expander in a single term: **kn*w!**.

A common error you may make is to use the root expander (!) without considering all the variations that may be generated. For example, if you enter **tax!** in most databases, WESTLAW will respond that this term generates too many terms. Think about all the words that have the root "tax":

taxes	taxpayer
taxable	taxation
taxability	taxied
taxonomist	taxonomy
taxicab	taxi
taxis	taxidermy
taxpayer	taxing
taxational	taxiway

To retrieve documents containing the terms *tax, taxes, taxation,* or *taxability,* use these terms in your query: **tax taxa!**. (Note: **tax** retrieves *tax, tax's,* and *taxes.*) In some cases, it may be safer to type in all the forms of the specific words you require than to risk getting irrelevant cases.

Universal Character (*)

The universal character represents one variable character. You can place the universal character in the middle or at the end of a term, but not at the beginning. When you place the asterisk at the end of a term, you specify the maximum length of that term. For example, **object**** retrieves all forms of the root with up to two additional characters. Think of the universal character as a ___ Scrabble® piece (Figure A1.1).

Figure A1.1 Using WESTLAW Can Be Like Playing Scrabble

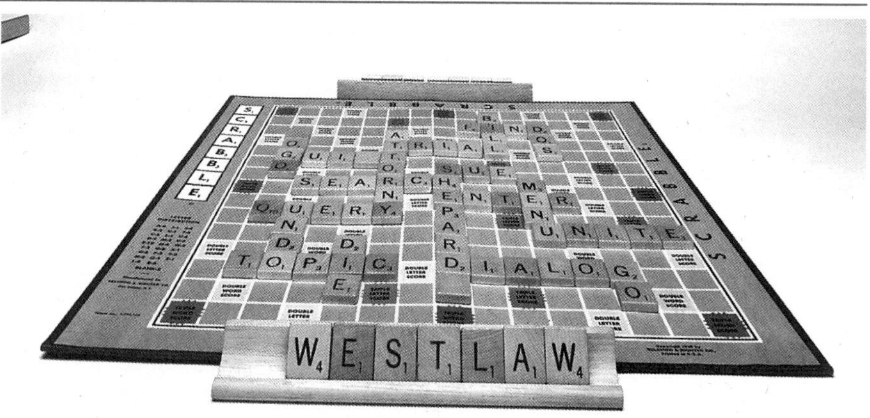

Phrase Searching

To search for a phrase on WESTLAW, place it in quotation marks. For example, to search for negligence per se, type

```
''Negligence per se''
```

Phrase searching should be used only when you are certain the phrase will not appear in other ways. For example, you would not want to use the phrase "blood alcohol" in your query because some cases might say "the amount of alcohol in the blood" instead. A more successful query would be

```
blood /3 alcohol
```

Words Too Common to Search: Stop Words

Some words, such as **the** or **with,** are too common to be searched on WESTLAW; these words are called stop words. If you enter a stop word, WESTLAW will display the following message:

```
Your query contains term(s) too common to be
searched.
```

If you receive this message, reformulate your query, leaving out stop words.

Alternative Terms

After selecting terms for your query, consider which alternative terms are necessary. For example, if you were searching **attorney,** you might also want to search for **counsel** and **lawyer.** You should consider both synonyms and antonyms as alternative terms. If you are searching for the phrase **good faith,** you might also want to search **bad faith.** If you are searching **admissible,** you might also include **inadmissible.** Remember to include only those alternative terms that are necessary to retrieve relevant documents.

Connectors

After selecting terms and alternative terms for your query, use connectors to specify the relationships that should exist between search terms in your retrieved documents. There are only a few connectors to learn—a few real words and a few computer words.

The OR Connector

Use the OR connector, represented by a space, to search for alternative terms. To use the OR connector, you can simply leave a space between terms or type the word "or." For example, the query

```
attorney lawyer counsel
```

retrieves any documents containing at least one of these terms.

The AND Connector

Use the AND connector (&) to retrieve documents containing two or more search terms anywhere in the document. For example, the query

```
seat-belt & mitigat!
```

requires that both seat-belt and mitigation, or forms thereof, appear in the document. In other words, you are interested in the issue of seat-belts and the separate issue of mitigating damages. Therefore, use the & connector if you want to retrieve two or more separate issues in the same search.

Be cautious in using the & connector in constructing your queries. In a 100-page document, for example, one term may appear on the first page, and the other may appear on the last. For this reason, you will often need to use more restrictive grammatical or numerical connectors.

Grammatical Connectors

Grammatical connectors require that search terms appear in the same grammatical unit (sentence or paragraph).

Same Paragraph (/p) The /p connector is the most widely used and versatile connector on WESTLAW. It requires search terms to appear in the same paragraph in a document. Many users feel comfortable with it since a paragraph is very easy to visualize. Paragraph searching is particularly popular since all of West's editorial enhancements, such as the synopsis, headnotes, and digests, are considered paragraphs. If you are not sure which connector to use, try /p first.

The query

```
pit-bull bull-terrier /p attack! bit*** injur!
```

retrieves documents in which the term *pit-bull, bull-terrier* or forms thereof appear in the same paragraph as *attack, attacked, attacking, bit, bite, biting, bitten, injury, injured, injure,* or *injuring.*

Same Sentence (/s) The /s connector requires search terms to appear in the same sentence in a document. For example, the query

```
design*** /s defect!
```

retrieves documents with the following sentences:

. . . liability for a defectively designed product . . .

. . . resulting from alleged design and manufacturing defects . . .

. . . the building was defective and the defendant was negligent in the design of the building.

You can use a +s connector to specify the order in which search terms should appear in a sentence. The +s requires that the term to the left of the connector precede the term to the right within the same sentence:

```
palsgraf +s island
```

Numerical Connectors

Numerical connectors require search terms to appear within a specified number of terms of each other. A numerical connector may contain any number from 1 to 255. For example, the query

```
attorney /5 fee
```

retrieves documents in which *attorney* appears within five words of *fee*. Therefore, the document containing the sentence

. . . caused the bank to incur attorney and trustee fees and expenses . . .

is retrieved because *attorney* and *fees* appear within five words of each other.

Numerical connectors are useful when you are searching for a phrase that may appear in various ways. For example, the phrase "forcible entry" may also be expressed as "used force to gain entry" or "entry was forced." The following query retrieves these alternatives:

```
forc! /5 entry
```

There are no magic numbers for specifying distances between words. In most searches, using a slightly smaller or larger numerical connector will produce similar results. As a general rule, however, it is better to use a grammatical connector when the number is larger than 9.